Myths of Termination

Psychoanalysis can make a huge difference in the lives of patients, their families and others they encounter. Myths have developed, however, about how psychoanalysis should end – what patients experience and what analysts do. These expectations come primarily from accounts by analysts in the analytic literature, which are often perpetuated in an oversimplified form in teaching. Patients' perspectives are rarely presented. In her book, Judy Leopold Kantrowitz seeks to address this omission. Exploring the accounts of 82 former analysands, she illustrates the rich diversity of psychoanalytic endings and ways of maintaining analytic benefits after ending; in presenting patients' experiences Kantrowitz provides correctives for some of the myths about termination.

Myths of Termination: What patients can teach psychoanalysts about endings is not a book that seeks to refute or support any specific idea about a best way of ending analysis, but rather to show that there are countless ways of having a satisfactory conclusion to the process. Nor is the author espousing any particular analytic theory. Kantrowitz sets out to show that an oversimplified view of psycho-analytic endings not only diminishes an appreciation of the diversity of psychoanalytic outcomes but may also interfere with the creativity of individual psychoanalysts. In this book, former analysands describe and illustrate how their analyses ended. They reflect on the effect of non-mutual endings due to external factors (moving, retirement, illness or death) or psychological factors (wishing to avoid facing some issue); the impact of post-analytic contact; and the ways in which they have held on to their analytic benefits after ending their analyses.

Myths of Termination confronts and refutes the myths about the termination phase of psychoanalysis that are passed from generation to generation. It is a refreshing and insightful study that will be welcomed by psychoanalysts and psychodynamic therapists, such as clinical psychologists, social workers, and others trained or in training to do clinical work.

Judy Leopold Kantrowitz, is a training and supervising analyst at the Boston Psychoanalytic Society and Institute and an Associate Clinical Professor at Harvard Medical School. She is on the Editorial Board of the *Psychoanalytic Quarterly* and has a private practice in Brookline, MA.

PSYCHOLOGICAL ISSUES BOOK SERIES

DAVID WOLITZKY
Series Editor

Published by Routledge

73. *Myths of Termination: What patients can teach psychoanalysts about endings*, Judy Leopold Kantrowitz
72. *Identity and the New Psychoanalytic Explorations of Self-organization*, Mardi Horowitz
71. *Memory, Myth, and Seduction: Unconscious Fantasy and the Interpretive Process*, Jean-Georges Schimek and Deborah L. Browning
70. *From Classical to Contemporary Psychoanalysis: A Critique and Integration*, Morris N. Eagle

Published by Jason Aronson

69. *Primary Process Thinking: Theory, Measurement, and Research*, Robert R. Holt
68. *The Embodied Subject: Minding the Body in Psychoanalysis*, John P. Muller and Jane G. Tillman
67. *Self-Organizing Complexity in Psychological Systems*, Craig Piers, John P. Muller, and Joseph Brent
66. *Help Him Make You Smile: The Development of Intersubjectivity in the Atypical Child*, Rita S. Eagle
65. *Erik Erikson and the American Psyche: Ego, Ethics, and Evolution*, Daniel Burston

Published by International Universities Press

64. *Subliminal Explorations of Perception, Dreams, and Fantasies: The Pioneering Contributions of Charles Fisher*, Howard Shevrin
62/63. *Psychoanalysis and the Philosophy of Science: Collected Papers of Benjamin B. Rubinstein, MD*, Robert R. Holt
61. *Validation in the Clinical Theory of Psychoanalysis: A Study in the Philosophy of Psychoanalysis*, Adolf Grunbaum
60. *Freud's Concept of Passivity*, Russell H. Davis
59. *Between Hermeneutics and Science: An Essay on the Epistemology of Psychoanalysis*, Carlo Strenger
58. *Conscious and Unconscious: Freud's Dynamic Distinction Reconsidered*, Patricia S. Herzog
57. *The Creative Process: A Functional Model Based on Empirical Studies from Early Childhood to Middle Age*, Gudmund J. W. Smith & Ingegerd M. Carlsson
56. *Motivation and Explanation*, Nigel Mackay
55. *Freud and Anthropology*, Edwin R. Wallace IV
54. *Analysis of Transference, Vol. II: Studies of Nine Audio-Recorded Psychoanalytic Sessions*, Merton M. Gill

DAVID WOLITZKY
Series Editor

53. *Analysis of Transference, Vol. I: Theory and Technique*, Merton M. Gill and Irwin Z. Hoffman

52. *Anxiety and Defense Strategies in Childhood and Adolescence*, Gudmund J. W. Smith and Anna Danielsson Smith

51. *Cognitive Styles, Essays and Origins: Field Dependence and Field Independence*, Herman A. Witkin and Donald R. Goodenough

50. *Internalization in Psychoanalysis*, W. W. Meissner

49. *The Power of Form: A Psychoanalytic Approach to Aesthetic Form*, Gilbert J. Rose

47/48. *Intelligence and Adaptation: An Integration of Psychoanalytic and Piagetian Developmental Psychology*, Stanley I. Greenspan

45/46. *Hysteria: The Elusive Neurosis*, Alan Krohn

44. *Symbol and Neurosis: Selected Papers of Lawrence S. Kubie*, Herbert Schlesinger

42/43. *Modern Psychoanalytic Concepts in a General Psychology: General Concepts and Principles/Motivation*, Allan D. Rosenblatt and James T. Thickstun

41. *Freud in Germany: Revolution and Reaction in Science, 1893–1907*, Hannah S. Decker

40. *A Structural Theory of the Emotions*, Joseph De Rivera

39. *A History of Aggression in Freud*, Paul E. Stepansky

38. *Schizophrenia: Selected Papers*, David Shakow

37. *Emotional Expression in Infancy: A Biobehavioral Study*, Robert N. Emde, Theodore J. Gaensbauer, and Robert J. Harmon

36. *Psychology versus Metapsychology: Psychoanalytic Essays in Memory of George S. Klein*, Merton M. Gill and Philip S. Holzman

34/35. *Freud: The Fusion of Science and Humanism: The Intellectual History of Psychoanalysis*, John E. Gedo and George H. Pollock

33. *A Consideration of Some Learning Variables in the Context of Psychoanalytic Theory: Toward a Psychoanalytic Learning Perspective*, Stanley I. Greenspan

32. *Scientific Thought and Social Reality: Essays*, Fred Schwartz

31. *Else Frenkel-Brunswik: Selected Papers*, Nanette Heiman and Joan Grant

30. *Psychoanalytic Research: Three Approaches to the Experimental Study of Subliminal Processes*, Martin Mayman

29. *Similarity in Visually Perceived Forms*, Erich Goldmeier

28. *Immediate Effects on Patients of Psychoanalytic Interpretations*, Edith L. Garduk

27. *The Effect of Stress on Dreams*, Louis Breger, Ian Hunter, and Ron W. Lane

25/26. *Information, Systems, and Psychoanalysis: An Evolutionary Biological Approach to Psychoanalytic Theory*, Emanuel Peterfreund

24. *Ego Boundaries*, Bernard Landis

PSYCHOLOGICAL ISSUES BOOK SERIES

DAVID WOLITZKY
Series Editor

23. *A Psychoanalytic Model of Attention and Learning*, Fred Schwartz and Peter Schiller

22. *Toward a Unity of Knowledge*, Marjorie Grene

21. *Prediction in Psychotherapy Research: A Method of the Transformation of Clinical Judgments into Testable Hypotheses*, Helen D. Sargent, Leonard Horwitz, Robert S. Wallerstein, and Ann Appelbaum

20. *Psychoanalysis and American Medicine, 1894–1918: Medicine, Science, and Culture*, John Chynoweth Burnham

18/19. *Motives and Thought: Psychoanalytic Essays in Honor of David Rapaport*, Robert R. Holt

17. *The Causes, Controls, and Organization of Behavior in the Neonate*, Peter H. Wolff

16. *Freud's Neurological Education and Its Influence on Psychoanalytic Theory*, Peter Armacher

15. *Dragons, Delinquents, and Destiny: An Essay on Positive Superego Functions*, Wolfgang Lederer

14. *Papers on Psychoanalytic Psychology*, Heinz Hartmann, Ernst Kris, and Rudolph M. Loewenstein

13. *The Influence of Freud on American Psychology*, David Shakow and David Rapaport

12. *The Formation and Transformation of the Perceptual World*, Ivo Kohler

11. *Ego and Reality in Psychoanalytic Theory: A Proposal Regarding the Independent Ego Energies*, Robert W. White

10. *Topography and Systems in Psychoanalytic Theory*, Merton M. Gill

9. *Activation and Recovery of Associations*, Fred Rouse and Richard O. Schwartz

8. *Personality Organization in Cognitive Controls and Intellectual Abilities*, Riley W. Gardner, Douglas N. Jackson, and Samuel J. Messick

7. *Preconscious Stimulation in Dreams, Associations, and Images*, Otto Potzl, Rudolf Allers, and Jakob Teler

6. *The Structure of Psychoanalytic Theory: A Systematizing Attempt*, David Rapaport

5. *The Developmental Psychologies of Jean Piaget and Psychoanalysis*, Peter H. Wolff

4. *Cognitive Control: A Study of Individual Consistencies in Cognitive Behavior*, Riley W. Gardner, Philip. S. Holzman, George S. Klein, and Harriet Linton

3. *On Perception and Event Structure, and the Psychological Environment*, Fritz Heider

2. *Studies in Remembering: The Reproduction of Connected and Extended Verbal Material*, Irving H. Paul

1. *Identity and the Life Cycle: Selected Papers*, Erik H. Erikson

Myths of Termination

What patients can teach
psychoanalysts about endings

Judy Leopold Kantrowitz

Routledge
Taylor & Francis Group

LONDON AND NEW YORK

First published 2015
by Routledge
27 Church Road, Hove, East Sussex BN3 2FA

and by Routledge
711 Third Avenue, New York, NY 10017

Routledge is an imprint of the Taylor & Francis Group, an informa business

British Library Cataloguing in Publication Data
A catalogue record for this book is available from the
British Library

Library of Congress Cataloging in Publication Data
Kantrowitz, Judy Leopold, author.
Myths of termination : what patients can teach psychoanalysts
about endings
/ Judy Leopold Kantrowitz.
pages cm
1. Psychotherapy--Termination. 2. Psychotherapist and patient. 3.
Psychoanalysis--Philosophy. I. Title.
RC489.T45K36 2014
616.89'17--dc23
2014004950

ISBN: 978-0-415-82388-3 (hbk)
ISBN: 978-0-415-82389-0 (pbk)
ISBN: 978-1-315-76153-4 (ebk)

Typeset in Times
by Saxon Graphics Ltd, Derby

For Sophie and Elliot

Contents

Foreword by Glen O. Gabbard   xiii
Acknowledgements   xv

Introduction   1

1   A short history of termination: The ideal versus the real –
    it ain't necessarily so   7

2   Developments in the ending of psychoanalysis: Insight,
    loss and mourning   24

3   Non-mutual endings   56

4   The effect of post-analytic contact   80

5   As time goes by: Ways of keeping analysis alive   106

6   Afterwards: What we learn   126

7   Reflections and reconsiderations   136

Appendix   152
References   158
Index   167

Foreword

Termination has always been a difficult subject for psychoanalysis. The word itself is so fraught with images of finality and death. Psychoanalytic institutes often find it difficult to attract enthusiastic instructors to teach seminars on the subject. Reading lists for such courses often include a host of articles that are decades old. These papers outline a theory and technique that are designed to guide analysts in the termination phase of their work, and to provide roadmaps for the neophyte analyst to demonstrate how the end of analysis 'is supposed to' occur.

Elsewhere (Gabbard 2009) I have chronicled my gradual awakening to the difference between the myths that are taught to candidates and the realities of termination in clinical practice. Few of my cases seemed to follow the termination pattern described in the classic articles on the subject. Moreover, I began to realize that little data had been collected on the subject. In fact, the literature was almost completely based on anecdotes.

In this context, the impressive new volume by Judy Kantrowitz that I am introducing is most welcome. She provides the field with systematic data stemming from the detailed interviews she conducted with 82 former analysands, some of whom are in the profession and some of whom are not. Her results confirm what experienced analysts have long known – namely, that we are prone to believe and accept received wisdom and myths that are handed down by our mentors to guide whether our analytic work is truly satisfactory. This body of knowledge is often in sharp contrast to the myriad ways that analyses end. While we have long known what analysts think about the appropriate way to terminate treatment, we have lacked systematic examination of reports from the point of view of patients. The collection of interviews that Kantrowitz shares with us fills that void.

The author makes a wise decision in letting her research subjects speak for themselves. In lengthy passages from the interviews, the reader will be struck by the emotional intensity of patients around the subject of termination and its discontents. Some feel deeply betrayed, while others feel the experience was one of great emotional depth and profound connection.

In reading the various accounts of former patients, what is immediately apparent is that analysis terminates in so many different ways that there is considerable irony that a 'standard' approach to termination permeates the literature on the subject. Candidates and analysts who have been puzzled by attempting to follow the 'proper' way to conduct a termination process will take heart when reading this volume. One can understand this discrepancy between writing and practice as simply one more example of a longstanding problem in the analytic literature – namely, that analysts tend to write about treatment in a way that does not reflect what they actually do in their consulting rooms. The literature on termination is no different to other areas of technique in that regard.

Among the findings of interest in the interviews are the following: very few patients experience the so-called return of symptoms during the termination phase; the majority of analyses discussed in the book ended unilaterally, not by mutual decision; 51 out of 82 of the subjects sought out further help from their analyst after terminating; post-termination contacts have variable results and are not necessarily predictable in their outcome; and not everyone internalizes the analyst and continues self-analysis even if they may have had a positive analytic experience with considerable improvement in their lives. Kantrowitz also found that intense grief is not necessarily a part of the ending or post-termination period of analysis. She reports that the most frequent complaint involved analysts who stepped outside of their professional role and are unaware of the negative impact such actions had on their patients. She also noted something that I have observed in my patients over my 35 years of analytic practice: namely, that some patients cannot experience the full benefit of the analysis until after termination.

This new work by Kantrowitz is a significant contribution to our field. Over the history of psychoanalysis, patients have often been regarded as rather questionable sources of information about their treatment experience and, in particular, about their analyst. The conventional wisdom has been that the patient's transference distorts the accuracy of their reporting about such matters. In the contemporary psychoanalytic zeitgeist, however, we have moved closer to the view of Bion that patients may be our best teachers. As you read this landmark contribution to the field, I suggest you listen to these former patients' words with an open mind and a keen ear. In these accounts that Kantrowitz has collected, we have a highly useful source of information about how analysis ends and about the impact those endings may have. We all owe a debt of gratitude to the author.

Glen O. Gabbard, MD

Acknowledgements

I am very grateful to the 82 former analysands who volunteered to tell me about their experiences in termination and its aftermath. Without them, obviously, there would be no book. Although I have not reported all their accounts in the final version, I learned something from each of them that contributed to my greater understanding of the process of termination and the meaning of analysis over time.

Many people have contributed to my writing. My writing group – Stephen Bernstein, Dan Jacobs, Malkah Notman and Judy Yanof – read the earliest drafts of Chapters 4 and 5. Steve Goldberg also read earlier versions of both these chapters as well as Chapter 6. Their comments and suggestions were helpful to me in sharpening my focus. Richard Zimmer contributed ideas to enrich the presentation in Chapter 5 on self-analysis and the organization of the opening chapter. Jay Greenberg helped me with the organization and focus for the material in Chapters 5 and 6 when the material was condensed for an article in the *Psychoanalytic Quarterly*. I learned a great deal from working with him. I am especially appreciative of the time and thought that Tony Kris and Shelley Orgel gave to this project. Over the course of several years as I worked on this manuscript, they read most of the chapters in one form or another and offered editorial suggestions. Tony Kris generously read the whole book in its near final version. I am lucky to have such skilled writers as devoted friends. The support and encouragement of all these people kept me working on a manuscript that I found daunting to hone sufficiently. I am grateful to Kitty Ross for the editing of this book. She helped me eliminate repetitions and develop the final organization. Her enthusiasm about this project also made me glad that I had persisted in what had become a difficult task of organization for me.

Other support in the process was not so directly focused on writing itself. I am deeply grateful to my family and friends who listened to me talk about this project and the difficulties I was having putting it together. My deepest gratitude is to my husband, Paul, who patiently accepted the long hours I put in at the computer writing and rewriting. He was interested in the work and supportive of me in the process. My children and daughter-in-law also contributed to my feeling that persisting in pulling together the material I had collected was a worthwhile endeavour. My grandchildren make me appreciate a sense of time and continuity as well as change – and bring so much joy in the process. My granddaughter was not born when I started these interviews and now she is a school girl. It is one of life's great pleasures to watch development. How we all grow and change is really what this book is about.

Introduction

Psychoanalysis offers a particular method for discovery and change. It is generally acknowledged that how this procedure will play out between any analysand and analyst is not predictable. However, writers and teachers of psychoanalysis may not always keep such unpredictability in mind when they speak about the process of ending an analysis. Various theories about how analyses end are generated. Expectations about the process, criteria and outcome of analysis may become over-simplified, idealized and mythologized.

I believe that some of the literature on termination, perpetuated sometimes in over-simplified form in teaching, has unintentionally created myths about how analyses end. Most often, it is not that a given author is claiming universality for a particular idea or observation about occurrences in the end phase, but that others believe it in this fashion and then both teach and speak of it as if it were universal. These myths create expectations about how analyses should end that may be passed from generation to generation, setting unrealistic goals and encouraging fantasies of completion that can adversely affect attunement to the individual analysand.

Repeatedly some analytic authors (Firestein 1982; Wallerstein 1986; Blum 1989; Golland 1997; Gabbard 2009; and Pulver, panel 2012) have tried to warn us about idealized, unrealistic expectations from analysis, and some teachers in analytic institutes do the same. They point out that internal struggles remain in all of us, analysed or not, throughout our lives. Even so, the idea of a 'perfect' analytic ending remains, and many analysts reveal this as a core belief when they discuss the subject in their presentations at analytic conferences or, more troubling, in their teaching of candidates.

An overarching point I want to make in this book – similar to conclusions by Schlesinger (2005), Salberg and many of the contributors to her book (2010a), and especially to Gabbard (2009) – is that generalizations interfere with our appreciation of both the complexity and specificity of experience. The danger lies in our wish for certainty – our wish to believe there is one particular way to conclude analytic work. If we can believe that something we read in the literature or learn in our analytic training is always true or should always be true, we gain a greater sense of security. But we also then are likely to feel a pressure to make our experiences correspond with this belief. This may result in a conviction that our patients and students should be able to behave accordingly. And if they do not, we may become critical of them or ourselves for failing to attain these goals. No one phenomenon characterizes endings, nor is there any one particular way analysts should manage termination or post-termination contacts. Even so, the interviews with former analysands, the data on which this book is based, suggest ways that analysts might be more aware of their patients' often unspoken vulnerabilities during termination as well as in post-analytic interactions.

Our field's history is replete with controversies; psychoanalytic leaders have insisted that their specific beliefs should be followed and other ideas disclaimed as deviant, misguided, unanalytic. Like Wallerstein (1988), I believe we can accommodate many seemingly divergent views, because our experience, as well as our data, supports the fact that people differ and that analyses differ. Some clinical theories suit some patients better than others. No single clinical illustration can be universally applicable, but it can disprove a theory that claims a particular phenomenon does not exist or that it invariably occurs. Pine (2011) has made a similar point about partial theories. The idea of partial theories generates controversies because some analysts believe they need to maintain the universality of the particular theory they subscribe to. I have previously written (Kantrowitz 2008) in support of Pine's view and offered an illustration of how different theories can be more or less useful at different points of an analysis as an analysand changes.

While there have been many theories over the years about the nature of a termination phase – what it should consist of, how it evolves and how it resolves – the material that is invariably used as supporting evidence consists of the concepts, theories and clinical experiences of the analysts' accounts of their patients. With rare exceptions (Craige 2002; Tessman 2003; Frank 2009), the views and experiences of analysands are not included. I am not suggesting that analysands' perspectives on their analyses are more 'accurate' than their analysts' – both are important in understanding a particular treatment and its outcome. But the paucity of patients' accounts contributes to mythologizing. Our views of the analyst's authority have changed over the years, and with that change we have increasingly recognized that analysis is a two-person endeavour. Therefore, representation of the analysands' perspective has become essential to our appreciation of the analytic process in which they are engaged.

Indeed, outcome studies reveal that patients and analysts can have different perceptions about the past treatment. In a prospective, longitudinal study of analytic outcome (Kantrowitz et al. 1987a), post-termination interviews indicated that analysts had more positive views of their analysands' therapeutic gains than either the analysands or independent evaluations. 'The lack of agreement among patients, analysts, and researchers' psychological test evaluations about the extent of improvement … points to the importance of multiple perspectives when evaluating the outcome of analysis' (Kantrowitz 1993). O'Malley, Suh and Strupp (1983) also concluded that therapists' outcome ratings were more positive when compared to those of patients and independent observers.

Since an individual analyst treats a relatively small number of patients during his or her career, and former patients may or may not report back about their experiences of termination and post-termination, the sample of knowledge about analytic endings and post-analytic experiences is relatively small. To my knowledge, reports from analysands who are not themselves engaged in clinical work are not part of the analytic literature. Moreover, while a number of analysts have written about their own experiences as analysands (Guntrip 1975; Little 1981), only a few (Frank 2009) focus on the ending.

The project I have undertaken and will describe in this book – studying the experiences of a larger group of former patients and gathering clinical material from their perspective – will attempt to correct this omission. My goal has been neither to support nor refute any particular idea about the 'best' way of ending an analysis but, rather, to show that there are countless ways of having a good-enough conclusion. In other words, I have wanted to dispel myths about the process of ending and demonstrate the importance of specificity (Becall 2010) in what occurs during this period for each patient. Beyond this general intent, I have obtained data, based on patients' perspectives, about specific topics that are frequently written about in the analytic literature and will suggest correctives for what seem to me to be faulty generalizations.

My information about termination and post-termination experiences in psycho-analysis comes from clinical interviews with 82 former analysands. These men and women are analysts, analysts in training, clinicians who are not analysts, and non-clinicians. I posted requests on the on-line bulletins and newsletters of various psychoanalytic associations and institutes and college health services, asking for former patients who would be willing to speak with me on the telephone about their experiences of termination and post-termination. My notice explained that the interviews would last one or two hours and that the material they revealed to me would be kept confidential and presented anonymously. Before the material was published, the participants would have the opportunity to read it and correct any inaccuracies. At the end of each phone interview I requested that the interviewee approach friends and colleagues who had terminated analyses, and who might be interested in participating, to contact me. Many of my subjects did this. They also suggested other venues where I could post notices about my research. In this way, the sample snowballed. Additional details about the project, as well as a summary of the data I gathered, are contained in the Appendix.

Since the aim of the interviews was to provide a wide sampling of how analyses end and what analysands carry away from the process, I did not focus in depth on any one analysand's account of treatment. These analysands offered material that stimulated my interest in each of them individually and a wish to know more about them and their analytic experience, but this was not the purpose of my interview. Therefore, I did not pursue these questions. My curiosity about them, like that of the readers of this study, will be only limitedly satisfied.

The patients' reports illustrated both the gains from, and limits in, each of their analyses and supported the idea that outcomes are always determined in major ways by the characteristics and conflicts of a particular patient and analyst, and the interactions between them. The interviews also shed new light on old theories about grief in ending and how grief is experienced by analysands who were analysts themselves, compared with those who were not analysts; the repercussions of non-mutual endings; the effect of post-analytic contact; and the development of a self-analytic function as an essential criterion for ending and a requisite for maintaining gains from the treatment. While some of my findings are quantitative, for example the frequency of certain kinds of experiences, most of my observations were qualitative.

The literature on analytic endings has been repeatedly and extensively summarized over the years (Firestein 1974 and 1982; Shane and Shane 1984; Blum 1989; Bergmann 1997; Salberg 2010a). Therefore I felt it was unnecessary to recapitulate it here in full detail. Instead, in Chapter 1, I will highlight the assumptions in the literature that have contributed to mythologizing the nature of ending and/or characterizing the termination phase and post-analytic experience in a particular way. In addition, I will indicate that while some analytic writers have tried for many years to address this problem, their cautions seem to have remained unheeded.

In Chapter 2, I present my subjects' descriptions of the termination period as well as their thoughts about their analytic work and what brought it to a close. Most of the reports emphasized that changes in the analytic experience occurred once termination was discussed. These included: new insights about the transference, emphasis on separation issues, new or recovered affect and recovered memory. Issues relating to separation, loss, grief and mourning were central to this material. The accounts made it clear that, just as each patient brought his or her own unique conflicts and life history into the analysis, the dyadic relationship unfolded for a particular individual in an unpredictable way. Individuality and specificity also predominated in the ending. I shall provide abundant material to counter the assumption that analysands who are analysts and/or clinicians find it easier to terminate than non-clinicians because of the expectation of future contact with their former analysts. Similarly, the interviews make clear that how and when grieving occurs is not predictable in the way the literature suggests.

In Chapter 3, I discuss the impact on analysands when endings are and are not mutually agreed upon. Most analytic authors do not specify whether a treatment (Novick 1982) concludes with both parties' consent or is unilateral. Novick believes that when clinicians read about termination of analyses, they most often assume the decision was mutual, but this conclusion may be unwarranted. Certainly, whether a decision to end is arrived at mutually or unilaterally makes a difference in how the analysis ends, and it would be misleading to make generalizations about the effects of an ending if it is not arrived at mutually. Surveys (Firestein 1974; Hartlaub, Martin and Rhine 1986) have determined that most analyses don't end with the patient and analyst in agreement that they have come to a satisfactory conclusion; rather, they are interrupted for varying lengths of time. Sometimes the analysand returns and resumes analytic work with the same analyst, and at other times seeks treatment with a different analyst, but on still other occasions the sense of an ending remains incomplete, at least in this respect.

Unilateral endings by the analyst were reported by 48 of the 82 former analysands. Some of these were dictated primarily by external circumstances, for example, the analyst died, became ill, moved or retired; other endings occurred primarily because of psychological factors. When psychological factors were primary, the analysts' decisions to end treatment, as well as the timing of announcing the ending, seemed to involve countertransference issues. This assumption could not be explored or verified in this project because my reports only include the analysand's perspective. I cannot know whether the analysts would have had a similar perception of these terminations.

There has been considerable debate in the literature about when, how, and how much personal information analysts should disclose when they are making the decision to end treatment. I will discuss various conflicting views on this issue and offer some suggestions about how to achieve more satisfactory partings when the ending is decided unilaterally.

While my interviews were focused on the ending of analysis, without exception the analysands also discussed their post-analytic experiences. Indeed, for many subjects, it was these post-analytic experiences that determined their decision to contact me. Chapter 4 provides clinical data about how analysands' internalized representations of the analyst, the analytic relationship and self-understanding were affected by different kinds of social and professional post-analytic contact. In certain cases, this contact disrupted the integration of the analytic experiences. In other instances, it seemed to consolidate a positive internalization. Some individuals, whose post-analytic contact consisted of a return to their former analyst as patients, reported that the renewed process expanded and deepened the earlier work; others were disappointed. The variety of the former patients' experiences emphasized the impossibility of making generalizations about post-analytic contact. But their accounts do suggest sensitivities that analysts should keep in mind when, and if, such encounters occur.

Toward the end of each interview, I asked the participant how he or she had kept the analytic experience alive after treatment ended. Twenty-three former analysands (slightly more than one-fourth of the sample) responded directly to this query. They offered vivid examples of how they had sustained and deepened their understanding of themselves. In Chapter 5, I describe the functions that analysts potentially provide for analysands and compare these with what analysands have been able to provide for themselves in the analysts' absence. In Chapter 6, I explore the issue of assimilation through self-analysis leading to insight, self-reflection providing affect regulation, and other ways in which the experience and benefits of treatment have been sustained.

In Chapter 7, I shall present an overview of my findings and discuss what we can and cannot learn from them. I acknowledge and discuss the multiple problems the data poses. These include the fact that the volunteers are different ages, had different treatment histories, different lengths of time in analysis, and different lengths of time since ending analysis. Their psychological strengths or vulnerabilities were not comparable, nor were their life histories and conflicts. Their reasons for volunteering were also different. It is self-evident that their experiences in analysis itself were also different and were responded to in different ways.

Throughout this book, I pay particular attention to the benefits and disadvantages of having accounts of the termination only from the patients' perspectives. There is no independent corroboration from the analysts or any other external source of assessment. While the analysands' views of their treatment are certainly a necessary, and far too often neglected, way of assessing clinical outcome, the absence of the analysts' views of the shared experiences means that these accounts are missing a major dimension of these narratives. Even so, I believe the data from this project can contribute to clinicians' appreciation of the impact on their patients of the ending of treatments. I believe this study may be instrumental in leading analysts to reexamine their thinking on many of our time-honoured theoretical assumptions concerning our patients' perceptions and feelings about the psychoanalytic process they have undergone and to appreciate more fully the individually determined variety of what occurs in its aftermath.

Chapter 1

A short history of termination

The ideal versus the real –
it ain't necessarily so

Today when we think of analysis, we assume a beginning, a middle and an end. But it was actually not until the 1950s (Reich 1950; Glover 1955) that termination as a phase of treatment was conceptualized. The most likely explanation for this is that early analyses had short durations. For the most part, patients sought treatment for symptoms they did not understand. Transforming 'what is unconscious into conscious' (Freud 1917: 455) would – and often did – alleviate the manifest problem. However, it was only when patients regained sufficient capacity to love and work (p. 457) that Freud considered that they had been returned to health.

Issues related to the transference both complicated and facilitated the process of analysis (Breuer and Freud 1895). Freud's recognition that unconscious factors affected both the analysand and analyst led to an appreciation that individuals who would be analysing others needed to know about their own unconscious conflicts and motivations. Because of this new understanding, training analyses began. At first these, too, were often very brief.

Ferenczi (1927) had originally believed that the process of ending analytic work would take care of itself. Neither analyst nor patient had to bring an analysis to conclusion; it would simply peter out on its own, dying of exhaustion. Later, however, Freud (1937) proposed more elaborated criteria. He stated that analysis could be concluded when the patient was no longer 'suffering from his former symptoms' and had 'overcome his anxieties and inhibitions', and when the analyst believed that the patient's specific difficulties would not recur because 'so much repressed material had been brought to consciousness' (p. 320). By the end of his life, Freud explicitly acknowledged the limitations of analysis, noting that 'bedrock' issues were unlikely to yield to analytic scrutiny. In addition, only those conflicts that were active during the time of analysis would be analysed. He was clear that conflicts that had seemed sufficiently quieted could be reawakened. He also reflected that analysts themselves were especially vulnerable to such a resurgence, due to their work with patients' unconscious. Enthusiasm for what analysis could reveal and change often led many of Freud's followers not to think too much about what Freud himself had viewed as the interminability of analysis.

In the post-Freud generations, there was agreement that, although the disappearance of symptoms was an important indicator of intrapsychic change, it was not a reliable criterion for whether such change had occurred (Firestein 1974). Glover (1955) expanded on the importance of having a termination phase, maintaining that without it, no analysis would be complete. The idea that a 'complete' analysis included a discrete termination period then followed.

Novick (1988) stated his agreement with Glover's view that the termination phase should be distinct from the rest of the analysis and assumed that most analysts would agree. Rangell (1982), for example, wrote that

> insight and working through occur simultaneously or in sequence from the beginning ... with small increments alternating with large reconstruction of traumatic events and constructions of developmental phases of the history – all coming to a peak some time during the heart of the analysis. What follows is a reworking and absorption of the entire process during the final segments, in which the phases of development and the web-like history become meshed. (p. 369)

He added that rather than new material emerging in the termination phase, the material deepens understanding and working through occurs (p. 347). Gilman (1982) concurred: 'The benefits of a designated, time-limited period ... are now well-established' (p. 471).

But other of their contemporary theorists of the period challenged this idea. Dewald (1982) noted that, while the termination phase had typical issues, apart from agreeing on a date to end, the treatment during this period should follow the kind of analytic work that had been characteristic of the patient. No special techniques were required. And almost ten years later, Novick (1997) changed his earlier view, observing that by the late 1980s there was disagreement about whether the termination phase was unique or necessary for all analysands (De Simone Gaburri 1985; Goldberg and Marcus 1985; Pedder 1988; Blum 1989; De Simone 1997).

Criteria for termination

In the 1950s and 1960s, especially in North America, the analysis of ego activities, especially ego defences, replaced the concern with modifying drives as an indication that treatment had been successful. By the 1970s, some notable North American analysts proposed that the last part of analysis should indicate a change in unconscious fantasy organization (Arlow 1969; Abend 1979, 1990; Boesky 1982), and this view flourished in other parts of the world (De Simone Gaburri 1990).

Over the years, analytic writers set forth a range of additional indicators[1] that an analysis had achieved its purpose and could end. These included: recognizing and managing resistances; resolving the transference neurosis through reaching and maintaining the oedipal level of relationship (Novick 1982) and the development of self-analysis (Hoffer 1950; Gaskill 1980; Novick 1982; Schlessinger and Robbins 1983; Kantrowitz, Katz and Paolitto 1990b; Bergmann 2005); experiencing de-idealization and disillusionment with the analyst and analysis (Rickman 1957; Novick 1976; Dewald 1982); belief in the analyst as a 'good object' who could confront the patient's acted aggression in the world and toward the analyst (Nacht 1962); more 'good hours' and a strong therapeutic alliance (Gitelson 1962); a deepened understanding and working through of the material rather than the emergence of new material, (Rangell 1966; Firestein 1974); and the capacity to tolerate uncertainty (Grinberg 1980).

Subsequently, a greater appreciation of developmental theory led to termination criteria focused on intrapsychic and interpersonal separation/individuation, autonomy from the drives, and increased differentiation of self. The goal of analysis was the internalization of a new structure to achieve a modification of self- and other-representation (Loewald 1988; Blanck and Blanck 1988) and self-cohesion (Kohut 1977).

Ticho's important distinction between life goals and analytic goals (1972) further refined termination. Analytic goals were to free patients from internal obstacles that impeded the attainment of their life goals, which might take longer to achieve. Once a developmental process that had been interrupted or distorted was resumed, it was assumed that growth and discovery of personal potential would occur. Kogan (1996) expanded on Ticho's idea by defining analytic goals as those shared by the patient and the analyst for the treatment, and life goals as those the patient wished to attain in life.

Decades after Ticho, the Novicks (2006) echoed his perspective, emphasizing the resumption of progressive development as an analytic goal. De Berenstein and De Fondevila (1989) refined ideas about progressive development. They made a distinction between aims that were general therapeutic goals – such as ego synthesis, sublimation and reparation capacity and an enrichment that affected the whole personality – and aims that were unique to each patient.

Despite such acknowledgements of the importance of specificity of the particular patient's goals, generic and idealized criteria still characterized what analytic candidates were taught. Gilman (1982) presented a survey of 48 successfully completed cases, based on reports prepared for graduation and certification from 15 institutes. Although his report supported the diversity in the nature and quality of the patient material, he continued to use language that overstated what had occurred. For example, 'For many of the patients who were working through Oedipal problems in the termination phase, termination signified the final relinquishing of the Oedipal object' (p. 468).

Even analysts who focused theoretical interest in this topic held inconsistent beliefs about the importance of the termination phase. For example, Novick (1982) pointed out that all criteria for a successful analysis were about cure, not about entering the termination phase. Less than a decade later, however (1988), he cited Glover as saying that 'unless there was an end phase passed through, it is very doubtful whether any case had been analyzed' (p. 378). As indicated above, Novick (1997) later changed this view.

Many ideas existed about what transpired during the last period of analysis. For example, some analysts believed that during the end phase the central themes returned (Ekstein 1965; Greenson 1965; Bird 1972). Others referred to the reoccurrence of symptoms (Firestein 1974) as well as a condensed revisiting of the transference neurosis (Buxbaum 1950), with a rapid oscillation between integration and fragmentation (Muslin 1995). Still others maintained that previous understanding was synthesized (Ekstein 1965) and unfinished business emerged (Calef and Weinshel 1983). Sometimes the last stage of analysis was characterized by the recovery of memory (Mahon and Battin 1981).

According to Bird (1972), during the last phase there was a sense of collaboration between analysand and analyst in the analysis of the transference, with an experience of the analyst as the 'Other' in the conflict. Cooper (2009) stated that not only could old conflicts and difficulties reappear, but previously unexplored and insufficiently worked through aspects of conflict could become manifest in the patient–analyst interactions. Orgel (2000) observed that an oscillation occurred between impulses to remain and to leave, as well as shifts in mood. Also evident were an intensification of transference reactions to separation and experiences of anxiety, as well as depressive affects stemming from losses at different developmental stages (Schubert 2000). Adolescent approaches to separation foretold and paralleled terminations patterns (Novick and Novick 2006).

Although so many ideas about the nature of the termination process were offered, Blum (1989) and Bergmann (1997) noted that a paradigm for ending analysis had never been developed. Many of the phenomena cited are likely in endings, but do not invariably happen.

Both Dewald (1982) and Siegel (1982) viewed ideas of complete resolution as idealized and unrealistic. Dewald stated that limitations always remained. Siegel emphasized that powerful forces can be released by real-life events that may not have been occurring at the time of analysis. There were many future challenges that the patient may not yet have encountered, such as marriage, raising children and growing old. Like Freud (1937), he believed that only those conflicts that were active when a patient was in treatment could be analysed during termination.

When I was an analytic candidate in the late 1960s and early 1970s, we were taught that we needed to assess patients' analysability before taking them on as supervised patients. It was assumed we would be able to make these assessments by evaluating the patients' reality testing, the nature and quality of their object relationships, their affect availability and tolerance and their motivation for psychoanalysis. It was also assumed that, provided the analysand showed enough ego strength to be analysed, problems in these areas would be resolved at the termination of analysis.

My CORST project, which was a prospective, longitudinal study of the outcome of psychoanalysis (Kantrowitz et al. 1975, 1986, 1987a, 1987b, 1989, 1990a, 1990b, 1990c; Kantrowitz 1987, 1993), revealed that these factors were not, in fact, predictive of analysability. The factor that had the highest correlation with a positive outcome was the patient–analyst 'match'. The vicissitudes of the 'match' could not be predicted at the outset. It could only be revealed in the course of the work. What is more, some matches that initially seemed facilitating could, as the nature of the issues of the analysand evolved, become impeding. The overlaps and clashes in conflicts and character and the blind spots that touched on the patient's difficulties – which the treating analyst could or could not overcome – these were the most important factors influencing the outcome of the treatment, provided the patient was able to tolerate the depriving aspects of analytic work.

Although the nature of the analytic relationship itself – for example, the candour between patient and analyst – had been a focus for some analysts in the 1950s (Weigert 1952), in the 1960s and 1970s many North American psychoanalysts taught that clinicians were interchangeable, blank screens (Glover 1964). The only personal factor that was presumed to have an effect on the treatment outcome was the individual's level of experience. My project demonstrated that when analysis was successful, the level and quality of object relations and affect availability and tolerance did improve (Kantrowitz *et al.* 1986, 1987a), and, as stated above, the variable most closely related to this improvement was a facilitating patient–analyst 'match' (Kantrowitz *et al.* 1989, 1990c). However, this did not mean that all difficulties had been resolved.

By the 1990s the nature and quality of the analytic relationship itself had become a main criterion for ending. For example, analytic trust – the patient's and analyst's capacity to hear, listen to, and respond to each other as separate people (Ellman 1997) – had developed. The change in focus in North America was due predominantly to Relational analysts, who conceptualized analytic work and its goals in different terms from those employed by classical analysts.

Whereas Freud sought to uncover buried, unconscious conflicts in order to attain greater mastery of impulse and freedom from inhibition (1937), Relational analysts focused on expansion, curiosity about affect states and deeper engagement in life (Salberg 2010b). Interpersonal analysts (Levenson 1978) had always regarded the patient–analyst relationship as central in analytic work. But it was not until the last two decades of the twentieth century that their views gained influence and were incorporated into the mainstream psychoanalytic movement in North America. I am inclined to think that the goals of Relational analysts with regard to termination are actually shared by most psychoanalysts today. It is the particular method by which one attains expansion, modulation of affect states, and deeper engagement in life and relationships that might still differ among various theoretical schools.

Increasingly, not only the nature of the relationship but the specifics of characteristics and experiences of the analyst have been taken into consideration in terms of how they approached ending analyses. Holmes (2010) linked types of endings to an analyst's particular attachment style. The analyst's personal history of separation and loss (Silverman 2010) and experience in termination (Salberg 2010b) are also now thought to influence the nature of the process in ending with their patients.

Mourning

While, as we have seen, there has been much disagreement among classical analysts about what criteria were required for termination, most maintained that mourning was a central and a necessary part of the termination process (Reich 1950; Balint 1950; Loewald 1962: Grinberg 1980; Dewald 1982; Cancrini 1988; Pedder 1988). Mourning was also thought of in terms of facing limitations of one's own omnipotence and omniscience and what analysis itself could offer (Milner 1965; Grinberg 1980; Novick 1982; Dewald 1982; Orgel 2000; Moraitis 2009). I will address this topic in Chapter 2.

In 1937 Deutsch described an absence of grief as the consequence of a child's having an insufficiently developed ego to be able to mourn and, therefore, becoming narcissistic as a self-protective defence to avoid the strain of a mourning process; she called this 'unmotivated depression'. Weigert (1952) stated that ending analysis is a painful process 'which calls forth the labor of mourning' (p. 467) that was avoided in all neurotic difficulties. Johnson, as described by Weigert, thought the importance of mourning, manifested in the analysand's grief in ending, reflected the loss of Oedipal fantasies. If the patient did not mourn, it was taken to mean that he or she was refusing to give up Oedipal wishes.

More recently, Craige (2002) observed that the final phase might serve as a trigger for evoking previous experiences of loss. Schlesinger (2005) believed that loss and mourning occurred throughout analytic work as patients relinquished symptoms and changed. In his view, 'Loss, especially unacknowledged loss', is the major reason patients come to psychoanalysis. 'When relationships dissolve, the tension of impending separation is painful; significant relationships do not dissolve painlessly' (p. 217). Patients may try to lessen the pain by putting off mourning, or they may 'analyse' the experience to diminish its emotional impact. Schlesinger's assumption was that resistance to termination is based on the dependency on the analyst – an assumption that maintaining analytic gains is also dependent on the analyst's presence. The process of mourning was therefore seen as necessary for making analytic gains one's own.

Tessman (2003) observed that although mourning had been accepted as a universal response to ending, this was not the case in her interviews with analysts about their analytic experiences. 'Our theories carry with them some degree of expectation vis-à-vis the analysand in so far as capacity to tolerate grief and mourning has long been proposed as a developmental achievement' (p. 237). The interview material in this project, which will be discussed in the following chapters, supports Tessman's statement.

Milner (1950) and Novick (1997) believed that candidates could bypass the process of mourning during termination because they would have future contact with their analysts. Both Milner and Novick stated that, as a result, candidates were handicapped in their ability to appreciate the process of grief and mourning experienced by their own analysands who would not have contact with them after the analysis had ended. Craige's survey (2002) of analytic candidates' experiences after termination provided a picture that contradicts this assumption. A large number of candidates had intense grief reactions in the year following the ending of their analyses. She did not find that the grief was related to earlier histories of loss.

This controversy illustrates my point: both Craige's observation (about the presence of grief) and Milner's and Novick's position (about its absence) can be quoted as if they represented the 'truth'. But are they, in fact, contradictory? Does Craige's data disprove Novick's and Milner's? Not all of Craige's subjects responded with intense grief. Craige did not claim more than her data showed. She clearly indicated that a specific percentage of her subjects manifested grief after ending analysis. And certainly I know from many candidates, supervisees and colleagues that their experiences of termination did not have the intensity of grief she had reported. So does that mean her data is false? I don't think so. These discrepant observations indicate that different people react in different ways: both the presence and the absence of grief can exist. My data supports Craige's findings that, for *some* candidates at least, grief is present after termination.

Mourning of the analyst as a 'real object'

In decades past, it was debated whether the patient was only mourning the loss of the analyst as a transference object (Granair, panel 1975) or the loss of the relationship with the analyst as well. Novick, writing 30 years ago, also assumed that when the analyst as a transference object is mourned, the transference wishes which are grieved come from all developmental levels. When analysts referred to grieving for the analyst as a 'real' object, he believed that they were referring to a revival of an early infant–mother transference that also needed to be mourned. It was necessary to experience disillusionment and de-idealization of this 'omnipotent, idealized, all perfect mother' (1982: 350).

Novick's idiosyncratic conception of the 'real' object and the transference object dated from the early 1980s, prior to the now generally accepted idea that the analytic relationship is a two-person, not a one-person, relationship. This assumption means, as previously described, that the analytic relationship is affected by the characteristics and conflicts of both the patient and the analyst and that actual aspects of the analyst as a person are therefore manifest in analysis (Kantrowitz, 1987, 1992, 1993, 1995, 1996, 1999; Kantrowitz *et al.* 1989). Not everything is transference. In this respect, analysands may also be mourning the loss of specific qualities of the analyst that were manifested in their particular analytic relationship.

Blum (1989) believed the analyst was primarily mourned as a transference object. However, he acknowledged that there was 'a unique intimacy … in the analytic situation' (p. 291). He thought that a real relationship developed in parallel with the transference. The patient appreciated the analyst's skill and dedication and might feel better understood by the analyst than anyone in the patient's life. In his view, 'Loss of the analyzing object (and analysis) is also mourned, but not in the depth and poignancy of the transference object loss' (p. 291).

Other analysts saw it differently. DeBell (1975 panel) emphasized that patients mourned the analyst as a real object; he thought it was a loss that could not be resolved by analysing it, but must be tolerated. Patients' mourning might not be overt, but when analysis was successful, he believed this could be successfully managed. Tessman (2003) maintained that pressure to de-idealize the analyst might be misunderstood as pressure to relinquish loving feelings for the analyst. Recognition of the 'actuality' of the analyst that held significant meaning for the analysand might facilitate de-idealization. When this change in perception was accompanied by continuing trust and loving feelings toward the analyst, the analysand's feelings of distrust toward the original objects that generated the traumatic affect might have been unconsciously transformed. Along with many other contemporary analysts, Tessman presumed that both a transference and a 'real' relationship existed. She illustrated how they are woven together, instead of trying to parse what was transference from what was 'real'.

There is data to support Tessman's view that both transference and the actual analyst are mourned. Lord, Ritvo and Solnit (1978) studied the responses of analysands whose analysts had died when they were in treatment.

> In this study, certain analysands with a definite sense of their analyst as a real person also gave the clearest evidence of a full-blown transference relationship and the most intensely felt mourning. When a transference-real person balance did not exist, however, mourning evidently did not occur. That is, when the analyst was experienced to an exaggerated extent as a transference object, the transference reaction dominated the analytic situation and interfered with grieving. At the other end of the spectrum, no mourning was reported in several instances in which the analyst's behaviour discouraged or masked transference reactions. (p. 195)

Before the 1980s, classical analysts focused almost exclusively on the patient when considering the process of ending. Balint (1950), who wrote of the analyst's experience in ending, was a rare exception. As noted before, Interpersonal analysts (Levenson 1978), by contrast, had always attended to the patient, the analyst and factors in the external world that impinged on the patient – in the analysis itself as well as the ending. In the last three decades, with an appreciation of the two-person nature of the process, analysts of almost all theoretical persuasions increasingly address their own experiences in analysis – specifically their own reactions in ending analyses with their patients (Mitchell 1993; Novick 1997; Orgel 2000). Relational analysts described the ending as co-created to suit the specificity of each patient–analyst dyad (Hoffman 1998; Salberg 2010b), giving an even greater weighting to the influence of the analyst.

Time, transference and the need for an ending

In analysis, time is not linear in the usual sense. The past is alive in the present. Schlesinger (2005), as previously noted, stated that there are many beginnings and endings during the work that anticipate the final ending and that serve as a partial working through of the feelings that are aroused. Analysis is intended to be time-limited, but in a certain way, once begun, time is suspended as the past comes to life and the analysand re-experiences a younger self. When analysands emerge from reworking conflicts and struggle with greater affect regulation and they feel ready to end, they not only revive experiences of earlier separations, they also may become anxious about future losses. Termination may arouse anxieties about death (Hoffman 1998; Bonvitz 2007), which can lead both patient and analyst to avoid facing a termination.

Even so, patients have the expectation that their analysis will eventually end. 'Emotional investments shift more and more toward life and relationships outside the analysis' (Orgel 2000). An ability to choose, 'to transfer the transference', develops (Ferraro and Garella 1997: 27), not simply new defences. 'If the feelings of mutual abandonment can be analyzed, and the relationship rather than the object is internalized, what results at the end of analysis is emancipation, but to a certain extent this emancipation is always only partial' (Loewald 1973: 15).

Layton (2010) expressed concern that these views of autonomy are 'cultural pathologizing of dependency and undervaluing of attachment' (p. 192) that 'perpetuate a lonely and omnipotent version of autonomy' (p. 201). Like Kohut (1971), she thinks North American psychoanalysts tend to deny and underestimate the extent of our mutual dependency. From this perspective, endings necessarily involve intense and painful grief. For Schafer (2007), termination is one of life's 'tragic knots', since it involves losing one of the most special relationships a person has ever had, while simultaneously recognizing that prolonging it is not realistic or productive.

Bergmann (1997) sounded a sobering and pessimistic note when he stated that, for many patients, transference love in analysis is the best love relationship that they have ever known. It is the best because it includes the potential for fantasy and idealization and because the analyst makes fewer demands than people in real life and asks for no reciprocity. So why would they ever want it to end?

Relational analysts Hoffman (1998) and Mitchell (1993) emphasized that the analytic relationship should not become a substitute for real life. Hoffman wrote that a developmental step could not occur without an actual ending; he saw avoiding such a step as avoiding facing one's mortality. Mitchell pointed out that 'ending is necessary if analysis is not to become a static alternative to a fully lived life' (p. 229).

More recently, some Relational analysts have expressed a concern that their more personal way of working may make endings more difficult. In descriptions of clinical work, both Glennon (2010) and Bass (2009) have raised the issue that patient–analyst relationships could potentially be experienced as satisfying enough to substitute for ones in real life. To quote Glennon: the 'glue or stickiness of the libido is firmer, more difficult to break loose from if the analyst allows himself or herself to be a real person known well beyond the transference and therefore more susceptible to being healthfully loved and missed as a unique individual' (p. 264).

While in certain ways analysands have almost always perceived their analyst as an actual Other, and not just as a transference figure, Relational analysts have been raising a concern about conscious and extensive self-disclosure as complicating the process of ending. Which of us has not had analysands who expressed the wish that afterwards they could be our friends or even lovers? Transference occurs all the time in life, not just in treatment, but analysis fosters conditions in which it can be understood. When more is known about the person of the analyst, does this make it easier or harder to sort out transference? 'Knowing' someone in the context of an analytic relationship is different from knowing him or her in the context of life. The data on which this book is based provides many examples with which to consider such issues.

Bergmann (1997) offered the same warning: if disillusionment is not confronted, the treatment may never end. While some patients required this continual engagement, he maintained that the question of an iatrogenically created dependency could not be ignored. The subject could not be sufficiently addressed in this present project, since the former analysands had all terminated (though some had returned or begun another treatment). A number of them reported having had to struggle with their analyst in order to stop. Sometimes interminable analysis may reflect the analyst's needs as much as the analysand's; sometimes, more.

Early in the history of psychoanalysis, Freud recognized that 'no psychoanalyst goes further than his own complexes and internal resistances permit' (1910: 145). Decades later, in 'Analysis Terminable and Interminable' (1937: 248–49), he stated that 'the special conditions of analytic work do actually cause the analyst's own defects to interfere' and recommended that analysis become 'an interminable task' for those who engage in analytic work. Freud proposed that analysts return for more analysis approximately every five years.

Most contemporary analysts, attuned to issues of intersubjectivity regardless of their particular theoretical orientation, are aware of the effect on their patients of their own psychic organization and internal conflicts (De Simone Gaburri 1985; Mitchell 1993; Kantrowitz 1996; Novick 1997). Termination revives the analyst's own inevitable wounds that accrue through the course of development.

> For the analyst, the pleasures and rewards of each termination are also accompanied by a revived necessity to face again the wounds inflicted by the developmental calamities of his or her own childhood – those we abbreviate as the loss of the primary object, loss of its love, oedipal defeat, castration, superego criticism, or awareness of death. (Orgel 2000: 732)

Davies (2005), who holds a dissociation-based model of the mind, believes there are multiplicities of endings between the self-states of the patient and analyst, which stem from different developmental traumas, conflicts and experiential meanings. She maintains that the way analysis ends affects the way it is remembered over time by the patient. Although most classical analysts have not stated this latter view explicitly, they also seemed to think that the ending significantly affected the analysand's view of the analysis. They agreed that what occurred during termination varied from patient to patient and was primarily dependent on the individual analysand's particular difficulties (Novick 1982; Blum 1989; De Berenstein and De Fondevila 1989; Hoffman 1998; Gabbard 2009; Salberg 2010a).

Confronting idealized assumptions

As we have seen, ideas about the ending of analysis have changed since the early days of psychoanalysis. A satisfactory ending is less likely to depend on the attainment of specific criteria. Nonetheless, it seems that approximately every decade some analyst raises concerns about generalizations and idealizations in relation to termination. In 1965 Ekstein wrote (p. 242):

> Many therapists are of the opinion that termination occurs when the goals of therapy have been met. For these therapists, termination is viewed as having an ideal final conclusion. However, others argue that termination should be thought of as a process that takes into account where the patient is and where he is going rather than just a fixed ending point.

Research data over the last fifty years have shown that not only is the transference neurosis not completely resolved when an analysis ends but that it is easily revived after termination (Pfeffer 1961, 1963; Schlessinger and Robbins 1974, 1975; Oremland, Blacker and Norman 1975; Norman et al. 1976). When analyses were successful, the solutions to the transference conflicts reached in the analysis were also repeated. At the same time, separation was more often seen as a developmental issue, which had been revived in termination, than as an opportunity to work through loss and mourn and internalize the analytic relationship (Klein 1950; Loewald 1962; Stewart 1963; Ekstein 1965; Firestein 1974; Dewald 1982; Rangell 1982; Pedder 1988; Frank 1999). It became increasingly common to view analyses as inevitably incomplete as a result of life factors as well as psychological ones (Wallerstein 1986).

Analysts with many different theoretical orientations now seem to agree that analysis *is* interminable. For example, Britton, a modern Kleinian, wrote (2010) that people have a primitive, archaic unconscious layer which remains after analysis ends. There is a continuous, lifelong cycle of fears that accompany integration and fears accompanying disintegration. Through internalizing the good experience they have had with the analyst, analysis enables analysands to feel hopeful and self-confident that recovery from fear and regaining stability is possible. I would add that this is no small achievement.

***

In 1974, Firestein reviewed the psychoanalytic literature on termination. From approximately thirty papers, he summarized the metapsychological and clinical criteria for deciding to terminate analysis:

> Symptoms have been traced to their genetic conflicts, in the course of which the infantile neurosis has been identified, as the infantile amnesia was undone. All symptoms have been eliminated, mitigated, or made tolerable. Object relations, freed of transference distortions, have improved along with the level of psychosexual functioning. The latter attaining 'full genitality.' Penis envy and castration anxiety have been mastered. The ego is strengthened by virtue of diminishing counter-cathectic formations. The ability to distinguish between fantasy and reality has been sharpened. Acting out has been eliminated. The capacity to tolerate some measure of anxiety and to reduce other unpleasant affects to signal quantities has improved. The ability to tolerate delay of gratification is increased, and along with it there is a shift from autoplastic to alloplastic conflict solutions. Sublimations have been strengthened, and the capacity to experience pleasure without guilt or other notable inhibiting factors has improved. Working ability, under which so many aspects of ego function, libidinal and aggressive drive gratifications are subsumed, has improved. (pp. 226–27)

Not only are these criteria idealized, but the way in which we conceptualize analysis and its ending has dramatically changed since this summary was published. It should be noted that, even forty years ago, these ideas did not represent the thinking of many contemporary analysts. Less than a decade after the summary above, Firestein (1982) published the results of a survey based on questions about termination posed to 12 New York analysts, each with more than thirty years of experience.

Most of these analysts cited improvement in relation to the patient's initial presenting problem as the primary criterion for initiating a termination process. They did not believe in a 'total cure'. Rather, along with a diminishing of symptoms, they looked for intrapsychic structural change, improved adaptation, better ways of coping with their problems and more satisfying object relations. It was assumed that instinctual wishes and conflicts remained, but that patients showed an improved balance between wishes, prohibitions from the superego and defences, especially a lessening of 'archaic and sadistic' aspects of the superego (p. 486).

While the state of the transference neurosis was central in assessing the readiness to end analysis, there was agreement among these analysts that the transference neurosis was not fully resolved during the course of treatment.

Some analysts stated that they assumed that the resolution would occur in the post-analysis phase. Given that the literature supported the position that ending an analysis should be a mutual decision, Firestein was surprised at the frequency with which analysts introduced the idea of ending.

The analysts in Firestein's survey were unanimous in their belief that their style did not differ during the termination phase. But they noted that patients' affects in this last period showed great variability, with both progressive and regressive trends. Some patients were mourning or angry; others were 'buoyant and optimistic'. This observation is important, since, as previously indicated, the literature had suggested that active grief and mourning were to be expected in the last phase of treatment.

Quinodoz (1993) offered clinical descriptions of buoyancy and elation in the last phase of analysis, as analysands finally felt capable of ' flying' on their own. His case reports support this earlier observation. The data on which this book is based also supports the variability of affect responses in endings. As we will see in the following chapter, not all patients are in a state of grief during termination.

At the other end of the spectrum, some analyses might not be able to terminate. As we noted earlier, Freud (1937) believed that some patients were constitutionally or functionally unable to sufficiently modify the intensity of the instincts with reliable ego-syntonic control. Although contemporary analysts would not frame the issue of interminability around the strength of instincts, many would agree that constitutional and/or developmental experiences, such as trauma, might leave a person unable to function independently. In contrast, continued supportive contact with one's analyst may enable such an individual to make a relatively successful adaptation to life.

Post-analytic contact

According to Firestein's survey (1982), attitudes about post-analytic contact also varied. Some analysts did not suggest that departing patients could contact them in the future; others offered this option on a case-by-case basis. A few analysts commented that at some point they had seen almost all their former analysands in consultation. Again, this is a noteworthy finding, since at the time it had been assumed that if a patient returned for additional treatment, it indicated either that the analysis was incomplete or that the renewed contact might interfere with its internalization. As a result, post-analytic returns had been discouraged (Schachter 1992).

However, even over 60 years ago, some analysts had had a different perspective on this issue. Buxbaum (1950) and Reich (1950) believed there were benefits in returning to one's former analyst. Schachter (1992) actively advocated periodic post-analytic contact as likely to enhance the continuation of both analytic gains and self-analytic work. In his view, this contact also enabled the analyst to better evaluate the previous analytic work and the patient to experience the analyst's continued interest in his or her well-being.

Data on post-analytic contact has been limited. Hartlaub, Martin and Rhine (1986) reported the findings from a survey of former analysands three years after termination. Two-thirds of the sample reporting 'successful analyses' initiated contact to rework termination issues. This contact served to continue de-idealization of the analyst, reactivate the self-analytic function or restructure the self–object representation. The restructuring included reporting significant accomplishments to the analyst and having him or her acknowledge these gains. In a more recent systematic survey, Roose *et al.* (2004) reported that 40 per cent of former analysands returned to see their analysts. Of those returning, 35 per cent came for a single office visit, 55 per cent had extended consultations or began psychotherapy, and 5 per cent resumed analysis.

As indicated in the earlier discussion about grief in ending, there had been agreement in the literature that termination for non-analysts was different from analytic candidates. Candidates were expected to have ongoing contact with their former analyst in the course of their professional lives (Limentani 1982). Sometimes the analytic relationship transformed into a friendship or a working relationship (Reich 1950). Buxbaum (1950) thought it usually took about a year for this shift in the relationship to feel comfortable. As previously stated, it had been assumed that since analysts-in-training had at least the possibility of future contact, they might be less able to appreciate the mourning their own patients experience at termination (Milner 1950; Novick 1997). But as also previously stated, Craige's study (2002) of analytic candidates' post-treatment grief contradicted this assumption.

Craige was also concerned that having regular contact with the former analyst could stimulate and reactivate the transference for the future analyst without providing a professional outlet to process the feelings. Levine and Yanof (2004) echoed this concern with data from a small anecdotal study. They noted how highly idiosyncratic post-analytic contacts tended to be: 'One size does not fit all' (p. 876). In Chapter 4 on post-analytic contacts, I discuss this topic at length and provide illustrations of both the positive and negative effects of these later contacts.

In an IPA panel on training (Quinodoz and Rocha Barros 2000), both Gibeault and Gomberoff observed that the particular problem in termination for training analyses was that the analysand-candidate and the analyst might collude in mutual idealization of each other and of the process of analysis. If these issues were not worked through, they could lead, after termination, to a shattering disillusionment as well as an inability to accept either personal limitations or the limitations of analysis (Quinodoz 1993). The implications were that, without the opportunity to reintegrate these reactions in an analytic setting, there could be serious repercussions for both the individual and the institute culture.

Writing in 1989, Blum again reminded analysts of the limitations of analysis and termination:

> The ideal of a complete analysis was championed by Ferenczi for future analysts, 'on whom the fate of so many others depends'. (1927: 84)

Therapeutic zeal found reason, and in degree, rationalization. Termination after thorough analysis was fused with a latent myth of complete analysis. (p. 282)

Disappointment and disillusionment are essentially universal, with rational and irrational sources. Analysts have repeatedly echoed Freud's caution about analytic outcome. There are the inherent real limitations of the patient, analyst, and the analytic process. (p. 287)

It became clear that there were some patients for whom the presence of the analyst and the continuation of treatment [were] the condition[s] for their adaptation or stability. Analysis could even become a way of life. (p. 288)

Many analyses are ended because of diminishing or vanishing returns, or the lack of new or enduring insight. (p. 289)

Analytic exploration, however, remain[s] essentially unlimited and interminable; we never reach the promised land. (p. 293)

Less than a decade after Blum, Golland (1997) took issue with the assumptions Freud had made about termination in his chess metaphor (1913). He wrote (pp. 259–60):

From the time of the end game metaphor until recently, the relative absence of study may have led to a sense that termination might, indeed, follow the metaphor. A few definable principles and variations would be available, as was seemingly true of analytic beginnings. Terminations would evolve, naturally, from properly conducted analyses; the phase would proceed from a mutually agreed-upon date and would include regression, reactivation of symptom complexes and a mourning process; the technique would be a continuation of transference and resistance analysis, especially regarding reactions to the fact of impending termination, with the only essential difference being the analyst's agreement to the actual date of ending. ... Despite the growing literature, which includes many warnings against a simplified view of termination, an idealized and simplistic view is, nonetheless, seen by some to obtain in practice.

Garcia-Lawson and Lane (1997) also cited the problem of generalized assumptions about termination.

While there has been an increasing acknowledgement that no clear criteria exist about how or when to end analysis (De Simone Gaburri 1985), the search for guidelines leads many analysts to treat observations and theories generated in specific treatments as if they could be applied to all treatments. These ideas persist, although it is now known that many analyses are interrupted and many patients return (Firestein 1974; Hartlaub, Martin and Rhine 1986; Gabbard 2009;

Pulver, panel 2012). The myths, nonetheless, continue to have a powerful impact on many analysts – on what they believe, how they practise and what they teach.

Even though in the mid to late 1990s analysts were writing about the diversity of material that occurred in ending analyses, analysts simultaneously continued to be taught and write about stereotyped, idealized processes. For example, Fonagy (1998) quoted the literature as if it were a fact: [An] '*inevitable* [my italics] part of ending is disillusionment with having achieved the ideal (Pedder 1988), and the loss of the object who has been the receptacle for projections (Steiner 1994)'.

Burland (1997), while reviewing case summaries written by 450 applicants for certification by the American Psychoanalytic Association, found that, despite variations in the way the analyses were conducted, the descriptions of each analysand's treatment experience were remarkably alike. They relived their past in the present; they had a similar range of affects that they struggled with in similar ways; they reported the process as healing.

Spence (1998: 643) wondered

> whether this concordance may stem from each candidate's need to appear normative and unexceptional and to generate an account that would maximize his or her chance of being certified. This kind of clinical summary would seem to be the likely outcome of conscious and preconscious narrative smoothing.

Over ten years after the volume of *Psychoanalytic Psychology* on termination (1997), in which articles by Golland, Novick, Bergmann, Garcia-Lawson and others warned about idealized assumptions in relation to analysis and ideas about the way it 'should end', Gabbard (2009) still believed it was important to urge caution about myths created around termination of analysis. He described the necessity to 'unlearn' things he was taught, such as, the emphasis on interpretative resolution of the transference neurosis to the exclusion of other kinds of interventions, the importance that all symptoms be gone before ending, the termination phase should last approximately one month for each year of analysis, a patient's wish to terminate always meant a resistance and should be treated as such, analysts were capable of being 'clear and objective' about when a patient was ready to terminate (pp. 578–79).

Gabbard wrote:

> Psychoanalysis, as a discipline, is about the idiosyncratic, the unique, and the overdetermined. It does not lend itself to reductionistic, etiological formulations or generic technical approaches. (2009: 580)

> Because of the anxieties about ending the treatment, we analysts are always in danger of selectively focusing on only one aspect of the patient, rather than holding the complexity. (p. 284)

Perhaps an idealization of grief and mourning haunts us as part of our exaggerated expectations of termination. (p. 284)

Working through the depressive position is a lifelong task. (p. 284)

[T]ransference is not destroyed or 'resolved'. (p. 284)

And Westen and Gabbard (2002):

Structural change in psychoanalytic treatment does not involve the total destruction of old object relationships that fuel the transference. Neural networks cannot be destroyed. They can only be superseded by the strengthening of new models of relatedness that merge in analysis such that old object relations are relatively weakened. (p. 586)

[E]ach patient must do analysis in the way that he or she must do it. Patients cannot avoid enacting an internal object relations' scenario that is revealing of who they are. We cannot legislate in advance how termination should unfold. (p. 589)

There are multiple scenarios that are 'good enough.' We must maintain humility about what we know and what we can achieve while respecting the idea that the patient may know better. (p. 591)

This discrepancy between idealized expectations and assumptions about termination as summarized in the literature and clinicians' descriptions of their actual experiences with patients was the stimulus for my project. What also needs to be highlighted, however, is that in the years after Firestein's summary (1974), the literature itself presented the striking contradictory stands that I have described. I will illustrate many of these contradictory positions in the chapters that follow.

Note

1 Symptom relief and the ability to make the unconscious conscious also remained accepted criteria for ending.

Chapter 2

Developments in the ending of psychoanalysis

Insight, loss and mourning

How do analyses end? Analysands who are not themselves clinicians are unlikely to be thinking about theory when they reflect on their analytic experiences. Clinicians who are not analysts may have theories about what occurred, but these ideas will be limited to their own experiences as patients and what they have read and been taught. Although analysts have also been analysands, with rare exceptions (Little 1981; Craige 2002; Frank 2009) their reports about analytic endings come from the standpoint of being the analyst, not the patient. We do not have much information on analysands' perspectives on this topic, though, as I indicated in the first chapter, some attempts to represent their views have become more frequent in recent years (Kantrowitz, Katz and Paolitto 1990a, b, c; Craige 2002; Tessman 2003).

With our increased awareness of the influence of our own subjectivity on our beliefs and perceptions, it would be hard to imagine that analysts' experience of their own analyses would not play a central role in how they theorize about analysis and its ending. Theories are personal (Spezzano 1998; Kantrowitz 2003); we believe in a phenomenon because we have personal experience of it – our patients', but especially our own. We have small samples, and since our perceptions are inevitably subjective, they are also inevitably skewed. The interview material I will present is based on patients' reflections about their analytic experiences. The accounts are intended to redress the tilt in our analytic literature, which has privileged analysts' perspectives. From these analysands' accounts, I hope to provide a way to think about endings that helps to free us from mythmaking (Gabbard 2009). In this chapter, I will focus primarily on ideas around separation, loss and mourning.

As previously stated, many analysts see mourning as a central part of ending. Analysands are expected to feel grief acutely when ending a deep, and often long, process of exploration of vicissitudes in themselves as well as their interactions with others. Leaving an analyst who has been both a central figure in the interaction and a companion in this process is, for many patients, very painful. Mourning relates to this loss and to the relinquishing of fantasies of omnipotence and omniscience about oneself and one's analyst and about what analysis itself can offer (Freud 1937; Milner 1965; Grinberg 1980; Novick 1982; Dewald 1982;

Moraitis 2009). According to Schlesinger (2005), mourning occurs throughout analysis; its culmination has been assumed to occur in termination, when the analysand comes to accept what he or she cannot have or be. Mourning in termination has been viewed as essential in order to gradually replace the loss of the object – the analyst – with an internalization of the analytic process and a changed self-representation (Loewald 1962). Mourning is also about the loss of the analytic relationship itself – all that the analyst represents in the transference and also the 'real' relationship (Blum 1989).

As indicated in the first chapter, some writers (Milner 1965; Novick 1982, 1997) believe that analysts cannot appreciate their patients' grief in ending because they don't have this experience themselves: after their own analyses are concluded, they have continued contact with their analysts in their analytic communities. One specific question, therefore, is whether and how experiences of grief in termination are different for analytic candidates and analysts than for analysands who are not clinicians and, therefore, unlikely to see their analysts again. Using the interview material from the 82 men and women who volunteered to discuss their experiences in ending their analyses, I will address this issue as well as the more general issue of the role grief plays in ending.

I remind the reader that the material I will present comes from a population of psychologically sophisticated people, almost all of whom have advanced educational or professional degrees. Of these, 43 were analysts or analytic candidates; 21 were clinicians, who had not been trained as analysts; and 18 were not connected with psychoanalysis or clinical work. The latter 39 subjects were unlikely to see their analysts again unless they made an appointment to return as a patient. My interviews provide data about the experiences of grief and mourning that allows us to compare those who are likely to continue to see their former analyst in non-clinical settings – that is, professionally or socially – and those who are not.

My sample of 82 is relatively large for psychoanalytic research. Because it is made up of volunteers, it has many limitations, some of which I referred to in the Introduction and will elaborate on later. But I do not believe that these limitations interfere with the point I want to make about many of the myths and generalizations that have characterized psychoanalytic lore.

In the context of presenting my overall findings, I will offer highlights from the literature, cited in the previous chapter, about characteristics of analytic endings. The issues of idealization, generalization and contradictions will be juxtaposed with my data about specific experiences of separation, grief and mourning presented in these interviews.

Freud (1913) initially thought of the ending of analysis as an automatic final phase, as in a chess game. Later (1937), he wrote of the inevitable limitations of analysis and its interminability. He had become aware that some issues were not likely to be resolved in treatment and that, for analysts, many issues might be re-stimulated by their work with patients. Conflicts that were dormant could not be ignited, so future treatment would often be necessary. The analysands in my study reported sufficiently diverse experiences in the last phases that there is no way in which terminations can be viewed as 'automatic'. Many of them returned for more treatment.

Freud's later appreciation that conflicts remained only partially resolved in analysis and can be rekindled is confirmed by follow-up studies (Pfeffer 1961, 1963; Schlessinger and Robbins 1974, 1975; Oremland, Blacker and Norman 1975; Norman *et al.* 1976). Life experiences as well as residual psychological issues contribute to this inevitable incompleteness (Wallerstein 1986). The analysands in this study presented corroborating material.

Glover (1955) viewed the end period as a time to analyse the transference neurosis; and, he believed, if this did not occur the analysis would be incomplete. Similarly, Bird (1972) and Cooper (2009) considered termination as a time when a new and important aspect of transference might emerge. The data I will present challenges an assumption in the literature that there is *always* change in ending.

While many of the analysands in this project described working in the transference and the centrality of a focus on analyst–patient interactions during termination, this was not the experience of the majority. Most of the participants reported a change in the period of the termination phase, but a change in the transference was only one kind of change. No one pattern characterizes the ending, and no one variable accounts for the changes the analysands believe occurred. Of the 82 former analysands, 66 reported changes during the termination as a result of ending itself. They highlighted the end phase of treatment as seminal to their sense of the total analytic enterprise.

The 16 analysands who did not report a change in the ending phase reported that termination was continuous with the rest of the analytic process. For these individuals, the termination phase may have been primarily a time for working through and synthesizing what had occurred during analysis (Greenson 1965; Ekstein 1965; Bird 1972). A relatively small number of former analysands referred to the reoccurrence of symptoms in the termination phase (Firestein 1974).

Many analysts believed that a capacity for self-analysis would develop as a result of the analytic process and that this capacity became a criterion for ending (Hoffer 1950; Gaskill 1980; Schlessinger and Robbins 1983; Kantrowitz, Katz and Paolitto 1990b; Bergmann 2005). Self-analysis is a concept that needs to be defined in order to be clear what we mean. It may be thought of as entailing very specific functions, or viewed in a more global way as any self-reflection that achieves some perspective on oneself.

In my study, most of the analysands had some ability to step back and look at what had occurred during the ending of their analysis, as well as some ability to assess the effect of analysis on them, but only a relatively small number demonstrated what is known as a 'self-analytic function' in the more restrictive sense of this term. I will discuss this material and explore the concept of self-analysis in Chapter 5. The interviews supported the view that the analytic process continues long after analysis ends; it is not just confined to the consolidation that is expected to occur in the year after its conclusion (Schlessinger and Robbins 1974; Firestein 1974).

Conflicts around ending were not only intrapsychic ones involving wishes to remain and to leave (Orgel 2000). Many of the struggles were expressed in interpersonal conflict with the analyst. Sometimes this appeared to be an externalization of one part of the self, but often the accounts seemed to describe a struggle with the person of the analyst. Contrary to expectations, it was often the analyst – rather than the analysand – who was described as resisting ending. The analyst, of course, might recount a different view of the ending. The idea, described by Hoffman (1998) and Bonvitz (2007), that termination could arouse anxieties about death, which might lead both patient and analyst to avoid facing ending, seems plausible. But only one of the analysands in my study expressed this as a factor or was conscious of it contributing to a delay in concluding analytic work.

As stated earlier, the role of mourning has retained its centrality in the process of ending an analytic experience (Reich 1950; Balint 1950; Loewald 1962; Grinberg 1980; Dewald 1982; Cancrini 1988; Pedder 1988; Orgel 2000). The distinction between mourning the analyst as a transference figure (Granair, panel 1975) and as a person with whom one has relationship in the process of analysis (DeBell, panel 1975) has drawn much attention in recent years. As stated in Chapter 1, Relational analysts such as Mitchell (1993), Hoffman (1998), Bass (2009) and Glennon (2010) have expressed concerns that the 'realness' and active 'relatedness' of the analyst as a person can be so central in the process that it could make it harder to end analysis and transfer these attachments to figures in the outside world (Ferraro and Garella 1997; Orgel 2000). And as I noted earlier, because for some patients the analytic relationship may be the most satisfying relationship they have ever known, they are reluctant to end (Bergmann 2010).

Given these concerns, it is noteworthy that in this sample there were relatively few examples in which the person of the analyst was the focus of loss. That is not to say that the personal qualities of the analyst were not important. Many in this group expressed strong feelings of appreciation and attachment to their analyst; but the positive aspects were a focus for far fewer than would have been expected. Rather, it was the negative qualities that received more attention. Whether these perceptions of negative qualities actually characterized the analyst or were primarily influenced by transference was not often something I could assess. As will be discussed later, strong unresolved affect in relation to analysis, and especially its ending, seemed a frequent motivation for volunteering to participate in this study.

As noted previously, it would be assumed from the literature (Milner 1950; Novick 1982, 1997) that analysands who were in the analytic field would experience less grief on ending. The assumption was not borne out in the reports from this sample. The grief in ending seemed no different for analysands who were themselves analysts and who would see their analysts later in the context of their profession than it was for clinicians who might or might not see their analysts at conferences or for non-clinicians who were unlikely to see their analysts again unless they returned to the consulting room. The intensity of grieving, like everything else, seemed related to the personal issues and histories of each individual and the interaction with the particular analyst.

There were considerable differences between the ways the former analysands in my study worked through loss, mourned and internalized the analytic relationship compared to the expectations described in the literature (Klein 1950; Loewald 1962; Stewart 1963; Ekstein 1965; Firestein 1982; Dewald 1982; Rangell 1982; Pedder 1988; Frank 1999). The range of experiences, the variability in depth and intensity, and the extent of resolution was vast. The discrepancies between the ideal and the actual are best appreciated when reading the analysands' experiences in their own words.

As described in the Introduction, the material I will present was gathered in telephone interviews of one to two hours in length from volunteers who responded to posted notices about the project or calls from others who had participated. None of the participants was my patient; I knew only two of the volunteers prior to the interview. My knowledge of the participants was, therefore, very limited. While talking about termination inevitably meant talking about their analyses in a more complete fashion, I would not presume to make inferences or interpret their experiences. I am presenting ideas about change as they have described them. Since many of the interviewees are themselves analysts or in other ways analytically informed, they used analytic terms. In all that I write, regardless of whether the material is in direct quotes, I am using the language that they applied about themselves.

While the analysands' accounts make it clear that no single variable accounted for the changes they believe occurred, most of them said that the ending brought about a new insight or an affect they viewed as important to their understanding of themselves. The majority described a complex revival of conflict and affect-laden experiences from different developmental phases, which could not be meaningfully limited to any single descriptor of change.

In earlier eras, Oedipal issues were thought to be the central problem to be resolved (Weigert 1952; Gilman 1982). I think most contemporary analysts believe that all developmental phases contribute to transference. Some specify that this is most apparent during termination (Schubert 2000). When the analysands in my study described their own transference experience, they tended to emphasize the role a specific developmental phase played in their analysis. It is unlikely that this emphasis meant they were unaware of other developmental factors that had come up during treatment – rather it suggests that they were viewing their experience from the perspective of their greatest perceived conflict or vulnerability.

I have organized their responses into broad categories based on the emphasis each person gave it. As you will see, the examples rarely illustrate only one issue. Since I asked each interviewee to describe his or her experience in an open-ended way, and did not ask about the presence or absence of any particular element, it is possible that many others would have stated that they too had, for example, a particular insight or change of affect, became aware of separation issues or experienced a recovered memory during termination. But if an interviewee did not bring up something spontaneously, I did not inquire, not wanting to lead or skew what he or she was reporting. Thus the reader should be aware that when I state a specific number of people reported material that belongs to a particular category, this might underestimate the actual number. In each category I will give material that best illustrates the changes that were reported.

Most, but far from all, changes occurred in a positive direction. Changes can be categorized as: (1) Recovered memory (reported by 2 people); (2) New insights discovered in the transference (reported by 20 people); (3) Recognition of separation issues (reported by 5 people); (4) Reworking conflicts through the analytic relationship (reported by 2 people); (5) Transference moved from displacement to the analyst (reported by 2 people); (6) Enactments (reported by 10 people); (7) Change in affect, new or recovered (reported by 37 people): anger, disappointment, and joy; (8) Grief and mourning (reported by most individuals as occurring at some point in analysis, most often in the ending). I will offer a few examples in each category to illustrate how these analysands think about their analytic work and what has brought it to a close.

1. Recovered memory

Knowing that analysis is ending creates an internal pressure that may bring previously repressed material to consciousness. Two former analysands reported the experience of recovered memory. One of them, FB, explained that she had suffered from sexual inhibition and had sought analysis because she felt helplessly controlled and demeaned in her marriage. During the termination phase, she believed that the imminent separation from her analyst and the safety of their relationship was the stimulus for recovering a memory linked to an earlier, unsafe experience when she was separated from her parents: While spending time at her grandparents' home, she was sexually abused by the gardener. The recovery of this memory allowed her and her analyst to better understand her sexual difficulties and her unfulfilling marital relationship. FB ended her analysis 31 years ago.

***

Insights about oneself rarely come from just one source or just one experience, even though some individuals may feel as if they do. Some analysands perceive new recognitions in their outside lives. Others make the discovery first within the treatment. For most people, however, new forms of self-understanding come gradually: There is a slow, almost imperceptible difference in the quality of relationships, modulation or availability of affect. I have organized the material around whatever factor seemed pivotal for the analysand.

2. Insights discovered in the transference

The participants in my study reported having two different kinds of insights about themselves during the termination phase. One was insight through a relived affectively powerful experience repeated from the past, which they understood differently when they connected it with their current experience in the transference. Obviously, the content of that experience depended on the nature of each person's particular conflicts, personalities and histories. Other analysands reported an insight about their separateness in relation to the analyst – a heightened recognition that the analytic pair involves two people with separate minds, subjectivities and experiences. These analysands perceived that this was a new development, not a repetition newly understood.

Twenty former analysands provided examples of reliving a past experience in the transference. I will describe three that illustrate conflicts organized around different developmental levels.

During the last phase of analysis, BK learned, 'but not from his disclosure', that her analyst was divorced. Through her belief that she needed to take care of him, she gained a new perspective on how she had felt she needed to take care of her father.

> Once we set a date for ending treatment, my feeling toward my analyst changed. In the course of termination phase, I learned he was divorced, but not from his disclosure. He and his family live in our neighborhood, but I was oblivious to the changes in their lives. During that phase of treatment, I worried what would happen to him. I was amazed he'd kept it contained from me. I had the fantasy I'd stay in treatment and take care of him, that I could bring joy to his life. Maybe this wasn't just a fantasy. He was the one to suggest I bring my infant daughter to analysis. I never would have asked. I think it was a joy to him to have a child there as he was separated from living with his children.
>
> This care-taking role was one I had assumed in my own life. I had to come to see that he was a grown man who could take care of himself. It wasn't erotic, but he replayed how I had felt I was an intellectual partner with my father, also a physician, in a way I thought my mother wasn't. It was a whole new experience to see I had a transference, something I couldn't identify in the years of analysis before the end phase. I realized then how my father expected me to take care of him and how my analyst didn't expect that. I was trying to be a good girl and was not clear what I wanted from my life. I didn't realize I had a choice about what I wanted for myself. It was eye-opening for me.

BK ended her analysis seven months before this interview.

TJ decided to end her treatment seven months before this interview. Once she made the decision to terminate, she discovered in the transference the ways in which she was caught in a mesh of hostile dependency that had existed in her relationship with her parents. She had believed she had to be pleasing to both her parents, whom she described as very controlling. She viewed her analyst as respectful and flexible, helping her to analyse and not idealize her. She went through feelings of disappointment in her analyst and in analysis during the termination phase, as she confronted their limitations.

> My analyst would let me go on and on about my anger in a diatribe … and I was distressed that my relationship with my mother was not improved and I was still anxious. I was seeing my analyst as another woman who needed me in inappropriate ways and would exploit me.

The recognition that TJ was turning ordinary disappointment about what analysis had failed to accomplish into a perception of her analyst as controlling and destructive allowed her to understand the manner in which she had separated from her mother and father. Her realization that she viewed her analyst as she had perceived her parents enabled her to restore her appreciation of her analyst. TJ then no longer saw her analyst as needing TJ to either idealize her or remain in treatment. I do not know whether this altered her view of her parents. I wish I had asked. Her termination occurred one year ago.

AI had completed an earlier analysis. Ten years later, in a conflict about having a career as a writer versus starting analytic training, she sought analysis again with a different analyst (because she was in a new geographic location). After about six or seven years into her second analysis, she started talking about wishing to terminate in a year and a half. Two months before the intended end, her analyst questioned whether she would be short-changing herself if she were to stop. On further reflection, AI agreed and continued for two and half more years.

> I felt like I'd been in analysis forever. I was concerned about the cost. I wanted to live my life more independently. I'd finished analytic training, published a book. But then my husband developed a serious illness. I felt I'd lost the person I relied on. I became terrified of losing my analyst.
>
> These were the separation issues my analyst had suspected. I felt the depth of my dependent needs. My mother was quite narcissistic, and my role was to be big and grown up. My father valued independence. I'd felt this tremendous need to see myself as independent. I felt I'd better act as if I were. I was the oldest, expected to be good and not need anything. I saw what I had warded off and felt it.
>
> My analyst put into words what was going on. I thought he'd find my dependency as unacceptable as I did, but that didn't happen. I went through a stage of being really frightened of my dependency, fearing the relationship would blow up, but he wasn't frightened of it.
>
> Having really felt dependent on my analyst and his accepting it, I felt ready to stop and felt good about ending. I became aware I had his voice in my head and I could do self-analysis, as I hadn't been able to do before. In the last months, I felt enormous sadness, grief – I couldn't stand it. I feared I couldn't be creative without someone as interested in my work as he had been, but

then I began to feel I had that capacity in myself and I began to feel excited – how momentous this was.

I terminated. I was fine, happy, and productive. Then there were a series of crises, and I was able to test out how I could use self-analysis. I analysed dreams and could find my wishes and feelings, knowing what I was reacting to. I thought of my analyst and I felt comforted. We had talked about it being fine for me to come back and see him if I needed to, but I didn't. I did email him to let him know our work had been helpful.

I'm more formal and less self-revealing than my analyst. He was more playful and open. But, I'm much more straightforward as a result of the work with him. He wasn't perfect – he would note my difficulty in being critical or angry with him, but on more than one occasion when I tried to express critical feelings he would respond in a way that seemed to deflect them. I told him this, he heard me, and it went better subsequently. With patients, I don't like being the bad object, and I have to struggle with them not liking me, not appreciating me, with things that infuriate me or make me sad, but I can, and I see how it deepens the work.

AI ended her analysis nine months before our interview.

BK, TJ, and AI are all themselves analysts. Each of them had an insight discovered by reliving an important affective experience from the past in the transference. The conflicts, organized around different developmental stages, had persisted over time and then were revived in the transference. The discovery of their ability to separate the past from the present involved a change in their perceptions of themselves as dependent – or the denial of this aspect of themselves as bad or shameful. They varied in the extent to which they describe grief and mourning as a central part in ending analysis. Only AI characterized her grief as intense as that reported in Craige's research (2002); even so, she did not describe it as persisting after the end of analysis.

3. Recognition of separateness

YA was one of two individuals I interviewed who specifically recognized that she had been denying her separateness from other people. She had insights about this difficulty prior to the last phase of analysis, but it was in the ending that she fully accepted that her analyst was differentiated from her and had a separate, individual identity. She was then able to feel more confident, independent and affectively connected with the people in her life.

YA was in her forties and had been in analysis for 15 years. She had begun treatment because she was depressed and 'felt lost'. She was successful in her work life and had good friends, but could not admit she wanted to be close enough to anyone to spend a life together. Although she was not aware of being dependent on her analyst, she thought she would have stayed forever if he had not initiated the termination by announcing he was going to retire in two years.

The first year I ignored his announced retirement. I didn't bring it up because I was in the full swing of doctoral work. Then he started saying, 'You're not talking about ending.' His persistence in bringing up my avoidance of the separation started what might have been the most important part of analysis. I began to see how I was not dealing with dependency and loss. It threw into relief how I was relying on him as a source of approval and how I feared a loss of his approval.

But I hadn't realized this at all. It was the relationship I had had with my mother that I was working through. I fundamentally had not completely separated and individuated from her or from my analyst. I was dependent on him and I feared his judgement, but I was not fully aware of the depth of this feeling. In the termination period, I came to see that as long as I didn't know about the realities of his life, I could pretend he was all mine.

The last months I sat up for the first time in years. There were a couple of really profound sessions where he wept – saying goodbye to me and to the analytic work as a whole. I got it that he had an actual personal connection to me. I took in that I could look at him in enough of an individuated way that I could really appreciate that he was grieving for others and the work, not just for me, without feeling competitively diminished.

I had been in analysis fifteen years, and when I stopped being a patient, I experienced an incredible growth spurt. I completed my dissertation three months later. I felt grown up. I felt I could take more risks with my own patients even if they weren't happy with me in the moment. Also I was happier in my romantic relationship. I think I had more libidinal energy free for investment. My erotic feelings for my analyst had been hard to talk about. I acknowledged them but incompletely. After the termination, I think I was able to put these erotic feelings more into a relationship with another person. Ultimately, though, that relationship wasn't right for me. It was not intellectually satisfying enough, and we had other practical problems – like wanting different places to live. So recently we broke up.

I've internalized my analyst. By and large I've become my own analyst. I'm still in supervision, and I can use that for personal work too. I observe what is going on. I feel my analyst there in a background way much of the time. I recognize that on one level I experienced a narcissistic wound that he chose to go away from me. It was a hurt that I processed in the treatment, which was very important because one of my central self-representations is that I'm not worth sticking around for. From the discussions leading up to the end of the treatment, I got that the other person had his own agenda, not related to wanting to leave me.

Seeing my analyst retire and create a new life for himself was also some important modelling for me. It made clear that it's okay to do what you want to do even if other people don't like it. It was extremely hard for me to say things that were wounding or created anxiety because I wasn't separate. It affected my work with patients.

I feel much more connected with my work now. I realized I didn't feel enough excitement about this man I'd been dating. But now I feel I'm attractive and unique enough. If it doesn't work out with him, it will with another.

YA ended analysis two years before the interview.

All of the interviews presented above specifically mentioned the experience of dependency that was stimulated by the ending of analysis. Separation is part of everyone's history. The end phase of analysis inevitably revives this experience, weaving together developmental threads with insights acquired in analysis to create a tapestry of a life. When separation and individuation are the central issues in an analysand's experience, termination can be the time when he or she affectively experiences the vicissitudes of this developmental step in the transference, as was the case with YA.

4. Reworking conflicts through the analytic relationship

What distinguishes the two former analysands I am about to describe from those above is that they were intellectually aware of their dependency. They were conscious that their inability to grapple with it had prevented them from moving on with their lives and making attachments to others. But it was only in the relationship with their analyst in the termination phase that they were able to struggle with the meanings of their dependency and free themselves emotionally. They each believe that the relationship with their analyst – rather than insights about themselves – was central in facilitating their capacity to grow.

CX's analyst had died during her treatment when she was in her thirties. She is now 80. She reported that the analyst who took over her treatment believed that she had done the central work in her analysis and needed to integrate it. In this second treatment, which was less intense and less regressive, her analyst helped her master her anxiety and dependency.

I was born in 1929. My mother was told by the pediatrician not to pick me up. My mother went on a three-month cruise with her mother during my first year; my father beat me and my brothers. I was pretty but terrified all the time of being rejected. I was not outgoing. ... I had some supportive therapy in medical school, but I wanted to understand more. So later I went into analysis. My analyst was very warm and nice, but I felt totally alone on the couch and in my associations; he was very classical. It was clear to me he had angina. I didn't know if he knew it. His secretary called to say he was in the hospital; the next day it was in the paper that he died. It was a sudden occurrence, as he'd never been ill before. His widow placed all his patients with other analysts.

I told the next person I didn't think I should be on the couch. I cried about my analyst's death for a month or two, but I realized this new person was much better for me. When I think of what happened in Dr S's quiet, book-filled office, I think of the first time I entered it. I knew, before either of us had spoken, that I had found the person I needed and that I would get well. This feeling always stayed with me, and gave the work we did together great intimacy and meaning.

My therapy with Dr S was very mutual and interactive – strikingly so for the years in which it took place – the 1960s. I told this exceptionally handsome and masculine young analyst that he was 'the best mother I could possibly have had'. I believe we were able, together, to create what had been so painfully missing until then. Alongside that, there were so many other changes – much greater sexual confidence and fulfillment, career success, happiness in marriage and motherhood, and a more solid sense of myself which I could bring to each personal encounter.

As the day of termination approached, I planned carefully for our last day. Having twice demanded tearfully that it be postponed, I was finally able to help it happen. I wore my prettiest dress, which I had bought for the occasion at Ann Taylor, and took a little extra time to ensure that my hair looked its best. It felt nice being there with him; we didn't say a lot, but we were at ease. I think we both felt that we had done such good work together – the very best that we could possibly have done. It was peaceful, but very poignant and sad also. At the end of the hour, I stood up and went up to him and kissed his cheek, as I had told him I would. He leaned down so that I could reach. He looked happy, but he did not say anything. I didn't either. I remember crossing the room and then opening and closing the door gently, while he stood quietly and attentively on the other side of it. I never saw him again.

I grieved a lot for him for almost nine months. Then I began to feel happier and stronger than I ever had. Wonderful things began happening with other people, and I was aware of growing and becoming more and more the person I hoped to be. Dr. S was always present in my mind – and is even now. Although more than forty years have passed, I still write him a fairly long letter every Christmas. Over the years, he has written back about ten times – warm, friendly notes full of appreciation for my accomplishments, as well as occasional delightful anecdotes about his grandchildren. The one I treasure the most ended, 'I think of you fondly. With love, Dr S.'

CX ended her analysis 39 years ago.

AR, who is an analyst, had seen several different therapists since his early twenties. He had had trouble making lasting relationships and felt dependent on being in treatment. After seven years of analysis, AR and his analyst planned to terminate in a year. Things were going well in his life, and he wanted time and money to do other things.

I felt I got an extraordinary amount out of analysis. I'd worked through the more difficult stuff, and we had established a relationship in which we really enjoyed each other. We went back and forth flexibly between lightness and heaviness, but the last year was dominated more by lightness. I decreased by one hour, which made it less intense. I was still examining issues – feelings of loss came up – but we talked about what type of contact would be possible after we stopped working together. I think it would have been much more difficult if we didn't know we'd have the opportunity for contact through the institute after ending. He made it clear I could come back any time – and I have seen him four or five times in the last two years after ending. But it *was* an ending, and it felt wonderful to end.

It was nice to have more time, more money. I felt better than ever before about myself, my wife, my marriage, and that sense pretty much has continued. I'd been very anxious and had trouble forming a lasting relationship with a woman. I was very shame-prone and shame-ridden. I was anxious about being seen and known. That really changed. I got much more comfortable with my feelings and thoughts.

Analysis freed me up in ways that were fabulous. It was something about the relationship. What we established enabled me to grow. It was very different from my previous therapies and very different from my relationship with my father. My analyst was very affirming. He was more personally engaged and responsive. It felt like a partnership. I could challenge him, and he didn't get defensive. He could acknowledge it when I let him know I felt he was unresponsive. Now I put myself out there much more readily. I get positive feedback and that keeps me going. I reflect on myself. I share with my wife. We talk to each other and support each other.

I got much more comfortable with my dependency, I'd been counter-dependent and self-sufficient in my behaviour. My mother was intrusive and needed me to gratify her narcissistic needs. I experienced her as anxious, so I distanced myself. I had anxiety about a woman's needs as being overwhelming, smothering. I had a certain closeness with my father, but he was more remote emotionally. I was similar to him in my distancing. I know there were key insights along the way but I don't remember them.

AR ended his analysis two years ago.

Both CX and AR emphasized their conscious difficulties with separation. CX described neglect and abuse in her family, while AR reported intrusion and lack of emotional support. They both acknowledged that analysis gave them keen insights about themselves, but they believe that it was qualities within the analytic relationship – being known, being seen, the sense of being well-matched and of having a partnership – that enabled them to take a previously delayed developmental step toward more autonomy, which they had missed growing up. CX talks of her second analyst as 'less warm' than the first and 'very firm'. AR talks about being able to be 'challenging' and his analyst as being able to 'set limits'. Both seem to be saying that some central aspect of themselves was affirmed in the context of self-exploration.

AR's account of the importance of knowing he would see his analyst after ending supports the viewpoint, frequently expressed in the literature, that analysts find ending less painful because they know they will have this contact (Milner 1950; Novick 1982). Other analysands, like AI and YA, who are also analysts, described intense grief. While CX, who is not an analyst, experienced intense grief during termination, she never saw her analyst again after her treatment had ended, but did not need this continuity to feel her sense of personal independence and emotional growth. The literature is not incorrect in citing that knowing one can see one's analyst again can make ending less painful; for some analysands, it is an accurate description. As will be seen from some subsequent examples in this chapter, the error is in generalizing and saying that it applies to all.

For all the patients described above, knowing that analysis was ending pushed issues of separation and separateness into centre focus. For five of them, separating from their analyst meant discovering previously unknown aspects of themselves. For the last two it was revisiting consciously known territory and having a different, corrective experience.

According to Alexander's concept (Alexander, French *et al.* 1946) of a corrective emotional experience, the analyst should consciously try to be different from whatever was perceived as the troublesome qualities of the parent. This theory was criticized in the psychoanalytic community because of its manipulative aspect. But if the aspect of role-playing is eliminated, I think most contemporary analysts would agree that successful treatment provides a corrective emotional experience. They recognize that the analytic relationship, as well as insight about unconscious aspects of the self, gives analysis its power to transform patients' sense of self and others and change relational possibilities.

5. Transference moved from displacement to the analyst

For two participants in my study, the analytic process did not focus on the analyst. The focus remained in displacement until they decided to end analysis.[1] But once they made this decision, they experienced emotional aliveness in the room in relation to the analyst. Here is the account of displacement reported by CF, who is a lesbian in a committed relationship in analysis with a female analyst.

> The termination phase was different from other parts of the analysis because it was working toward a specific goal of ending. I had come to understand that I was in love with my mother and she was very manipulative. My father was an alcoholic. I took his place and wanted to be her partner. So I saw her as a superior person, always right, and it was my responsibility to make her happy. During the last four years of analysis I was emotionally connected to a woman at work. It didn't become physical, but she became the person where my feelings played out and got understood in analysis. My analyst and I were in a power struggle. I felt passive and fought it; I felt I needed to be in charge.

I left analysis many times. One time, within a year after leaving, I'd fallen in love with a woman who was straight and a social worker, just like my analyst. I couldn't do it directly with my analyst, so I did it that way. I returned to analysis and brought it back into the treatment.

The last phase of my analysis was more intense and challenging. I was deeply connected to my analyst, yet I was leaving voluntarily and addressing that. I had many insights during this phase related to separation. I felt that I was losing my mother forever. I'd never been able to speak honestly to her about my feelings toward her because I was afraid of losing her. So in termination, it all went to my core; my guts were turned inside out. Suffering and mourning stayed with me for a long time. In this last year, I got clear that my analyst really cared about me. I felt I could leave because we'd have that caring bond between us, and I didn't have to please her or stay.

CF, who is not an analyst, ended her analysis six months before this interview. She had understood her conflict in other personal relationships, but in the last phase of analysis she experienced it directly in relation to her analyst. Her awareness of feeling 'deeply connected' suggests that these intense feelings existed previously but had been defended against. While she reported feeling intense grief in the last phase of analysis, she did not say whether these feelings continued after ending.

6. Enactments

Ten individuals reported that, in the ending of analysis, they enacted in the transference important conflicted parts of themselves that they had not consciously understood or explored previously in either displacement or the transference. The following example comes from EO, who had begun her analysis because she recognized her anxiety about separating from her child. For years she leaned on the advice and support of her analyst in both her childrearing and her clinical work. She appreciated the way her analyst thought and also her attitude toward her work. Over the course of a ten-year analysis, she thought she had integrated her analyst's inner strength as part of herself.

Then her analyst told her that in six months she was going to move to another country and proposed they continue the analysis on the phone. EO did not feel comfortable with this arrangement and felt she was ready to terminate. The analyst did not accept this and interpreted it as resistance and a hostile step against her. After a period of weeks of telephone sessions, EO insisted on stopping.

It was a very traumatic termination. I learned a lot from it. It helped me see I was in a transference relationship with a countertransference; it was my image of my relationship with my mother all along. I saw how I was paralysed and afraid of my analyst. I did all I could do in this relationship. I saw how it was problematic and complicated – a traumatic relationship that I had had with my mother was being repeated.

At first I was traumatized and depressed. I couldn't get through it. But after a long piece of self-analysis, I saw in a clear way. I felt enlightened. I questioned my unconscious choice of her and of continuing with her for so many years. I understood that I had idealized her and that I had tried to trust her and follow her line of thought. But I couldn't anymore.

She influenced me in many ways. I learned from this. I learned how easy it is for an analyst to become domineering and how necessary it is to be mindful of this.

EO ended analysis two years ago.

When unconscious conflicts have not become conscious during analysis, the ending may sometimes push them into consciousness, as it did with EO, who lost the idealization of her analyst and felt empowered. For some other participants in this study, however, insight did not occur until long after termination. Later analysis, later contacts with the former analyst, or life itself may make analysands more aware of their conflicts. So ending itself is not always the percipient for further growth. The interviews did not provide the facts that might help me account for these differences.

7. Change in affect, new or recovered

Anger (1): Sexual boundary violations

Since the analytic method invites the patient to develop an erotic transference for the sake of self-understanding and greater freedom of desire, both the process and the patient are abused when an analyst takes advantage of this state. That desire can be stirred, that it may also be an experience of love for patient, analyst, or both – of course such feelings can occur. But it is never acceptable to act on them, nor is it possible to underestimate the damage they can cause.

Patients who have become sexually involved with their analysts may find it difficult to trust or love again. They may come to distrust themselves and their capacities to accurately assess others, especially those in positions of authority. They may also come to fear their own power to seduce. If they are in the mental health field, their sense of identity as a clinician can be compromised.

Three analysands reported sexual boundary violations related to the ending of their analyses. In one instance, the analyst initiated a sexual relationship with an analytic candidate, AS, during the last year of her 14-year training analysis with him and it continued after termination. AS reported that the affair began after a crisis occurred in the analyst's family. She said that initially she was gratified by his desire for sexual intimacy with her, but she ultimately felt that she was being used by him for his own needs and ended the relationship. Subsequently, AS sought treatment with a different analyst to understand and work out what had happened. She reported that this experience was helpful.

Two other analysands left in fury when they discovered their analysts had been sexually involved with another patient. RZ discovered that her analyst had been sexually involved with another patient who was also her friend, and she immediately left treatment. This case will be discussed in the following chapter on non-mutual terminations.

The experience had significant repercussions on these patients' feelings about analysis and being analysts. All three had other successful analytic experiences afterwards. Two of these patients, nonetheless, explained that they were profoundly affected by the boundary violation. It limited the extent to which they could fully give themselves over to these subsequent treatments.

Anger (2): Short preparation for analysts' move

Three of the people I interviewed felt furious, betrayed and bereft when their analysts failed to tell them in a timely fashion that they were moving. I have already described EO's reaction to her analyst's move leading to her understanding an enactment. I will offer one other example reported by DH, who was a candidate at the time of this analysis and had been in analysis for 12 years.

> I heard that my analyst was retiring in three months. I said to him, 'Why did I not learn from you that you were leaving?' He said that he thought I knew from other candidates that he was retiring. I was much older than they, did not socialize with them, and did not hear the gossip. I was really angry. He said, 'You're sad, not angry'. I thought he was denying his importance in my life. I asked for a referral. He said I should wait for a year because the transference was red hot. I was furious. Thinking about his responses gave me the opportunity to go back to early losses and the meaning of his not being able to handle my feelings. I felt betrayed by him.
>
> My analyst said it would take a year to work on the transference before we could be friends. I was pretty depressed, but I worked my way out of it, but I didn't go to anyone else at that time.

DH's analysis ended 15 years ago. His analyst was trained at a time when ideas about what sort of personal information an analyst should share with a patient were more rule-bound and followed stricter criteria for abstinence and neutrality than they do now. Eventually, DH had another analysis, which he described as very helpful.

While the idea of 'sufficient time' is often different for each person, analysts are not always enough attuned to the intensity of their analysands' attachments to them. The impact of being caught by surprise – of not knowing important information that others know, of making a unilateral decision to stop treatment – is probably painful to most analysands and can be devastating to some. The analyst's retirement or relocation from one city, state or country to another is a reality that the analysand has to grapple with, but the analyst's non-defensive acknowledgement of its negative consequences for the patient can lessen some of the pain of this loss. All this will be explored more fully in the next chapter on non-mutual endings.

Anger (3): Intolerance for analysts' limits

Two of the individuals in my study ended their treatment in anger at the analyst's setting limits – one because her analyst refused to have a sexual relationship with her; the other because her analyst would not see her for a reduced fee after she had used up her inheritance. A third individual threatened to end treatment because she was angered by her analyst's refusal to read her literary work. She came to understand that the behaviour toward her analyst repeated what she believed her mother had done to her by constantly threatening to leave. Two of these former analysands, neither of them analysts, acknowledged gains from their treatment and expressed deep regret that they ended as they did.

Coming to accept limits is something one hopes analysis can help patients achieve. In these examples, this did not happen. Since I do not have the analysts' accounts of what occurred, it is not possible to know how they tried to help their analysands understand the limits they set. Often patients can learn a great deal about themselves in these circumstances if their analysts help them contain and express their anger – and other emotions too. But sometimes this is not possible.

Anger (4): Struggles about ending

Nine of the individuals in the study felt that the end phase of their analyses were marred by their analysts' refusal to accept their wish to stop. Three of them were able to resolve this contention, but six were extremely unhappy that the ending had spoiled what had otherwise been a positive experience.

AM, who ended a 14-year analysis five years before our interview, described a situation in which she recognized a painful repetition during the ending that she did not share with her analyst:

> I wanted her to accept that I wanted to stop and work with me on finishing, make it a good goodbye. I was aggravated because she kept interpreting why I should stay. I had a frustrated feeling because she wouldn't let me go. So it *wasn't* a good goodbye. She felt I had more work to do, but I felt, 'I don't care'. She was excellent, but I was ready to go. I set a date. The analysis was good, but why couldn't there be an end?
>
> I needed to talk with someone so badly, to be heard, and I did feel heard by her for many years, and it was important. My father hadn't listened, and in the end part *she* didn't listen. I didn't say to her then that it was a repetition. So was I not a good patient?

AM seemed to have gained insight into what occurred in her analysis and how it was a transference repetition. But the insight did not afford her a relief. Her affect experience was one of distress that was not resolved before she ended – a painful repetition that served to confirm, rather than diminish, her sense of not being heard or understood. The ending brought a negative transference to the foreground – a repetition that, according to AM, the analyst did not recognize. It is not clear why AM chose not to share this awareness with her analyst, and I regret I did not ask. AM blames herself. She views herself as 'not a good patient'; it seems as if she was too hurt and angry to try to work things out.

This example seems a cautionary tale. Analysts need to remember that analysands' reactions to their dyadic interactions usually rekindle something old. This is, of course, what we mean by transference. AM's report might be an instance where staying with a relational focus interfered with reworking a pivotal emotional experience from the past. Again, of course, we cannot know what would have happened had the analyst made the link between the past and present and – equally important – had the analysand been willing to provide important information that was within her awareness. It deprived them both of a 'good' ending.

As is noted in the analytic literature (Davies 2005), the ending of an analysis affects the way the experience is remembered and internalized. When there is contention about the ending, anger may become a more dominant affect. In addition, the state of the analysand's life at the time of ending makes a difference. If analysands have developed important, emotionally rich relationships with people in real life and/or have places of emotional investment outside the analysis, they are more likely to feel positive about ending compared with those who have not done so. I will discuss this further in the following chapter.

Although most of the people I interviewed believed that their analyses had been valuable, several felt that their analysts' strong confrontations in the end phase about their unresolved problems meant that they had been inadequate as analysands. They felt especially criticized when the analysts raised these issues as reasons why the analysis should not end. In later chapters I will provide an example of this reaction from HH, who, like AM, did not tell his analyst his feeling of being injured during the termination phase.

The patients described in this section left analysis with unresolved anger or disappointment. In some instances, they could not accept actions by the analysts – either because the analyst had not been able to maintain an analytic role or the analysand had not been able to accept the limits of that role. In other instances, the unresolved anger occurred in the context of an analytic struggle, which might have recapitulated earlier negative experiences that the analyst had not recognized. If the analyst *had* understood what was occurring, he or she was not able to communicate this effectively enough to the analysand. I think the former patients' wishes to recount such experiences are continued attempts to find some outlet for anger and disappointment. These feelings of distress can persist for many years.

When the analytic pair can work out their struggles, positive changes in affect can occur. One study participant reported that she felt gratitude and appreciation during her termination when she and her analyst could finally agree on her remaining in analysis because she herself wanted to stay, rather than because her analyst insisted that she do so.

Anger (5): Recapitulation of transference

The next example illustrates an observation noted in earlier eras: symptoms that had appeared earlier in the analysis probably recur in the termination phase. Four people reported this experience.

AU had been caught in an angry rebellious struggle with her mother during her teenage years. After an initial period of delight in her analysis, she found herself living out her rebelliousness with her analyst. She missed hours, didn't call to cancel appointments and acted on all her wishes not to be there – just as she had behaved with her mother. She came to understand both the recapitulation and meaning of her behaviour and settled into a deep and productive analysis that lasted 16 years. During termination, her anger and her wish to distance resurfaced. Her wish to leave was as intense as it had been in her adolescence and in the early part of her analysis. But unlike AM described above, at the end phase she was able to talk about it without enacting it.

> At the end of analysis I'd have a conscious thought I don't want to go to my session, but I didn't act on it. Things were going well. I thought, 'I want to leave. I'm done.' It was very intense in my thoughts. I started talking about stopping a year before I left. I felt the patterns in my life that bothered me had changed. Intimacy was better. I'd gotten to a really good relationship with my mom, though it had been very difficult. And it was also now much better with my siblings. I was able to get married. The termination itself was very difficult. I felt like I was going through everything again – in thoughts though, not actions. I was scared, worried if I was making the right decision to stop. Saying goodbye to her felt very intense.

AU's analysis ended one year ago.

Disappointment (6)

Many of the former analysands refer to their disappointment in the way their analysis ended, and for some individuals this feeling dominated the termination. Often, disappointments came from the perception that their analysts were insufficiently aware of how their own wishes, needs or conflicts impinged on the analysands. I will give some examples of these in Chapter 4, when I discuss post-analytic contacts. Patients also felt let down when they believed their analyst had a blind spot or was in denial about something of importance in his or her own life, such as illness, which the analysand, but not the analyst, recognized. DH, who felt he was not given sufficient notice about his analyst's moving, illustrated this point. Some analysands described being disheartened at the ending in relation to enactments on their part that the analyst had not understood or acknowledged. The reports emphasize recognition of these disappointing experiences in the ending. I cannot tell whether what was described is a new recognition or an actual new behaviour during the ending. Another kind of disappointment came from analyst's self-disclosures, which occurred specifically in the last phase of analysis.

Disappointment (7): Unwanted self-revelations

Three people I interviewed expressed explicit disappointment that, in the termination phase, their analysts began to tell them things about their own lives. For example, AU's analyst told her about the death of his child, believing she would find out after the analysis ended. AU believed her analyst was suggesting she would have sought out information about him, which she thought she would not have done. Having this information inhibited her from expressing her anger toward her analyst, but the analyst was skilful in recognizing and addressing this. While AU was basically very positive about her analytic experience, she saw the analyst's self-disclosure as unnecessarily complicating the ending. This may well be described as a countertransference enactment: the departure of the analysand experienced as the death of a child.

Another study participant, MS, whose narrative follows, described the analyst's talking about herself as a distraction. Because the analyst had been so helpful and kind, MS felt unable to bring up this subject, as she did not want to introduce negative feelings in their ending of a six-year analysis. In addition, she felt that the analyst had let her end treatment too quickly, basing the termination on MS's forthcoming wedding rather than on some deeper internal readiness to stop. Afterwards, the marriage became problematic, and MS believed that the analyst never helped her focus sufficiently on her choice of partner. It is not clear whether MS had an awareness of this as a neglected focus during the treatment, which ended 15 years ago.

> My feeling about the ending is that I wasn't done. My analyst started talking about *her* own analyst when we were ending. It was too much information, and I didn't want to have it. I felt the boundary was unclear. But I never told her that. I couldn't. I respected her as an analyst and valued the work we had done, I was aghast that she had done that.
>
> I was disappointed in the ending. The whole last year she'd tell me personal information, and it really did distract me. I was critical of her that last year. I invited her to my wedding and she didn't come. She put that boundary in, but not the others.

These former analysands experienced their analyst's self-revelations in different ways. AU thought her analyst assumed she would seek out information about him, which she believed was a misperception of her; therefore she felt hurt. MS felt her analyst's self-revelations distracted her from her focus on herself, especially since she thought she had more work to do and was not ready to end treatment. Both felt very disappointed by these self-revelations in their analyses.

There is no way of knowing the analysts' views on these matters. Perhaps their self-revelations reflected their wish to be known as people in their own right. They might have wanted their patients to think of them as they thought of themselves. Perhaps they felt a transference stress that needed to be relieved before the treatment had ended. Since both AU and MS were clinicians, their analysts may have believed that the self-disclosures would serve as a transition in their relationship to future colleagues, whose worlds might later overlap with their own. In any event, in hindsight one can only wish that the former analysands could have expressed their feelings of anger and disappointment within the context of the analytic relationship. It is possible that having the opportunity to report these experiences to me allowed both women to discharge pent-up negative feelings and a sense of satisfaction at having their view of events on record – a possible act of revenge, however anonymous.

Joy after working through depression (8)

Eleven of the former analysands reported they had experienced a new sense of lightness and joy during the termination phase. This occurred despite moments of sadness about leaving their analysts who, they believed, had helped them achieve so much internal growth and independence. All these individuals had childhoods in which trauma or deprivation had prematurely forced them to become self-sufficient. They were bright and resourceful. Their external adaptations worked well. The reason for seeking analysis was most often some depressive feeling. Once in treatment, their self-sufficiency eventually gave way to the previously warded-off feelings of dependent longing.

AR, who was described earlier in the section on recognition of the primacy of separation in the context of the analytic relationship, stayed for eight more years. Another analysand who had also left, returned to treatment and remained for another six years. Each of these analysands had been in analysis for so long that they were afraid they would never be able to leave analysis. When they initially tried to, or did, terminate, they became intensely depressed and returned to analysis. In some cases, the analysand returned to the original analyst; in other cases, to a different one. When this second analysis – or second period of analysis – ended, they reported a feeling of elation. They had never expected that they would be able to both function with such self-confidence and feel so autonomous. Three former analysands presented variations on these themes.

UT, who was 56 at the time of our interview, had sought therapy in her early thirties before beginning analytic training, because she wanted to feel more comfortable and emotionally 'safe'. Her therapy hours had gradually increased from one to two to three to four to five times a week. She did not appreciate 'how many levels there were' until she was in analysis. Gradually, she used the treatment in a fuller way. She realized her marriage was unsatisfying. She divorced, was single for a number of years, and later remarried. Her first analysis terminated after 11 years.

She began her second analysis as a candidate. This analysis had two parts. In the first phase, she was in classes with her analyst, which she later realized had been an intrusion. The second phase, which lasted six years, was more successful.

> I had a great desire to live life on my own. I had a wonderful marriage and a wonderful child. I felt my analyst had helped me achieve this positive feeling. But I think the scared part of me wasn't attended to enough. I had dreams of diving into water and of sharks being there. I was excited and scared. I set the date six months before actually stopping. But the question of how I would really know if I were ready to stop was there from the beginning.
>
> I bought my analyst a bottle of wine to share with his wife in celebration. At graduation, I again felt both happy and scared. The analytic community is small, and I wondered how I would navigate with him in it. Six months after terminating, my father died. I realized I was holding onto Oedipal stuff in relation to my analyst, and it was hard to be in meetings with him. My father's death had been sudden and sad beyond anything I had anticipated. I was worn out, devastated. I wanted to be back in analysis. Though my functioning was fine, I went back for another six years.
>
> The first year or two of this second phase of analysis, I didn't go to study groups or functions where my analyst might be. I needed to keep my analysis separate, to deal with loss, de-idealization, sexual hang-ups and find my own desire. The feeling in this analysis was very different from before, where I felt I had really been a pseudo-adult and trying to please. Not having my analyst in multiple roles in relation to me, to privilege him as my analyst was very important.
>
> There were years of complaining, 'If only you'd ... whatever', of dealing with disappointment and feeling the glass was half empty. The new material at this second ending was the gratitude I felt. My feelings for my analyst changed. I wasn't so disappointed. We talked about terminating for two years, with an intense focus on ending in the last two months. I had found his feet of clay, but I felt fondness and regard for him. I knew I had to go and was ready to go and had dreams that confirmed that.

Her analysis ended nine months ago.

Once UT terminated, she found she liked being alone in her own head and the autonomy of doing this work on her own. She felt confident and got feedback from colleagues that she was doing well with patients. She found an increased ability to interpret her own dreams, and to do self-analytic work.

I feel that that I'd stopped second-guessing myself. I feel a solidifying of my own mind. I find anxiety in my dreams but it no longer feels crippling. I feel I have a capacity to weather what comes. With my patients, I am bolder in relying on my knowledge of myself as their content gets inside me and stimulates a countertransference. When I see a collusion, I am aware of my own history, of my reluctance to individuate. I become aware of what we are avoiding, and I can help my patients hold their more vulnerable parts.

I seek consultation and am less desirous of being pleasing. It's great to be on the other side of the fence. I don't have to be a shaker and mover, and analysis doesn't have to be my whole life. I have my own life with my husband, my daughter, yoga – that's the best – to make my life my own.

AZ, a male analyst now in his sixties, had a ten-year analysis, beginning in his thirties, in which he started to think about ending three years before the actual end. He was successful in his life and relationships but experienced a deep level of suffering, knowing something was not right. He had consulted with an analyst at a time before he was planning to become an analyst. Less than a year into the treatment, his analyst died.

I was successful in real life – I was growing professionally, had a wife and child – but at a deeper level I was suffering and lonely. I thought I could do it alone, but I knew I couldn't. It was the death of my first analyst that helped me make the connection to my father's death when I was fourteen. I was conscious of my loneliness but unconscious about its connection to the loss of my father. My parents came from Poland. They were survivors of the holocaust. Everything was okay, and nothing was okay. I wasn't bleeding, but many parts of me were bleeding.

I entered analysis with another analyst – this time a woman. It took me ten years to understand what was troubling me. I was the only son. My mother needed me too much. This isn't a projection; it was really true. When I came for the first interview with my second analyst, I knew I wasn't on solid ground, though I didn't understand why. My analyst asked for my earliest memory. It was my mother showing me ground outside our window. Later I understood it was the ruins outside the ghetto in Poland. It took me years to understand 'the ruins'.

When I felt ready to stop, I had this metaphor that it was like coming to the frontier in the West and I was ready to settle. Solid ground. I knew I was leaving analysis but not really leaving her. She was in my heart, and I could talk to her in my mind – very clear, very intimate to know someone is really present. I didn't go through a sense of death. It was so different from death. I knew death from the armed services. This was not it, not mourning. Death and ending were very different.

I was very satisfied with my family life, with my professional life. I felt alive with my life. It was very different from before. I appreciated the way I had changed. I felt freer to think for myself and to speak openly. I felt really independent and at the same time really there and connected. It was time to go on, to go out, to be on my own. The journey was over. I was in analytic training. I knew what to expect in the end phase, and it happened. I had outbursts of being idiotic at work and at home in ways that hadn't happened for years, but they didn't continue. It didn't make me worry either when they were happening. I remember thinking that this was part of life and that I had the ability to talk to myself. It was a very good time.

Six years after terminating my mother died. My mother had been very sick, so initially I felt a sense of relief. I thought I was doing okay, but gradually I began to realize I was out of contact with myself, and it was affecting me more than I realized. At that time I was also nominated for an important professional position. I knew that it was overload, that I was being asked to do something beyond my capacity. I felt I couldn't do it alone.

Ten years after terminating I went back to see my analyst. We met once a week for a year. It was very productive. It was easy to come back. I was so much less defensive and defended. I understood how connected I had been to my mother. At the time I had a clingy, crazy patient who'd call all the time, needing me like my mother had. My analyst and I opened all this up. I got another deeper look at what all this meant for me after her death.

It was very clear again when I knew I was ready to stop. But this time I was not so young, and she was not so young, so we both knew that maybe there wouldn't be a next time – but that wasn't a reason to continue. I didn't think my analysis or my life would have a happy ending, but they have. I feel on solid ground now, and those feelings of suffering that I didn't understand aren't there now – and they weren't when I stopped either time.

AZ's first analysis with the second analyst ended 17 years ago. The brief second period ended six years ago.

AH, not a clinician, had been seriously enough depressed at an earlier time to consider hospitalization. He had had two analyses. He ended his second analysis after five and a half years. He made the decision to stop analysis four to five months before ending. By that time, he felt strong and confident as never before. He felt a profound feeling of thanks.

When I ended the first analysis because I had moved, I had hoped that understanding could rework my character and keep me from repeating my father's life. Ending the second analysis, I felt independent, that I could make my own way. I had found work I loved. I'd cut the umbilical cord. I found and married a woman I love. I feel I have a strong marriage. Before analysis, I had been passive in relation to women. ... I learned how not to parent from my parents.

Toward the end of my analysis, I felt my analyst as more a peer than an authority. He wasn't a god-like figure anymore. I felt I could make my way on my own. I'd internalized my own toolbox. I felt a proud feeling – Wow, I really did it! Analysis saved my life – not in the sense that I was suicidal, but in how I came to be different. Both analysts did that.

AH terminated 18 years ago and has not gone back to see his analyst.

We have seen in these patients, as Quinodoz (1993) noted, that termination may be accompanied by the quality of 'buoyancy'. Departing patients may have a stronger sense of independence and a feeling of truly being themselves. He emphasized that this feeling did not represent omnipotent or manic independence, nor did it express an indifference to the analyst. The awareness of personal responsibility, the ability to rely on and think for oneself, contain one's affect and accept one's own vulnerability may often encourage a sense of freedom that also allows interdependence with others.

Loewald (1962, 1973) describes this as an internalization of the analyst and the analytic relationship. The analysand takes and reconstitutes the relationship with the analyst, who is given up as an actual person with whom the patient interacts, while seamlessly assimilating traits, attitudes, or stances that the patient and analyst have in common. This internalization of supporting qualities is never acquired once and for all, but at termination the analysand can feel 'the pleasurable sensation of managing to "fly with his own wings" because he feels he has acquired a self-supporting capacity that makes him independent of the object which he needed until then in order to "be carried"' (Quinodoz 1993: 172).

As Quinodoz and Loewald both emphasize, the ability to rely on oneself and think for oneself develops over the years of analysis. Capacities are never totally stable acquisitions. We all need other people. For different reasons both UT and AZ had to prematurely relinquish their dependent ties, and the attempt at separation plunged them into a depth of depression greater than before. The analytic work that followed enabled them to access and resolve long-buried issues of dependent longing and conflict in a way that had not previously been possible. Both these patients regressed, giving up their self-sufficiency for a period of time to experience what they had escaped from and defended against. The presence of the analyst as a steady figure of affect containment, as well as an object of transference for the reliving of past disappointment, pain and conflict allowed them to fly with their 'own wings', to borrow Quinodoz's metaphor. The analysands could then carry their analysts with them as introjects, making the separation less sad and creating a feeling that they were less totally alone. It should be noted too that they had found meaningful, intimate relationships outside of analysis.

When analyses have been long and hard, there have been periods of intense grief for some patients, like those just described, often precipitated by abortive attempts to stop. When the final ending comes, the balance of their feelings may well be joy rather than grief, though for most of these 82 volunteers it was an admixture of these states.

Limentani (1982) noted that the catastrophic reaction that sometimes occurs at the end of analysis may be due to the analysand's fantasy of fusion with the analyst, which is only apparent when he or she becomes conscious of the separateness between them. It is not until the analysand faces the loss of the analyst that the warded-off anxiety about separation, the revival of traumatic loss or absence, may become affectively alive.

It can be speculated that it was the interruption of this fusion with the analyst that the analysands who described having joyous ends may have experienced when they made their first unsuccessful attempt at termination. The depression that followed enabled them to unearth and then rework in the transference their intense dependent yearnings, resulting in their being able to separate self from other.

Sometimes weekends, cancellations, vacations or other interruptions of the analytic schedule were sufficient stimuli to revive analysands' affective memories of loss and unmet dependent yearnings and fears of abandonment. Similarly, misunderstandings, disappointments and other ruptures in the relationship could arouse the grief connected with dysphoric, traumatic or affective early loss or the absence of early objects of attachment. Schlesinger's idea (2005) that endings are continually occurring in treatment is related to these suggestions.

The 11 patients with joyous endings did not report that any of these more limited separations or ruptures created affective distress. Perhaps this is a trick of memory. Perhaps, as a result of their analysis, they returned to a state of independence, are now more firmly grounded, and wished to report the experience. But it is also possible that these former analysands had learned to tolerate absence or mistreatment in their early years and trained themselves not to react to breaks in regular contact or misattunements. They may have dissociated or walled off their affect in a similar, but less extreme, manner. It was only the actual or anticipated loss of contact with the analyst that disrupted their functioning and plunged them into depressive despair. Their lack of grief in ending may not only have been the previous working through of grief, but also the return to a state of independence, now more firmly grounded, which has a functional pleasure.

Grief and mourning

If grief in ending has not been experienced before, it is also a new affect. But I am treating it as a separate topic because of its centrality as an expectation of concluding analytic work.

Most analysands reported feeling some sense of sadness and grief in the closing phase of analysis. Some, like those just described, grieved intensely before the actual ending. For others, the ending itself was especially painful. In this study, most of the analysands who emphasized intense grief in ending had a history of significant losses or separations. These results are contrary to the findings in Craige's (2002) study, who did not find a relationship between earlier loss and separations and the extent of the candidates' grief during termination. In my project, 12 participants who elaborated on their grief in the final phase of treatment had significant earlier losses, separations or what they viewed as constitutional depressive issues. Two others, who were analytic candidates, experienced intense grief only after termination. They will be described in Chapter 4 on the effect of post-analytic contact. Each of the 11 analysands, previously discussed in relation to joyous endings, had significant periods of grief in the final phase of treatment, and they mourned. The difference is that they ended with joyous affect, not grief.

Here I will provide two accounts of candidates in analytic training who experienced intense grief in termination during their analyses. Only one of them seems similar to the descriptions in Craige's reports.

AW, whose ending occurred long ago, had a history of significant loss and separation. His father had been in the armed services for several years when he was three. His parents divorced when he was seven, and he permanently lost touch with his father after that. He had difficulty sustaining meaningful relationships. He would make close ties but then withdraw with no sense of sadness or regret. In his analysis, which he had ended 30 years ago, he had come to understand this pattern and its origin. Once he decided to terminate, he was flooded with sadness and grief that he had never felt before.

> I was forty when I started analysis. I had early childhood loss. Then there were lots of people I cared about, but I didn't keep in contact. In analysis I didn't care about separations. The big thing was when that changed and I started to keep relationships. I feel analysis made me more colourful in my imagination. Earlier I was afraid to get close to suicidal patients. I got freer empathizing and getting to their despair. … The termination was rough. I felt real sadness that I hadn't before. I had psychosomatic symptoms. I'd choke and fall asleep on the couch. I could get in touch with repressed emotions of grief from my grandparents' death in my adolescence. The longing was for my father whom I really never knew … so much feeling previously unknown.

AW's analysis ended 30 years ago.

ST had wished to be in analysis for years but feared humiliating attacks and being shamed during the treatment. But after deciding to become an analyst himself, he finally began an analysis. He described himself as an 'intellectualizer' who was compliant. The early work centred on his being deferential and his discovery of how angry he actually was. Having promised himself he would say all that came to mind, he did just that and was surprised at how kind, supportive and non-retaliatory his analyst was.

> I felt he gave of himself; it was transformative to have learned something and, whatever it was, I'd learned it for me, not because it was a requirement. After the first few years I was deciding to terminate, but then I couldn't imagine not being in analysis. Two years before ending, I felt I'd made substantial changes and could stop, but realized I was in too much of a rush. My analyst was very explicit about the thought that something was going on when I pushed to stop, that I was avoiding something very big. It was the grief. I was avoiding the

terrible feelings of loss if I stopped. Then I worked on that, experiencing a depth of pain and longing I'd never previously known.

Later came a period when I really felt ready to stop. In the last six months almost the entire hours were given over to talking about termination. While earlier I'd been talking about my life, now everything was about leaving my analyst and what it would be like, what the final hour would be. There were feelings of loss, abandonment ... I wanted to move on. Other times there were powerful longings, as if the end had already occurred, anger that he'd let me go, wondering about how he felt about my leaving. Things shifted around quickly and intensely. Thinking about what I'd gotten done and what hadn't gotten done and wondering if it would get done.

I realized I was thinking of stopping as a real death. And then I realized that my analyst would go on and I'd go on. That led me to wonder how could he go on without me? The thought of who would he replace me with led to my competitiveness and its exploration. I was sure ending would be very difficult. I'd wondered if I'd be devastated by grief, but I wasn't at all. I have a quiet reflectiveness now, but not grief.

ST's termination occurred a month before the interview.

ST's account parallels Craige's report that former analysands who experienced this intensity of grief were without a history of actual loss. ST is the only one, in this section, who did not report a history of separation, loss and trauma. Like the analysands described with joyous endings, he too experienced intense grief and dealt with issues of separation in a new and intense way when he tried to end his analysis. He did not describe joy in ending. But at least at the time of his interview, one month after ending, he was no longer in a state of grief.

While experiences of grief and mourning were reported by almost every person I interviewed, and are characteristic of most of the endings, they were not always as intense as the literature has suggested. Issues of grief about separation and the process of mourning were not particularly prominent in Kramer's (1959) clinical exposition of termination. And going against the general assumption that grief always accompanies termination, Arlow (1969) questioned the significance of mourning in the end phase of analysis. But their perspectives are rarely cited. Do the analysts who write about the intensity of grief have a higher percentage of analysands who fit the category of intense mourning? Are these analysts writing about their own sense of loss? Are the patients' experiences of grief connected with the extent to which their grief gets explored and analysed during analysis and in the end phase? I suspect that the experience of grief varies greatly, as does the way it is remembered over time.

In this study, some analyses had ended many years ago and grief may have faded from their memory. But the lack of focus on grief was also characteristic of many analyses that had ended within the last year. Notably, however, for five of the 20 individuals who stopped analysis so recently, their sadness had a poignancy, an acuteness, that was not so typical of those who had ended years before.

Since many of my interviewees have had other analytic experiences, one wonders whether the intensity of affect may lessen in later experiences of treatment. I do not know that grief and the process of mourning were absent for these individuals. The earlier mourning process may have been satisfactory enough to ease the acuteness of grief. Grief may have occurred in a previous experience of ending an analysis or in trying to end the one they reported. Or they may have experienced, explored and reworked their grief in many smaller, incremental ways during the analysis. In addition, some patients may need considerable time to build trust and attachment, while others may give themselves over to the first experience, and if the revived, inevitable disappointments are not addressed sufficiently to work through the pain, then they may retreat from allowing so much vulnerability. Some analysands left their analyses in anger or remained defensively self-sufficient and unchanged in termination. They did not express grief or describe experiences of mourning. Dysphoric affect of rage or disappointment dominated and perhaps obscured grief, but certainly replaced it consciously. When there is no grief due to anger, disappointment or defensive self-sufficiency, it would seem there is unfinished analytic work.

In contrast, those with joyous endings had specifically explored grief in relation to earlier experiences of separation, loss and disappointment and in the context of the analytic relationship, but they did not describe feelings of sorrow or loss in the concluding phase. After long, hard work, they really wanted to conclude their treatments. By the time of the actual ending, joy in mastery and feelings of being independent and competent were dominant. There descriptions seem related to Quinodoz's ideas (1993).

Conclusions

Here are my general conclusions about developments that occur at the end of analysis.

1   My findings do not support the assumption that intense grief is necessarily part of the ending or post-termination process of analysis. Nor do they support the assumption that there is a difference in the experience of grief at termination between analysts, non-analytic clinicians and non-clinicians. This finding is in line with Craige's data that candidates are not immune to the experience of grief. Until her study, the literature suggested that analysts and non-analysts had notably different grief experiences on termination because they knew they were certain (or likely) to have later contact with their analyst (Milner 1950; Novick 1982).

2   The end phase is not always notably different from the rest of the analysis. In my study 20 per cent of the former analysands did not report any special features of the end phase. While these terminations may have been characterized more by synthesizing and reworking previously explored

themes, none of the individuals in the study actually offered this conceptualization.

3   The intensity of grieving seemed related to the personal qualities and histories of the particular analysand and his or her interaction with the particular analyst. As was true with other issues related to what occurs in psychoanalysis and how it ends, the individual nature of each former analysand and each analyst are what stood out.

4   While many former patients expressed strong attachment to the analyst as well as an appreciation of having him or her as a companion in the process, only a small number emphasized the loss of the relationship with the analyst as a person. The lack of focus on the loss of this relationship was more frequent than might have been anticipated from the literature, and was a surprising outcome. Perhaps some of the interviewees felt the importance of the analyst as a person was implicitly understood. Or possibly they imagined that thoughts of loss of the actual person were not acceptable, believing that their attachment itself was only transference. If this was the case, maybe they actually 'transferred the transference' (Ferraro and Garella 1997: 27) to the other important individuals in their lives.

5   In discussing the termination phase, many of these former analysands focused on their need for self-sufficiency. Allowing their dependent yearnings in the relationship with their analysts was central to the work. For others who did not give themselves over in this fashion, it is not possible to tell whether the holding back was a result of the psychological conflicts and organization of the analysand, the analyst, or their interaction – or a combination of these variables.

It does not mean that these former analysands did not gain from the analytic experiences. But it does suggest that the idea of intense attachment, idealization, disillusionment, acceptance of limits and limitations leading to a secure sense of separateness, together with grief and mourning leading to an ability to separate while continuing to love the now-more-realistically-perceived other, may be another one of those analytic ideals – a sometime occurrence rather than an expectable outcome.

6   The majority of the sample believed that they had had very satisfactory experiences and valued their analyses and their analysts. A number of them described a wish for post-analytic contact – a topic I will elaborate in the next two chapters.

7   When patients said they were unhappy with their analyses, they specified the personal qualities of the analyst they believed had interfered with the process. The most frequent complaint was about analysts who seemed unaware of the impact of their actions on their patients, for example by stepping outside their professional role by making unwanted self-revelations or resisting the analysands' wish to end treatment. Analysands' descriptions of believing their analysts were not letting them leave were more frequent than thinking their analysts were ignoring their wishes to stay. Again, we need to keep in

mind that their analysts might have a different perspective on what occurred. While some analysands did offer poignant descriptions of their wishes *not* to end, these were proportionally far fewer than the literature would lead one to expect.

8   The way an analysis is experienced, assimilated and represented is likely to change with time and the analysand's later life experience. So the accounts presented here are more a snapshot of how an analysis is now seen rather than the whole story or the enduring 'truth'. In addition, there are always two participants in any analysis and, therefore, two points of view; the analyst's perspective, which is usually given in the literature, is not part of this study.

9   With respect to the representations of the end phase of analysis and the experience of grief, my expectation was that the differences in both the analysand's age and the length of time since ending would have led to greater discrepancies in their experiences of grief than were apparent. Most, but not all, of the analysands who had ended within the last year thought of their analysts with a greater frequency, but not all were actively grieving. If it is true, as Schlesinger (2005) has suggested, that endings occur throughout treatment experiences, then perhaps the memory of grief fades as its affective intensity diminishes and the relationship and the analytic process are internalized. Even so, some analysands, like AW who ended analysis 30 years ago, continue to describe grief as acutely painful. Optimism about what might be possible due to positive changes in the analysand also did not seem to be so different for younger analysands with many years before them as it was for the older analysands. The study has left many questions unanswered. As with analysis itself, we are left with the fact that there is always more to be understood.

Note

1   The displacement is a defence against awareness of an unconscious, repressed experience from the past.

Chapter 3

Non-mutual endings

Whether the analysis ends by mutual agreement or by a unilateral decision affects the way the analysand experiences not only the ending and its aftermath but an overall sense about the analytic endeavour.

There are times when the analyst has little choice about ending an analysis, even if the timing is not desirable for the analysand. Illness is the clearest illustration of this necessity. The analyst may also move or retire. The extent of the analyst's ability to decide what and when to tell the patient will vary depending on the particular circumstances. How the analyst informs the analysand is likely to have long-term reverberations. Limentani (1982) stresses that unexpected endings can disrupt, and sometimes even destroy, basic trust in the analyst.

Even when the patient is the one who moves, the decision is not always primarily under his or her control. For example, the patient's job or a spouse's job may require a relocation.

Analyst or analysand may also unilaterally initiate ending an analysis for primarily psychological factors. Either may come to the conclusion that the treatment is not progressing and call a halt to the meetings. Or either may decide that enough has been accomplished and propose stopping. External and psychological factors may be interwoven. For example, an analyst who is aging may no longer have the energy to persist in a treatment that seems stalemated. When the analyst suggests ending and the patient does not feel ready, the patient may think that the analyst has given up hope for further progress and feel humiliated and angry, believing he or she has been a failure as an analysand.

When the patient is the one to initiate the decision, if it is based on the sense that he or she can go no further it is likely to be accompanied by a sense of disappointment. And when the analyst is not in agreement with the patient about ending, the patient is also likely to have a sense of guilt and a feeling of being disappointing. When patients leave in anger, experiences of guilt and concerns about being disappointed and disappointing are heightened. Under these circumstances, it is unlikely that the analysand will feel the sense of increased connection to people and autonomy that one hopes would accompany the ending of analysis. According to Novick (1982, 1997), non-mutuality in ending inevitably interferes with analytic gains.

The first non-mutual ending reported in the literature was Freud's presenting a termination date to the Wolf man (1918), with the intention that an awareness of the finiteness of time would overcome his resistances and end the stalemate that had occurred. We know from follow-up treatments (Brunswick 1928) that what had seemed to be a successful strategy at the time turned out to have failed to relieve the analysand's symptoms and psychic distress.

For many decades, there seemed to be an assumption in the literature that it was the analyst's responsibility to decide when to bring an analysis to a close. Hurn (1971) and Brenner (1976) believed it was the analyst's job not only to initiate termination but to impose it. And their view seemed to prevail in Firestein's survey on termination (1974), which indicated that a large number of the analysts initiated the ending of treatment. These results are not so remarkable since the analysts in his survey came from the same analytic community as Brenner, who was a central and influential teacher and analyst at the time. Here is evidence of the effect of teaching.

As always, however, there were some analysts who proposed a different stance that anticipated contemporary views. Fleming and Benedeck (1964) had already emphasized the importance of mutual agreement about the ending of an analysis. And beginning in the early 1980s, with a diminished deferral toward authority more prevalent, contemporary theory no longer endorsed the idea that analysts should unilaterally decide to end an analysis based on psychological factors. In Gilman's survey (1982) of 42 cases, for example, 'in only two instances did the first mention of termination come from the analyst' (p. 465). Instead, mutual discussion and consideration of what the analysand was gaining from analytic work would probably be recommended; ideally, a decision about continuing or ending would emerge from a joint exploration of this topic (Novick 1982, 1997; De Simone Gaburri 1985; Goldberg and Marcus 1985; Hoffman 1998; Gabbard 2009).

External factors posed a different problem. When analysts are ill, they have to decide what, if anything, to tell their patients about their illnesses. But the issue of self-disclosure itself remained controversial. Abraham Freedman (cited in Schwartz and Silver 1990) believed that the analysand should be told if the analyst is seriously ill. Other analysts (Abend 1982; Lasky 1990) maintained that they should disclose as little as possible to preserve analytic neutrality. This belief was based on an idea that the more factual information a patient was given, the more likely it was to contaminate the transference distortion (Dewald 1982). Deciding what and how much to reveal should be determined by the stage of the analysis, the diagnosis and the particular analysand's need for truth (Dewald 1982).

It should be noted that while these ideas about the importance of individualizing the kind and amount of information the analyst communicates were compelling, many analysts, following their own psychological needs, did not follow them. Sometimes the reasons for not individualizing communications were based on theoretical convictions, but many times they were strongly influenced by the analyst's psychological needs; it was not always so easy to separate the two. In both situations of illness and geographical relocations, what to tell the patient, and how to tell it, seemed to be influenced by countertransference factors (Weiss 1972; Beatrice 1982; Glick 1987; Martinez 1989) as much as – if not more than – by theory.

Endings that occurred because of the analysts' geographical relocation, most often unavoidable, may have considerable impact on analysands (Dewald 1965; Schwartz 1974; Beatrice 1982; Glick 1987; Martinez 1989; Sherby 2004). How and when analysts conveyed this information to their patients might be as, or more, important than the actual fact of the move itself. In this respect, the situation was similar to an illness. Not unexpectedly, there was disagreement about whether the analysand should (Schwartz 1974; Martinez 1989) or should not (Dewald 1965, 1966; Weiss 1972) be informed in detail about the reasons for the analyst's move.

In reviewing the analytic literature, Novick (1982) found that the number of 'prematurely terminated cases ranged from a low of 31 per cent to a high of 72 per cent' (p. 331). In my study, 48 of the 82 former analysands, close to 60 per cent, reported that at least one of their analyses had ended unilaterally. In 25 of the analyses discussed in this project, the endings were initiated by the analysts, and 23 by the analysands. Fifty-four per cent of the endings (26 out of 48) were ended primarily for external reasons.

I will report the experiences of these 48 former analysands who had one or more of their analytic experiences end by a non-mutual decision. While many of these analysands were angry and disappointed, and sometimes became painfully self-critical, these endings did not invariably prevent analytic gains as the literature suggests.

I

Analyst initiates ending – for external reason (28)

1. Analyst moves (6)

EO and DH, both quoted in the previous chapter (pp. 38–39 and 40–41 respectively), discovered that their analysts were preparing to close their practices and move. They felt betrayed that they had not been told and distressed that they had not been given adequate time to work through the separation and termination. DH was able to express his fury and disappointment about the move, but he felt his training analyst had not taken responsibility for what he had done (or, in this case, not done). Nor had his analyst understood that three months was too short a time for DH to process and grieve his loss. He reported that eventually he had another analysis that was very helpful.

In contrast, four other analysands felt they benefited from their analysts' moving. WN was told about the move six months in advance, and she was relieved. She had been in analysis for over seven years, and, while it had been helpful initially, she felt she had reached an impasse. WN felt that her analyst's approach made her feel criticized rather than understood and that he was not willing to listen to clarifications based on what she assumed were countertransference issues. She also felt that her efforts to communicate her experience to him had not improved the situation. WN had been unable to extricate herself and the analyst's move gave her an excuse to stop.

Two years later she began twice weekly treatment, which she said she had found extremely helpful. She and her analyst were able to address 'primitive, dark places without too much fear' – issues that were not engaged in her earlier analysis. It is not possible to tell from this report whether the first analyst was not as skilled as the second, whether the patient was more ready to do analytic work at a later date, or whether the differences reflect issues of the match between patient and analyst.

Unilateral endings, while never desirable, can sometimes lead analysands to insight and emotional growth. A patient can value the analytic experience but have very different feelings about the analyst by the time of the ending.

I remind the reader that EO, who had been in analysis for nine and a half years, regarded her analyst as a source of wisdom in both her personal and professional life. After her analyst moved, EO found the phone contact, proposed by her analyst, unsatisfactory and wanted to terminate. Her analyst interpreted EO's reaction as both resistance and hostile. At that point, EO realized that she was repeating the experience she had had with her mother, who had also had trouble letting her go. Although the termination had been traumatic, EO believed she had grown through it.

YA (pp. 32–34) was told by her analyst that he was planning to retire and move in two years' time. At that time, she had been in nine years of analysis and four years of therapy. Like EO, her analyst's moving facilitated her separation, but the ways in which their analysts dealt with ending were in sharp contrast. EO's analyst resisted the ending while YA's analyst kept her focused on the impending termination when she was avoiding it, staying with the patient's pain about the fact they were ending. This enabled her to acknowledge previously unrecognized dependency and lack of differentiation. Also, unlike EO, YA ended with positive, appreciative feelings for her analyst.

When an analyst moves or retires, it usually forces an ending for which the analysand is unprepared. However, these examples illustrate how such non-mutual endings can be managed with greater or lesser sensitivity to the analysands' feelings. Nonetheless, as EO's account illustrates, even when there is a traumatic ending in which the analyst is unaware of countertransference interference leading to an enactment, insights and feelings can sometimes be effectively worked through independently of the analyst, resulting in an internalization of the analytic process.

When an analyst moves or retires, they have obviously thought about this decision for a time before telling the patient. So there is a way in which the analysand may sense, or imagine, that the analyst has not been fully present for the analysand during that period of analysis. This retrospective awareness may also cast a light on the previous experience and affect the analysand's experience of the entire treatment.

2. Analyst becomes sick or dies (15)

Fifteen former analysands in my study, all of whom had had more than one analysis, reported that their analyst had become ill or died.[1] Three analysands whose analyses were near completion did their grieving with the analyst, who acknowledged the imminence of his or her own death. Two others whose analysts died suddenly were helped to mourn the loss, and continue their analytic work, with a new analyst.

BD's first analysis, which lasted 14 years, was completed before his analytic training and other professional commitments. While living in another city, he had a period of analysis with a second analyst as part of his training. He considered this analysis very unhelpful and initiated the ending. When he returned to his home city, he re-entered analysis with his first analyst.

During this last period of analysis, BD's analyst told him when he became ill and was dying. They continued his analysis by phone for several months. BD was able to grieve and mourn his analyst. He believes this analyst influenced him in very positive ways both personally and professionally. When he is in a dilemma, he thinks of what his former analyst would say. These thoughts make him continue to feel close to him as he does his work. BD never returned to treatment following his analyst's death, which occurred more than ten years ago.

By contrast, JW, whose analyst's illness caused an interruption of her treatment of four or five months, did not experience him as sensitive to her needs either then or in the last part of her analysis. For the previous five years, she had been trying to end a 25-year analysis. She had sought a consultation to help her. She wanted her analyst to be involved in the process of ending.

> When my analyst came back, I said I really want to stop. That was four or five months before I left. ... He died six to eight months after I stopped. I set the date and I followed it. It was what I called a 'do-it-yourself termination'. My analyst did not agree to it, but did not argue against it ... It was excruciatingly painful. I couldn't be with him while he was dying. I couldn't say the kinds of things I needed and wanted to say to someone who was dying. So he was disappointed in me, and I was disappointed in him in the end. ...
>
> He had a tumour. He was very matter of fact about it. They were doing radiation, and it was unknown what would happen. At one point I said how painful this was, and he said I'd just have to trust he'd be okay. I think he was in denial. I went to see someone to help me have the courage to terminate. I found that my dying analyst was not the only analyst with whom I could make a deep connection, that there were other analysts who would listen and not overpower me with their theories. It opened up much greater possibilities

for me. It took a long time, but I finally decided to do analytic training. I went to another analyst.

The process of ending treatment was already a difficult one for JW, and she experienced increased complications because of her analyst's illness. When she read this material to give permission for its publication, she added, 'I asked the consulting analyst why I found myself so much better able to talk and make use of her. She said something very important – that I seemed to have acquired a great deal in my previous analysis and was mourning its loss. So moving on, ending one analysis, did not mean I had to reject it all.'

Ending treatment because of the analyst's death presented the analysand with a precipitous loss and an inability to influence the time of ending or its length. In addition, it deprived her of the analyst's guidance in the process of termination. The particular meaning of the loss for an analysand would depend on the gains that had been made and what was being explored at the time. None of the participants in my study elaborated on the specific meanings that these unexpected endings stimulated for them. JW was fortunate to have a consultant who helped her appreciate what her analysis had given her prior to her analyst's illness and regain a perspective on her analytic experience.

Three other analysts became ill and did not discuss this situation with their analysands. It is not clear if they themselves were aware of the state of their health, but the analysands believe they were in denial. The analysands also felt left on their own to struggle with the unacknowledged illness and deal with their disappointment in their analyst as well as with their loss. The difficulty of extricating themselves from the treatment was further complicated by their having to deal with the incomplete analytic work on their own.

3. Analytic communities' ways of dealing with analysts' illness or death (7)

In three other instances, the communities of the analytic institutes were secretive about illnesses of the treating analysts and unsupportive to the analysands who were candidates at the time of the illness or death. These analysands had to deal with their analyst's loss as well as their institute's lack of communication and support.

In one example, BB, a former candidate, was met by silence from her institute when she inquired why her analyst was cancelling her appointments and not returning to work. When he died, no one would talk with her about what had happened, nor did they refer her to anyone to discuss it or help her with this unexpected end to her analysis. Two other former analysands had almost identical experiences.

In a fourth instance, the institute informed the then candidate, AP, that she would have to stop seeing her analyst because he was unstable and was being removed as a training analyst. After a number of confusing communications with the institute, AP was ultimately told that she needed to inform her analyst of his dismissal from his position. According to AP, this was the first time he had learned of this decision.

> All the rage and pain that his three mature colleagues couldn't face in telling him was heaped on me, a vulnerable candidate at the height of a positive transference after six helpful years of work with this analyst. I never recovered a positive view of my institute. ... I was so shocked to be asked to lie to my own analyst for two weeks while they kept delaying confronting him. I never lie to anyone, but I was given no choice. The whole thing was handled very destructively for me and for my analyst.

CR recounted being painfully isolated after her analyst's death. She was planning to begin terminating her training analysis when she noticed her analyst was ill. He began to miss sessions. He told her he was having surgery and would return to work several months later. When he did not come back, she called a colleague who told her he had metastatic cancer. She wrote and wished him well, and then he telephoned her.

> I knew he was very ill and expected to die. I was very sad. He said that I was ready to end and that when he came back we'd set a date. He had tears in his voice. That phone call and what he said meant a lot to me. ... He died, and his wife called and told me. The funeral was very powerful. None of the analysts talked to me – only one of my TA supervisors made eye contact. I realized he was my analyst's analyst.
>
> No one called to see how I was doing. I tried to talk with a number of people. Taking classes, I'd bring it up, but there was no response ... I stopped practising as an analyst. I was always torn between the arts and therapy.

Later CR returned to treatment with an analyst who confirmed that the analytic community did not know how to deal with an analyst's death. She experienced this acknowledgement as supportive of her experience and found it comforting.

In two other situations mentioned earlier, the analytic institute or community was supportive and facilitating when the analysts died abruptly. KB was helped to find a new analyst by the analytic institute. And CX (pp. 34–37) was contacted immediately by her analyst's wife, who was herself an analyst. She referred CX to another analyst who helped her mourn the loss of her analyst, integrate what they had done, and successfully complete her analytic work.

Having one's analyst become ill or die during the course of analysis inevitably causes distress for an analysand. But when the analyst denies this reality and/or the analytic community fails to communicate with or offer support to the analysand, the difficulties and distress are compounded. In this study at least, when there was support from the community, analysands were better able to deal with the loss and continue their own analytic progress and development.

Analyst initiates ending – for non-external reason (4)

AT had a history of medical trauma as well as a histrionic mother with wide swings in mood. A series of therapies had not been successful in relieving her depressive feelings. Her five-year analysis was very stormy. AT thought she was borderline, but her analyst didn't share this view.

> I think my analyst was a geek, not someone I'd be friends with, but he did an absolutely fabulous analysis with me. He literally saved my life, but I had to figure insights out on my own after stopping. … I didn't decide on termination; my analyst did. I wasn't thrilled with this, but it wasn't wrong. I said I was afraid to terminate but thought I probably should. We'd done much of the work. But any time would have been hard.
>
> I thought he stopped because he was worn out with me, and maybe he thought I'd never terminate on my own. I'd been going five days a week. My guess is I would have wanted to go another year. I worked really hard that last year.

After termination, AT integrated the work she had done in analysis. Using the self-analytic skill she had developed in her treatment, she attained insights about herself that changed her sense of herself and others. But this is a tale to recount in Chapter 5.

While AT's analyst was the one to propose the ending, they worked collaboratively for another year. But such collaboration does not always occur. As I will describe later in this chapter, some analysands react with feelings of injury and are unable to express this, making the ending unsatisfactorily incomplete. In the previous chapter, there were several descriptions of analysts who resisted their patients' wishes to end. Here I will illustrate one analyst's proposing an abrupt ending when her analysand brought up his wish to end his analysis.

AL had begun a second analysis when he found himself unexpectedly facing a crisis in both his marriage and his career. He considered his previous analysis satisfying and successful and would have returned to his analyst, but for various reasons this was not possible. Initially, the second analysis was helpful to him, because re-engaging in the analytic dialogue allowed him to articulate his difficulties. However, the longer his analysis continued, the more dissatisfied he felt. His central issue, why he had tolerated for so long being treated badly, wasn't analysed. Instead his analyst seemed to treat him nicely, behaving like a good friend and colleague who wanted to be helpful and encouraging, rather than a professional who would explore his unconscious motivations.

In retrospect AL thinks that the very situation that had precipitated treatment was, at least in part, being repeated in his second analysis. His analyst offered extensive tales from her own life and chatted about her own work or about colleagues they both knew. He found himself focusing on what she was interested in rather than following his own associative ways. Even though he was still intensely involved in the analytic relationship with his analyst, he felt more and more at a loss with her analytically, and often ended his sessions perplexed or dissatisfied.

After a holiday break, he was vaguely disgruntled throughout his session and wondered aloud where all of this was getting him. To his surprise his analyst proposed ending his treatment. He said that he too had thought of eventually terminating and would consider it in the upcoming months. She responded: 'Why not stop it now?' AL said he was flabbergasted and tried to reflect on what it would be like to terminate. But when she reiterated her suggestion about ending immediately, he thought that if she wasn't willing to analyse and work with him on his complaints and questions, it would, in fact, be better to end it right away. So he said okay, got up and left.

This sudden ending was painful for him, but AL eventually found a senior analyst with whom he worked through his experience of this sudden ending.

AL's description suggests that he felt the abruptness of the ending was his analyst's retaliation for expressing the wish to end treatment. While it is the only example I will give, it is not the only instance in which this occurred.

Analyst ends based on analysand's life changes (1)

MS, who had a history of incest and alcoholism in her family, came to analysis because of an eating disorder. Her symptom disappeared quickly once she was in analysis. She developed a sense of confidence and strength and was able to find words to express her feelings.

> My analyst and I talked about terminating because I was getting married. It was a period of great intensity. She had been in my life six years, and I was losing her. I did get married before we ended, but I think I knew I had made a poor choice in my husband. Now I think I could have used more analysis. But it was also a good time in that I'd developed interests and more self-esteem. I'm sure I was sad and missed her, but I focused on myself and the excitement of moving on – though I had some anxiety about being without her.
>
> A year and a half ago, which was twelve years after stopping, I called her and she suggested we get together socially. She had invited me to an open house, but I never went. I was too anxious. Then this year, I went to her house for lunch. I didn't feel so scared any more, and I wanted to have a relationship. I was having trouble in my life and angry that we'd ended too soon. The very day we were meeting my husband was threatening suicide. I thought I could use her support and did.
>
> Maybe it's childish, but I blame her. How could she let me marry him? I feel she didn't help me enough on my choice of partner and too much of our decision to end was based on my getting married.

MS did not tell her analyst about the anger and disappointment she had experienced at the ending – though perhaps her thoughts about this have clarified in retrospect. She did not return for treatment, despite her regret and belief there was more she needed to understand. Instead, she chose to have a social relationship with her former analyst. This choice will be discussed more fully in the next chapter on post-analytic contacts. It is clear that the social relationship did not resolve her negative feelings.

II

Analysand initiates ending – for external reason (15)

Analysand moves (8)

Eight of the analysands in my study moved during their analysis. In two instances, there was distress about the relocation. Six of the relocations took place for positive professional or personal reasons that were not connected with the analytic process. According to the literature, when analysands end their analyses because they are moving for a better position, pleasure in this accomplishment is often the predominant affect (Glick 1987). If the move is for a spouse's job, ambivalence may be much greater.

In two instances, the former analysands were regretful about their relocation. For SR, it was not only, or primarily, about the loss of the first analyst and analysis, but about a total world she had grown up in and loved. The first analysis also engaged her in an erotic transference that was never revived in her latter analysis.

The other former analysand, FM, an analyst who will be described in more detail in Chapter 5, moved because his child's schooling required it. His analysis ended over 50 years ago, but he still feels it is an active force in his life. Many years after the move, at the time of a life crisis, he returned to a psychoanalytic therapy for a year and a half. This treatment helped integrate his insights with his behaviour.

> My analyst thought my progress was sufficient, even if not I could find another analyst. It was two months from deciding to leaving. There were certain things she thought I didn't get to, and she was right ... I continued to do self-analytic work and learned a lot through my patients.

JS was happy about her move for personal and professional reasons but was sad about leaving her analyst. She believed she had completed a very successful treatment, which had allowed her to separate from a fused relationship with her mother, who had pushed JS because of her precociousness as a musician. She believed her mother's vicarious pleasure in her success prevented JS from recognizing her own wish for independence and having a more balanced life. It was her unconscious blocking for a few moments in the midst of a concert that had led her to seek analysis. She thought her analysis transformed her life.

After moving, JS reported that she would periodically return and meet with her former analyst. Ultimately, she found a therapist where she lived. Later, when I contacted JS about permission to use this material, she added:

> The therapist I saw after the move really helped me to maintain what I learned from my analysis as well as facilitated even greater insights. So he had what I would term the same kind of power and importance – just of a different nature.

Moving, when it occurs because of the analysand's initiative, did not seem to stimulate feelings of abandonment in the individuals in this study. My findings are in accordance with the literature that it is *the meaning of the move* to the analysand that is most relevant. However, those meanings may be more complex than they appear. The interruption of a valuable analytic experience – unless it is replaced by another that is felt to be as valuable – may lead to more regret and sense of loss than was initially anticipated.

Analysand initiates ending – for non-external reason (25)[2]

Analysands who end their analyses for psychological factors may not always communicate their reasons. In this study, there are also times when analysands wish to end and analysts resist, as I described in the previous chapter.

Sixteen participants in the study left their analysis angry or disappointed. Four have been described above – three in relation to their analysts' unacknowledged illnesses and one in reaction to her analyst's move. One other initiated the ending of analysis ostensibly based on external realities, but later she recognized there was unfinished work. This patient will, therefore, be considered as having ended for a psychological reason.

1. Analysand leaves because of analyst's sexual boundary violation (3)

As described in Chapter 2, three interviewees ended their analyses when they learned that their analysts were having a sexual relationship with another analysand. Two of the women could only decide to stop treatment when they recognized that their analysts were also exploiting them in non-sexual ways. Both of these individuals were fortunate to have had subsequent analytic experiences that they viewed as successful.

The issue of sexual boundary violations was discussed in the previous chapter (pp. 39–40), but I will repeat here that such abusive experiences are likely to have a long-lasting effect on the nature and quality of later relationships, as was the case with RZ, previously mentioned in Chapter 2. RZ was a clinician in analysis with the same person as a friend with whom she felt very competitive. She had an idealizing transference to her analyst – an idealization she recognized she had felt in relation to her father. Her analyst had told her that her friend 'didn't hold a candle' to her. RZ left treatment the day she learned her analyst and this friend were having an affair. Her description is a powerful reminder of the reverberations that occur when boundaries are violated.

> I felt I needed more treatment desperately. I sought numerous consultations and couldn't connect. I finally worked with a woman once a week until I moved. Then, I worked in a clinic at a frantic pace, often working well more than a full-time schedule. After three years, I went into analytic training. The forefront issue was a conflicted relationship. I probably worked out the first treatment more in supervision and writing. I thought I'd put it behind me.
>
> I don't think I realized how much it affected me until I moved again. I finished my training in a different city. I didn't realize how much analysis had been spoiled for me until then. I didn't allow myself to feel deeply immersed. I think the first analyst was sad that I left. I had such conscious rivalry with this other woman, but I never thought it could really happen. With the next two analysts – two women – I felt deep respect and gratitude but not transference. The first woman was very savvy. I was much freer. I took everything with a grain of salt, felt much freer to argue with her. Leaving didn't feel like a big deal. In the third analysis, the woman was smart and very plain-spoken. I trusted her, was fond of her, but she felt like a friendly mentor, helpful, but I never allowed her to become that important. … I didn't feel special to her or her to me.
>
> I feel I understand in a deeper way the importance of the breach. I understand the vulnerability patients feel, but I almost envy my patients. I lost something of the freshness of this work. It's bittersweet. I'm in study groups. I think about, talk about, write about my work to stay clear about what I'm doing, but I don't think I can work on it in analysis any more. I think I underestimated the attachment I made to my first analyst. I was in shock and denial. The first analyst captured my relationship with my father – so idealized.

I will repeat what I wrote in the previous chapter, as I do not believe this point can be over emphasized: 'Since the analytic method invites the patient to develop an erotic transference for the sake of self-understanding and greater freedom of desire, both the process and the patient are abused when an analyst takes advantage of the patient's vulnerability' (p. 39).

Analysands who have a sexual relationship with their analysts or, in RZ's case, who know that her analyst has violated his ethical responsibility with another patient may find it difficult to trust or love again. They can come to distrust themselves and their capacities to accurately assess other people, especially those in positions of authority. They can come to fear their own power to seduce. And if the patient is in the mental health field, his or her sense of identity as a clinician may be irreparably compromised. That desire can be aroused, that it can be experienced as love for the patient, the analyst or both – all these things are certainly possible. But it is never acceptable that either physical passion or emotional attachment should be acted on.

2. Analysand leaves because of inability to tolerate the analyst's limits (3)

The examples that follow have already been referred to in Chapter 2. Here I will supply more detail.

CH abruptly left her analysis when she understood that her analyst was not going to have a sexual relationship with her. She recognized that he was holding to the boundaries in analysis, and she could not tolerate the frustration. She does not indicate how her analyst interpreted her wishes. A second analysis helped her accept that she would not get everything she wanted, but, again, she left abruptly, wanting to 'just live life'. And again she did not elaborate on how her analyst handled the situation. CH recognized her difficulties with frustration but did not seem to have gained any perspective on her behaviour. But in a later contact, when I requested her permission to publish this account, she had clearly become reflective and asked me to add:

> Over time I came to some vague understanding that my need to flee was a way to reverse my father's abrupt 'dropping' of me – his emotional withdrawal and angry, critical stance towards me when I finally refused his overtures when I was fourteen. *My* abandonments of my male analysts could also be interpreted as expression of anger towards my father, which became generalized towards men. I could defeat my analysts and refuse their good fathering.
>
> I left my second analyst because I was better, and analysis no longer had the imperative it had held for me in those earlier years. And I worried that those years of psychoanalysis with male analysts were partially substituting for a relationship with a real male partner, which I did not have much of while in psychoanalysis. Post-analysis I am three years plus into the best romantic relationship of my life. *Not perfect* at all! But *waaaay* better thanks to psychoanalysis.

SS's analyst had been reluctant to treat her because she had originally seen her in couple's therapy. SS was a poet, and during the course of the analysis, her analyst refused to read her poetry. SS did not specify the manner in which her analyst had understood, interpreted or talked with her about this refusal. Throughout the analysis, SS threatened to leave. She understood that she had repeated in her relationship with her analyst the experience of rejection she had had with her mother.

> I knew I was doing to her what my mother did to me. I'd say, 'I need you to help me do something different.' So I acknowledged it. I thought I was meant

to let it all out, and then we'd figure out how to deal with it. But as a couple, we couldn't deal with it. My analyst *never* told me she was only in her first year of training when I became her patient nor that she had never conducted an analysis before mine. She was always very squirrelly about her credentials. I inquired repeatedly about all these things, and she would not answer the questions. ...

I went on Zoloft a year into the analysis, and this dramatically affected everything that happened. Without the intervention of medication – which my analyst, a social worker – was against and which she repeatedly interpreted as a defence against her, I believe I would have become more suicidal than I already was and would have found it impossible to leave – ever – what was clearly a problematic analysis conducted by a novice.

When I left, I immediately experienced relief, peace, clarity. My life changed once I disengaged from what I felt was a mutually destructive process. Then I could see her more clearly. A month or two later, I was regretful. I felt it was unseemly and unkind and saw it as a pattern of something I'd done in my life. It helped me to think about it differently. I went back to see her a few months later. When I went back, I did not go back for analysis – it was once a week sitting-up psychotherapy, with the specific goal of re-terminating.

But some of the pattern repeated itself. When SS asked her former analyst to return the journal of her analysis that she had left with her, her analyst told her she had shredded it. Her analyst could not explain to her satisfaction why she had done this.

Eventually I realized I was not the right patient for her, and she was not the right therapist for me. But this time I told her calmly that I had gotten things from her but I should stop. ... I felt it was another relationship in which I'd failed. But I did have gains from analysis. I felt the analytic setting and its demands had forced me to straightforwardly acknowledge feelings of chaos and dependency in me. I could libidinize them before – great sex! – but it affected my personal relationships. After analysis I could look at feelings and not feel chaotic. I suspect it was a bad match.

Sometimes what an analysand wants in the relationship with the analyst cannot be transformed into something that can be understood, and the analysand cannot withstand the tension of the ungratified wish. Other times, an enactment is occurring that is partially understood, but it still cannot be tolerated. The tension is increased when analysands feel their analysts have been unable to recognize or acknowledge the part they play in what has transpired. It is not possible to know from SS's report if the analyst explored the meaning of SS's wishes or the decision to set the particular limits that she did. SS ended analysis three years ago and has not returned to treatment.

3. Analysand leaves after analyst resists the wish to stop (9)

As reported in Chapter 2, nine study participants struggled with their analysts about their wish to end treatment. Three were able to negotiate their endings in a way that ultimately seemed mutually satisfactory, but six remained contentious.

HH, mentioned briefly in the previous chapter, described his feelings about the struggle in ending his treatment, which he was unable to express to his analyst.

> My analyst confronted me more directly about what I needed to do. It brought up more anxiety. It made me feel I'd not progressed as much as I felt I had. He was not really in favour of my terminating; he felt I needed more. I didn't directly tell him how I felt. I didn't tell him enough of what I felt about this. … I still have unresolved negative feelings. I don't know that I would have been able to tell him. I felt angry, but underlying it was a sadness. I have a need to be a good boy. You feel you want to hear from your father, 'Go and conquer the world.' Anything less makes you feel less.

Six of these former analysands were left with anger and discontent feelings about both the analysis and the way it ended. While most of them expressed positive feelings about what they had gained from analysis overall, their more elaborated descriptions of their treatment experiences have a negative cast and emphasize what they couldn't say.

For some interviewees, the struggles with their first analyst had remained unresolved. BG wanted to end treatment with her non-training analyst in order to begin her training analysis. She reported that the first analyst opposed this and warned her that she would be humiliated during the interview process if she took this step.

> After about six years I wanted to stop. I wanted to become an analyst and I wanted a break. My analyst was not a training analyst. She opposed my stopping, and that marred the last few years. I had always assumed that she needed me for the hours required to become a TA, although this has never been confirmed, obviously.
>
> She told me she would be a TA soon, but fortunately for me she wasn't a TA soon enough to be *my* TA. I used that fact to stop with her. I told her I wanted to start classes as soon as I could, and I also used that reason to stop. She told me my worst fears were true – i.e. that in a 'good interview' my most shameful things would come out. She also said that if I broke off with her, 'It would get out.' I applied to be a candidate and told her. She didn't oppose it then. She'd get into fights with me. I'm very good at getting people to fight with me. I asked her if she'd consulted with anyone about me and our conflict, and she said no.
>
> I was afraid to stop with her. I felt the analytic community would disapprove. But if I had been as I am now, I would have done it. I'd have left.

... She'd harp on my difficulties as she did about breaks. She'd rub my nose in things. This is a new thought: I knew she was angry and felt disapproving of me. It matched my relationship with my mother, so I just accepted it.

Until I was no longer seeing her, no one in the analytic community would discuss with me my wish to terminate in spite of her opposition or encourage me to get consultation about the situation outside the community. After I ended, people did speak freely to me, and it has always seemed clear that they didn't want to say anything at the time for fear that I would quote (or misquote) them back to her, and risk making an enemy of her. She was seen as cold and not very well liked in the analytic community.

Eventually, BG insisted on ending and entered an analysis that she found very different and deeply rewarding. She also became an analyst.

The account of BG suggests she was able to make analytic gains with one analyst and not another. The response of BG's first analyst, as BG described it, seems determined by countertransference and possibly personal issues. This may have reflected the analyst's personal dynamics or abilities. But these issues may also have been exacerbated in the patient–analyst match. I remind the reader that the analysts might report different perspectives.

4. Analysands leave treatment abruptly, with unfinished work (1)

NP abruptly initiated the end of her nine-year analysis, rationalizing that external demands in her life – babies and her work – required it. Later she came to realize the psychological component in her decision.

> I couldn't figure out how to come even one time a week. Even as I was open, I realize now I was holding back. I wasn't connecting deeply. That ending was abrupt – only two to three weeks' notice. I hadn't dealt with the issues really. I didn't understand the pattern that I could help others but not myself. ... I felt I was never measuring up. ... I didn't feel so connected to my daughter until she was three and a half or four. I saw her as a pushing-away person too. Only when I saw this, and spoke to her from my heart to her heart, did it become clear to me that I wasn't really connecting to others. No one would have thought it.

Fifteen years later, NP returned to treatment ready to face and work on the issues that she had turned away from in her earlier analysis. Her original ending reflected a character defence of which she was unaware at the time. Her capacity to recognize this tendency in herself – 'that I could walk out like I didn't know him – it was a shock that I was like this' – eventually led to her return to treatment. The process of her self-scrutiny and the insight derived from it will be illustrated in Chapter 5.

5. Analysand leaves after analyst proposes ending (11)

Four former analysands struggled with anger and disappointment, seeing themselves as not being 'good enough' at analysis.

BE had had two earlier analyses that she believed had not been helpful. She offered this version of the sequence of events leading to her ending of a 12-year analysis:

> Somewhere in the last two–three years, I don't know exactly when, I first reduced from four to three, and then to two times a week frequency, and in the last year, to once a week. I reduced the sessions as my money was running out. So perhaps, in a sense, the last three years were a kind of beginning termination process.
>
> Here's how I remembered how the sequence of termination events unfolded. In my last year at one session, my analyst said something to the effect of, 'You are doing well, so perhaps you can stop soon.' I did say, 'But who am I going to talk to?' Of course he did not answer. For me, anticipating the break of this intense, important relationship was frightening. However I do remember – I am not sure exactly when – that I indicated that being on my own was going to be a true test of how much I had grown and would be able to handle.
>
> A couple of months or longer after that, I gave my analyst a list of all the sessions I had seen him for about the last two–three months and asked him to fill out an insurance form listing these sessions. The following week when I asked him for it, he indicated that he had not done it. I think it was at this point that I felt truly rejected and pushed away. It felt to me, in my regressed state, that he wasn't taking care of me because he didn't want me any more. I did express my anger that he hadn't done it and felt that he knew that I was low on money.
>
> These thoughts fuelled my anger. However I didn't express to him that I felt that he didn't want me any more, because these feelings were so painful. I barely could express them to myself. So shortly after the insurance incident, perhaps a week or two, I left the analysis, which probably seemed to him abrupt. I did have written contact with him about three times after that, letting him know how I was doing, but I never mentioned those feelings of being unwanted.
>
> After leaving the analysis, by means of self-analysis I became more aware and able to work on those feelings of rejection. I thought the intensity of those feelings could be linked to the birth of my sister at age three and a half, when I must have felt uncared for by my mother and not enough of a woman for my father because I couldn't have babies. It is likely that the feeling of being uncared for could go back to my infancy. My analyst at certain points in the analysis underscored that my mother might have been depressed during my infancy, and this could have impacted on my self-esteem, and probably I

would imagine some degree of narcissistic rage. I know from stories and pictures that I was an alert, curious, and precocious infant and toddler – so facing an on-and-off worried, depressed mother most likely was deflating and distressing.

I feel that in some sense the unfolding of the termination process of my analysis was an enactment on my and my analyst's part. I think those feelings of being uncared for and unwanted perhaps were on a non-verbal, more unconscious level. One could ask why, in a week, he didn't fill out the insurance form when I had so carefully written it for him.

BE's analysis ended 13 years ago, and she did not seek further treatment. Her description of the ending indicates that she had acquired considerable insight about herself and her struggles. However, she was also left with residual conflicts and low self-esteem that she was ashamed to communicate to her analyst – at least in part because of unresolved self-criticism. Again, her reluctance to communicate conscious feelings is highlighted. Shame and humiliation are particularly difficult for patients to bring up in treatment because they seem to be experienced as facts about themselves rather than as feelings that can be analysed and understood.

Analysts would need to be aware that their analysands are distressed by the suggestion that analysis could be ended at that time. In order to be appropriately responsive, they would need to explore the patients' reactions as well as possibly to extend the length of the work. While there are non-verbal ways by which patients indicate their upset, in the situations reported in these interviews the analysts did not seem to recognize these communications, if they occurred.

In another example, although the analysand had been upset by her analyst's proposal to end the treatment, the analyst was responsive to her analysand's wish to extend the termination period by exploring and, to some extent, resolving her patient's feelings.

***

Discussion

Let me begin the discussion with the caveat that what is presented here is the truth of the patient's subjective experience as each reported it. As I have repeatedly indicated, it is not an objective truth any more than the analyst's report would be. As analysts, we certainly appreciate the importance of how the patient experiences things, but we must always keep in mind that the other member of the dyad may see it differently. I reiterate that research has told us that the perspectives of the analysand and of the analyst are not always the same (Kantrowitz et al. 1987a; O'Malley, Suh and Strupp 1983).

Three things stand out in this data on unilateral endings. Perhaps the clearest and most important finding is the impact of what is *not* told, whether by the analyst or the analysand. When analysts do not inform analysands about their illnesses or plans to retire or move, it adversely affects the ending.

Similarly, when analysands do not communicate their experiences of hurt, disappointment or anger about how the termination is being handled, the likelihood of having an opportunity to work it out differently is decreased and a satisfying outcome is unlikely.

A few analysands were unable to work out their difficulties with any of the analysts they saw. Another few found that the first analysis profoundly affected them, for better or worse, in ways that later analyses did not. It is not clear whether it was the impact of a first experience or the nature of the patient–analyst match that accounted for the great significance of the initial analysis.

Second, while non-mutual endings are not desirable, and certainly not recommended, these findings indicate that they are not necessarily always as disruptive of positive assimilation of an analytic experience as the literature suggests. Nor do they inevitably lead to dissatisfaction with the overall analytic experience. Many of the study participants have been able to maintain a balanced perspective on what they have and have not gained from analysis. Others who located the difficulty within the particular analytic dyad were later able to find another analyst with whom they had a very satisfying experience.

Third, with time, some interviewees reported a more positive perspective on their analyses. This was also true of some individuals who reread what they had told me only a few years earlier. For some, but not all, of the former analysands who amended their initial presentation, this newer and brighter view seemed related to positive changes in their lives. They credited psychoanalysis with these changes and that altered their view of their analysis.

I will explore each of these findings in great detail below.

I. Communication

Withholding information by the analyst

It is understandable that when someone is seriously ill, he or she may be in denial of the illness. However, many study participants experienced disappointment, a loss of trust in their analyst, having expected that their analyst's emotional capacities to share and not deny would be greater. Having to deal with this disappointment and negotiate an ending to treatment without the aid of the analyst affect their feelings about their analytic experience. When, in addition, the analytic community neither communicates with nor supports the patients during the illness of the analyst or afterwards, it may leave them with bitter feelings about the psychoanalytic field itself. CR, for example (p. 62), gave up her aspiration to become an analyst.

While we need to respect our colleagues' privacy, we need to find a way to not leave their patients to struggle alone with these painful, difficult situations. Note that the two accounts describing how the analytic community dealt with the patient directly and supportively after the analyst's death had very positive outcomes.

When an analyst is sick but not necessarily going to die, the situation is more complex. Abend (1982) and Lasky (1990) present concerns about how knowledge of the analyst's actual state of health might interfere with analytic work. But I think we have learned that transferences are far more robust than previously assumed. Details about the analyst's health are not necessary and may be burdensome, but some communication about the seriousness or non-seriousness of the illness and the expected date of return is likely to strengthen the analytic relationship rather than interfere with it. The anxiety and loss of trust that may follow being told nothing will surely do far more damage to the analytic relationship than providing factual information.

While illness may raise ambiguities about what is told and when, moving or retiring should not. As illustrated in the former analysands' accounts of finding out from others – or not being told in a timely fashion – that their analyst is closing his or her practice, the lack of direct communication creates a loss of trust and a feeling of betrayal as well as anger that may have longstanding consequences. In contrast, when the analyst is straightforward about his or her intention to end because of a move or retirement and gives sufficient notice, it may enable the analysand to do deep analytic work around separation as well as many other issues.

Not communicating their feelings and reactions by the analysands

Most analysts make the assumption that their patients are telling them, or will try to tell them, what they are experiencing. The examples of patients not saying all they were feeling or thinking were numerous, as was their pain involved in silencing themselves. When analysands feel rejected, as they often do when their analyst makes a unilateral decision to end the treatment, their sense of humiliation and shame makes it even harder for them to share their deepest feelings. A striking number of former analysands in this project also reported that they believed their analysts were unaware that they felt as they did. Here I repeat a few quotes:

> AM: The analysis was good, but why couldn't there be an end? I needed to talk with someone so badly, to be heard. My father didn't listen, and in the end part my analyst didn't listen. I didn't say to her then that it was a repetition. So was I not a good patient?

> AK: If I disagreed with her, she would never say she had a role in it. So I learned not to bring it up. She told me she was moving six months before she moved. I bit my tongue to not say I was relieved. I was worried it would be used against me. ... I fault myself for not being strong enough to say, 'I want to and am going to leave.' She thought I was aggressive, but in the end I was

compliant. I didn't want it to be that I was leaving her because of my problems, because I was messed up.

BE: I felt he didn't care about me and wanted to get rid of me. ... I felt rejected and hurt, as if he didn't like me. I didn't tell him how I felt. ... As a little girl I was punished for not being grown up enough by my father. It was the height of the Oedipal time. I felt I was not measuring up. I was ashamed to say that to my analyst. I felt I should just leave and deal with it.

HH: He confronted me more directly about what I needed to do. It brought up more anxiety. It made me feel I'd not progressed as much as I felt I had. He was not really in favour of my terminating; he felt I needed more. I didn't directly tell him how I felt. I didn't tell him enough of what I felt about this. ... I still have unresolved negative feelings. I don't know that I would be able to tell him. I felt angry, but underlying it was a sadness.

It should be noted that it is not only their feelings that these analysands did not communicate; some of them also did not report their insights about the transference itself, as doing so was too humiliating. BE believed she needed to be a big girl and tolerate her feelings as she had done as a child. HH believed he needed to be 'a good boy' to get his father's approval. As analysts, we need to keep in mind that our patients may not be telling us everything. The ending – when the press of a now-or-never feeling exists – may also make some communications harder. Patients – especially ones who tend to be self-critical and experience shame – are likely to worry about their last impression.

2. The effect of a non-mutual ending on the analytic experience

According to the literature, a non-mutual ending, unilaterally decided upon or forced by the analyst, is likely to be more painful for the analysand than one that is mutually agreed on. The distress, however, will vary depending on the particular analysand and the analyst and the particular way the decision is communicated (Dewald 1966, 1982; Limentani 1982; Goldberg and Marcus 1985; Glick 1987; Martinez 1989; Hoffman 2009). This proved to be true in my study.

In eight of the 48 analyses that were terminated unilaterally, four ended by the patients and four by their analysts, important insights were stimulated by unexpectedly introduced terminations. These analysands were not happy about the management of the ending, but they nonetheless viewed their treatment as successful and were pleased with what they accomplished. Moreover, as noted above, when reviewing their initial negative descriptions several years later, an additional four analysands expressed a more positive perspective on their analyses and acknowledged gains they had achieved. Approximately 44 per cent of the group that had non-mutual endings went on to have another analysis that they reported as successful. This finding seems notable, but it must be remembered that the sample, though large compared with most psychoanalytic surveys, is small in terms of actual numbers and is also self-selected. A larger, randomly selected sample might not support these findings.

A few analysands believe the unexpected ending had unanticipated benefits One example is CX (pp. 34–37), whose analyst died and who then had a second treatment that enabled her to understand and integrate aspects of her self that she had not previously understood. While such understanding might have come in the first analysis if the analyst had lived, CX believed that the second analyst worked with her in a way that was more attuned to her needs. A better example is YA (pp. 32–34), whose analyst's retirement encouraged her psychological development, pushing her to understand her denial of dependency and appreciate her separateness as a person.

3. The effect of time

A number of analysands were able to appreciate the full benefit of analysis only after its ending. JS (pp. 65–66) moved and was unable to find another analyst in the community where she relocated. Eventually, she had some analytically oriented therapy that was mainly supportive. However, she found over time that the insights from her analysis were not only sustaining but also deepened.

NP (p. 71), who abruptly ended her analysis with little feeling about stopping, came to understand previously unrecognized aspects of her character and conflict. She eventually returned to her analyst with great appreciation and respect for their work together. Both HH (p. 42) and BD (p. 60), who initiated the ending of their treatments, felt their analysts were disappointed in them. In the aftermath of analysis, they each came to understand what they had brought to the transference. Post-termination contact enabled HH to restore positive feelings for and from his former analyst. This situation will be discussed in more detail in Chapter 5.

Similarly, EO (pp. 38–39), whose analyst moved and wished to continue the work by phone, came to recognize a transference dependency and the repetition of a maternal relationship in the struggle over termination. Although she ended with disappointment and anger towards her analyst, over time in her post-treatment self-analytic process she recognized that she derived great insight and benefit from the work. In addition, she felt that her increased sensitivity to the use of influence and power has made her a more attuned analyst.

Further thoughts

Non-mutual endings and past history

When ending of analysis is not mutually agreed upon, for whatever reason, there is an added complication in terms of what the unilateral decision meant to the analysand. For five of the six former analysands who had a history of trauma, the non-mutuality of the ending recapitulated in some manner their previous painful experiences. EO and AT were able to do meaningful self-analytic work in its aftermath. They both felt helped by their analytic experience in ways that continue to reverberate over time. Other former analysands, while acknowledging significant gains from the analytic work, had persistent feelings of distress, which ranged from disquietude to significant disruptions of previously beneficial experiences – perhaps an echo of their past painful experiences.

Time and timelessness

Analysis creates a sense of timelessness. The past is revived in the present to be re-assimilated. While the length of analysis is based on individual need, the experience is meant to have a limit in time. Either the patient or the analyst can lose this perspective. This chapter reports cautionary tales about impositions of endings, but there is a need to keep in mind the idea of termination and the idea of time passing and life continuing to move on.

Analysts can introduce the idea of ending. Awad (2006) suggests introducing the idea of termination to confront a patient who denies the passage of time and refuses to change. Presenting the idea of termination not as a unilateral decision but as a way of making patients aware of the idea of termination may increase their ability to step outside the transference and consider analysis in relation to the rest of their lives. Kris (1992) makes a similar point: the analyst must help the analysand to be mindful of the idea of termination. As Schafer (2007), Salberg (2010a) and Bass (2009) all emphasize, analysis is intended to be an aid to living, not a substitute. Most of the former analysands reporting in this project seem to agree.

Alternatively, analysands can introduce the idea of ending. In this project, many patients felt they had to struggle with their analysts to end the treatment. They believed they were ready and that their analysts were not. Not only were their analysts not responsive, they obstructed their wishes to end. A sample that is based on volunteers always has certain biases built in, biases based on why people volunteer. We cannot know how representative is the feeling of being kept from ending. Undoubtedly, feeling held back when ready to leave generates strong feelings that these former analysands wished to express and have known by others.

While we are limited in the generalizations we can draw from this very diverse sample, we can conclude that recounting experiences of anger, hurt and outrage at analysts' behaviour is a motivating factor for volunteering. It may help these former analysands recover from their sense of previous helplessness. Telling their side of the story with a potential for having it published may have given them a sense of empowerment that could be reparative. It is likely that the motivation to have their residual distress on record accounted for such a large percentage of individuals, almost 59 per cent of the sample, presenting non-mutual endings. Certainly their accounts will help analysts become more alert to ways that they might present unilateral decisions about ending or communications related to illness.

Analysts must remain acutely attuned to their analysands' reactions to ending. At the same time, they must be mindful of their own countertransference and other personal feelings that may lead them to hold on too long or too tightly or, alternatively, to let the analysand go too quickly without adequate exploration of the meaning of the ending.

Notes

1   When an analyst dies unexpectedly, the analysis, obviously, ends traumatically; it is not a matter of a unilateral decision. Nonetheless, the analysand is left alone to find a way to deal with the impact of the abrupt, unprepared for ending.
2   In four instances, external and non-external reasons are interwoven; thus, they are listed in both categories but counted only once in the total number of non-mutual endings.

Chapter 4

The effect of post-analytic contact

My focus in this chapter is how patients' contact with their analyst after termination affects their feelings, thoughts and representation of themselves, the analyst, the analytic relationship and analysis itself. It is necessary to specify the context of this contact. Returning in the role of a patient is different from meeting in a professional setting, which is also different from having a social interaction. What occurs when the patient and analyst meet again in any of these situations may facilitate the assimilation of analytic gains or disrupt it. This is especially true when analytic treatment has ended badly, as post-treatment contact may either be healing or add to the injury.

As previously discussed, the situation for former analysands who are analysts or analysts in training is different from the situation of those who are not, since those in the field of psychoanalysis are likely to see their analysts in a professional or social setting after ending treatment; whereas for others, future contact with the analyst is unlikely unless they return for consultation or a continuation of treatment.

Return as a patient

As stated in the Introduction, it had long been assumed that after termination the analysand internalized the analysis and worked through the loss of the analyst and the analytic relationship (Parres and Ramirez 1966). Both the consolidation of the analytic work (Roose *et al.* 2004) and deep mourning for the analyst (Craige 2002) required the treatment to end. In decades past, because it was thought that a return might disrupt the resolution of the transference neurosis and its post-analytic consolidation (Firestein 1969, 1974), it was believed that a return meant that the analysis had been incomplete. While contemporary analysts appreciate that the process of analysis is never entirely complete (Bonvitz 2007), the previously idealized vision of analysis influenced analytic thinking and teaching long after there was evidence that a 'complete' analysis was a myth.

Tessman (2003) writes:

> It was traditionally assumed, that the analysand's individuation from the analyst requires definitive separation, which in turn was then expected to usher

in the necessary libidinal renunciation. This assumption may underlie some of the divergence about how patients who seek out their analysts for further contact have been thought about. Such patients have been characterized as still having particular difficulties, such as deficiencies in the capacity for internalization, a history of severe early losses, unanalysed separation anxiety or primarily pre-Oedipal problems (Schlessinger and Robins 1974, 1975; Lord *et al.* 1978; Blanck and Blanck 1988; Luborsky in Schachter and Johan 1989).

The power of such implanted beliefs is illustrated by Hartlaub and his research group (1986). They had all shared

> a fantasy that after a successful analysis the patient would not need further contact with the analyst, or, conversely, that re-contact somehow cast doubt on the completeness of the analysis. The fantasy existed although none of us could ever recall ever actually having been taught this. (p. 894)

The fantasy reported by Hartlaub and his researchers supports the concern about mythologizing in our field that I hope more data will help to decrease.

It should be remembered, as stated in Chapter 1, that even in the earlier days of analysis, there were contradictory beliefs endorsing the benefit of future consultation with one's former analyst (Buxbaum 1950; Reich 1950). Firestein's survey (1982) also indicated considerable variation in analysts' views concerning future visits to their former analysts after termination.

Informal conversations among analysts indicate that contemporary psycho-analysts most often believe that returning to the previous analyst or another analyst is beneficial if an individual encounters post-treatment difficulties. They are usually in agreement with Schachter (1992), a long-standing advocate for post-analytic contact, that patients and analysts should decide together about post-analytic returns (Schachter 2009). As also indicated in Chapter 1, follow-up studies (Hartlaub, Martin and Rhine 1986; Roose *et al.* 2004) on post-analytic contact corroborated Schachter's beliefs: a large percentage of the analysands who reported successfully completing treatment returned to rework termination. Contrary to earlier beliefs, they reported that telling their former analysts about their accomplishments – and having these achievements acknowledged – facilitated their assimilation of analytic gains.

Post-termination contact between analytic candidates and their analysts

In Chapter 1, I summarized the analytic literature, which presents a consistent view that ending analysis is different for analytic candidates than for other analysands because candidates will probably have future contact with their former analysts in a professional or social setting (Milner 1950; Limentani 1982; Novick 1982, 1997). The problems candidates faced in making the adjustment from being an analysand to being a colleague were either minimized or not recognized, or if they were, they were not part of the analytic literature.

The data from Pfeffer's studies (1959, 1961, 1963) and others (Schlessinger and Robbins 1974, 1975; Oremland, Blacker and Norman 1975; Norman *et al.* 1976) were not yet available to make analysts aware of how easily transference is revived. For the same reason, they had not considered the possibility that social or professional contact could reawaken transference reactions as well as feelings related to the specific qualities of the analyst and their relationship – and that former analysands would have no place to process their reactions. The former analysts must also have had reactions to these contacts, but that is not data I can provide in this study.

Early in the history of psychoanalysis, Freud had cautioned, '[N]o psychoanalyst goes further than his own complexes and internal resistances permit' (1910: 145). In this statement he was acknowledging that powerful though analysis was, it could not remove all psychological vulnerability. Toward the end of his life Freud wrote about the limits of analysis and the particular problem this posed for analysts. In 'Analysis terminable and interminable' (1937), he stated that 'the special conditions of analytic work do actually cause the analyst's own defects to interfere', and he recommended that analysts return for more analysis approximately every five years. Thus, he concluded, analysis is 'an interminable task' (pp. 248–49).

Craige (2002) echoed and reinforced Freud's warning (1937) that being an analyst inevitably stimulated and kept alive conflictual aspects of the self. She extended his perspective in her recognition of the reactivation of transference and other complex responses to continued contact with the former analyst in a non-treatment setting, believing that contacts might complicate the process of mourning. While, unlike the 'ordinary patient', analytic candidates have additional intellectual preparation for the development of a self-analytic function to sustain themselves after analysis, because of post-analytic contact they were faced with re-encountering their former analysts as complex, real people, no longer idealized figures. Former analysands who were not themselves analysts were not likely to be confronted by such painful de-idealization.

As I have pointed out earlier, other analytic writers assumed that the likelihood of post-treatment contact would only have the gratifying effect, for the analysand, of not having to contend with the loss of the actual person of the analyst (Milner 1950; Novick 1982). These writers expressed a concern that, as a result, analysts might be insensitive to the experience of loss for their patients who were not themselves clinicians. Craige's data (2002) and my own in this present project indicate a lack of support for this as a general concern. In my study, the four former analysands who described the most protracted experiences of grief after ending were all in analytic training. Of course, some individual analysts might not be sensitive to their analysands' feelings of loss because they themselves had not experienced it in their training analyses. But I believe this is a personal dynamic issue rather than one related to the expectation of future contact. Most contemporary analysts are aware of the intersubjective nature of analytic work and are attuned to issues that a patient's conflicts and distress may stimulate in them.

While most analysts now seem to recognize that it is unreasonable to expect that analysis can resolve all problems and that its inevitable incompleteness may be a source of great disappointment, these expectations of 'completeness' never entirely disappear. They leave analyst and analysand vulnerable to a multitude of post-analytic difficulties depending on the specific issues of each analytic pair. I will repeat the more general warning about this issue offered by Gibeault (2000) and Gomberoff (2000) in an IPA panel on training (Quinodoz and Rocha Barros 2000): unless unrealistic expectations of the analyst, the analysand and analysis are addressed and sufficiently worked through during the course of analysis, its ending and in post-termination consolidation, they might collude in mutual idealization of each other and the process of analysis. Moreover, the analysand can be left with an inability to accept personal limitations or, alternatively, a devastating disillusionment.

**

While post-termination relationships are likely to occur when the analysand is an analyst or is in analytic training, the way in which the former analyst manages this contact makes a difference. Levine and Yanof (2004) 'discovered that post analytic relationships within the institutional setting are conducted in highly idiosyncratic ways that vary from institute to institute, analyst to analyst, and analytic dyad to analytic dyad' (p. 876). Their data was drawn from anecdotal accounts collected by 16 analysts in a study group. All the accounts indicated the continuing effect of transference on the part of the former analysands, and most specified problematic reactions that could not be resolved because there was no longer a professional relationship in which to process them. The authors acknowledged that the reports might have been skewed, as the examples had a problematic and negative cast.

In contrast, Schachter (2005) believed that the negative cast of Levine and Yanof's findings misrepresented the experiences of most former analysands, whose post-analytic contact often supported further assimilation of analytic gains and, when it did not, often resulted in the individuals' returning to treatment. Based on her interviews with analysts, Tessman (2003) also suggested that the benefits of analysis could be deepened when post-analytic contact with the former analysts was positive. Her data, like Levine and Yanof's and mine, came from volunteers and, as I have emphasized earlier, the motives for volunteering inevitably colour what is presented.

Depending on the culture and size of the institute, the former analysand might not only see the former analyst at meetings but might also be on committees or teach together. As I have noted above, what these contacts mean to the former analysand is rarely if ever discussed in the literature. The changed relationship opens the potential for enactments of fantasies of intimate contact – 'friends, colleagues, co-workers, or even lovers' – as well as the continuation of omnipotent or hostile fantasies. Professional and ethical restraints may be weakened (Novick 1997). The persistence of idealization owing to the suppression of negative feelings, or the reverse – a reaction against the analyst – both pose hazards (Pedder 1988).

Schachter (2005) expressed concern about changing the nature of the relationship. 'Post termination meetings', he observed,

> will rarely develop into a friendship, and when this occurs it requires major changes of both patient and analyst. The risk for the former patient is that the friendship may founder and leave the former patient without either friend or analyst, but with unanalyzed negative feelings. (p. 218)

Schlesinger (2005) maintained that there was no such thing as an ex-patient. He warned about the 'temptations some therapists and patients feel, when no longer restrained by strictures of the therapeutic relationship, to enact their desire to allow a fuller friendship or even a sexual relationship to flower.' His view was that nothing should interfere with the ability of former patients to return to treatment if they should wish to do so. But the 'essential reason' was that the 'purposeful, but mostly not reciprocal, intimacy of that relationship, with its built-in power differential, precludes forming, a new, untrammeled, and reciprocal relationship of any depth. Therefore, the possibility that the therapist, even inadvertently, exploit the patient's transference cannot be ruled out' (p. 221).

As I have pointed out previously, Quinodoz and Barros (2000) cautioned that, unless the former analysand had an opportunity to meet with the former analyst to reintegrate the reactions that had been evoked by their contact, there might be untoward consequences for both individuals, the institute culture and, by extension, the field of psychoanalysis.

Hoffman observed (1998) that:

> The very fact that we usually maintain the analytic frame even after termination to the extent that, for example, we do not become friends with or socialize with our patients in the usual sense, indicates that we want to preserve rather than undo the special kind of presence in our patients' lives that the analytic situation fosters. (p. 120)

He went on to say that when analysts wished to develop 'more mutual and egalitarian relationships' with former patients, the previous asymmetry of the therapeutic relationship makes the 'mutuality matter … in an intensified way' (p. 121), which helps them develop a view of themselves as creative and deserving of love. In other words, Hoffman was emphasizing that – because of the transference, abstinence and neutrality in the analytic relationship – when the former analyst conveyed a wish for an ongoing mutual contact with a former analysand, it was not only an affirmation and an expression of positive regard, it also had an especially intense meaning.

As part of her study of analysts' representations of their own analysts, Tessman (2003) reported on the wished-for and actual effect of post-analytic contact between analysands and their former analysts. At best, post-analytic contact in post-analytic social or professional settings offered an opportunity to synthesize an idealized image of the former analysts with more ordinary aspects of their character – an experience that was enriching for the former analysands. Other former analysands, however, wanted to preserve the essence of the analysis and not dilute it with a later contact. On some occasions, it was the analysts who seemed to need 'continued love or loyalty' (p. 277), which created problems for the former analysands. At other times, if the analysts maintained an analytic stance of abstinence and continued the asymmetrical relationship, former analysands could feel diminished.

Many of Tessman's subjects mentioned that the emotional intimacy of analysis could not be replicated in casual meetings or social relationships. Others were puzzled by the discrepancy between their perception of the analyst as a person during the analysis and the way they perceived him or her afterwards. When the analyst was seen by them as better as an analyst than as a person, it did not normalize their experience. In fact, on occasion it 'spoiled' analytic gains.

Like Tessman's subjects, the former analysands who volunteered to talk to me about their experiences of termination and post-termination described many variations in their reactions to post-analytic contact. My hope is that the data from this project will help analysts accept that, while we are engaged in an enterprise that has a structure and basic assumptions about maintaining our integrity in our interactions with former patients, there is enormous variability in the specific ways in which analysands internalize the analysts' functions, the analytic relationship and the post-analytic interactions.

We are clear that a sexual relationship between analysts and their analysands is against the ethics of our profession. I have discussed this subject in Chapters 2 and 3 in relation to reports by two of the former analysands in this project, AS and RZ. Most, but not all, analysts believe that we should remain a resource for our former analysands should they want to return; and that precludes a social relationship. But based on the data from this study, many different relationships actually occur.

The literature suggests that analysts are most often wary of changing the nature of the analytic relationship into more than casual interactions. Nonetheless, depending on the particular culture of the institute, there may be many situations where former analysts are together with former analysands. What these contacts mean to the former analysand is most often unknowable. It depends on the character and conflicts of the analysand and the analyst and the particular culture of their institute with respect to both what is acceptable and what facilitates or interferes with the assimilations of gains from analysis.

In what follows I will consider how post-analytic contact may help or may hinder former analysands in the process of working through feelings about analysis and the analyst, as they try to make their achievements in treatment part of themselves in the analyst's absence.

***

As is clear from what I have described above, there are three types of post-analytic contact. The first involves social contact; the second involves professional contact in a non-clinical setting; the third is returning as a patient. Obviously these forms of contact are very different.

Before presenting this material, I want to remind the reader that the subjects in this study are all volunteers and, as I noted at the end of the previous chapter, strong affect, especially when it is not adequately resolved in the analysis, is a motivating factor for wanting to recount a past experience. When reading these accounts, it is important, on the one hand, to take reported distress seriously and view the stories as cautionary tales, and on the other hand, not to over-generalize from this material and assume that post-analytic contacts are primarily disruptive.

Although I have said this repeatedly, I also wish to remind the reader that in the material that follows, I am reporting accounts from the analysands' perspectives only. The observations of the analysts, who might have a different viewpoint, are not included. Much about what transpired in these encounters remains unknown. As I have said before, I have chosen to present the analysand's views, not as the 'truth' of what occurred but because it is the view that is not often represented in our literature. And, as also said before, when I use analytic terms, I do so because the interviewees, who are often themselves analysts, have introduced them. I do not have sufficient information about the people I interviewed, or relationship with them, to presume an independent analytic perspective.

Post-analytic contact in social and/or non-clinical settings

The reports of social contacts with former analysts described in the narratives that follow may make us mindful of the powerful impact of those contacts, for better or for worse, in relation to the specific vulnerabilities of each former patient.

Thirty-four of the 82 participants in my study reported on post-analytic contact with their former analysts in a social or non-clinical setting. Thirty-one individuals who are in the psychoanalytic field offered specific examples of post-analytic social and/or professional contact. Five clinicians who are not analysts and 12 who are not clinicians also described the effect of this type of contact.

To the best of my knowledge the effect of social contact between an analyst and a former analysand who is not an analyst has not been documented in the analytic literature. Some reports, though not numerous, do exist about post-analytic social contact between analytic candidates and their analysts (Craige 2002; Tessman 2003; Levine and Yanof 2004).

Negative social and/or professional contact

Eighteen individuals described experiencing disappointments with their analyst that involved contacts in social settings.[1] The disappointment stemmed from their disparate experiences of the analyst during the analysis compared with the analyst afterwards.[2] These perceptions were often related to specific conflicts and the characterological organization of the former analysand.

In the broadest terms, some former analysands felt the internalized relationship had been disturbed when their former analyst shifted from his or her analytic role by initiating social contact or by reassuring them rather than helping them understand post-analysis distress. Other former analysands were pained when their former analysts continued to adhere to their former analytic stance. In these instances, it seems that the former analysands had a negative representation of how they were regarded by the analyst, which they had not had at the end of treatment. The examples that follow illustrate these experiences.

Experiences that undermined analytic gains

Six individuals (four of them analysts) felt that their former analysts' initiation of social and/or professional contact after the analysis disrupted, or could disrupt, their analytic gains. In all instances, the former analysts treated their former patients as friends, inviting them to social events or requesting their views or assistance in ways that they experienced as interfering with their wish to maintain the professional relationship. I will provide two examples.

BC, an analytic candidate at the time of her analysis, believed that her analysis had been very helpful in many ways but that certain issues had been insufficiently addressed. She described that her analyst prematurely wanted them to become friends.

> I was a good girl – masochistic – and certain aspects of my relationship to authority were not dealt with enough in the transference after the first years. I was too compliant. It was a paternal transference. I felt so protective of my father that I couldn't confront it, and it didn't get worked out. … It took a year after stopping to get used to not being in analysis and to develop my own self-analytic capacity, but I also felt good.
>
> It was a while before I wanted my analyst in my life in another way. I felt he pushed for contact before I was ready. Two years after termination, he invited my husband and me to dinner along with others from the institute. I declined. A year later he repeated the invitation, and we went; but it felt like a mistake. It was too soon. I felt angry that he didn't keep himself available as an analyst. At a party, he confided feelings about his relationship with his daughter that I would rather not have known. It made clear certain aspects of his countertransference. I felt I'd become his favourite daughter at the institute, as I had been my father's favourite daughter. Up until that point I never felt I had a particular role for him. This occurred three years after analysis.

BC's analysis ended 19 years ago. Later, when she had a case that stirred countertransference issues, she went to see him for help.

> It was four years after terminating. I had a woman in analysis with a depression and suicidal fantasies, and an enormous sadomasochistic transference. I felt my supervisor was not getting the case. My former analyst said he thought I was doing fine, nothing more. I felt pushed away. I wondered about seeing someone else, but it didn't seem like a good time to start another treatment. I soldiered on and worked it out.

Eventually, her feelings settled down.

> Later, through the years, I had much more contact with him. By six or seven years after analysis, I began to feel comfortable and able to chat. Another time I called to discuss something at the institute that was upsetting me. He was tactful and helpful. ... Now I do a lot of self-analysis. I have a very close friendship with another analyst. We can say anything to each other, and I do that. My husband also knows me very well and is helpful. So between the two of them I talk about most important things.

BC described the evolution of her feelings about both her contact with her former analyst and her assessment of what she had gained from analysis. Negative feelings toward him in his role as analyst, which seemed not sufficiently addressed in analysis, emerged in its aftermath. She wanted him to remain in his analytic role until she had worked through her leave-taking. She objected to his insensitivity to her needs while continuing to value the work they had done together. But as her capacity to do self-analytic work increased, she came to feel differently about having contact with him in later years and came to view her analytic experience as more satisfying.

Her former analyst became a colleague who could be helpful. She also came to appreciate how she could continue a pleasurable process of self-analysis apart from the relationship with him. She was moderately disappointed in post-analytic contact, and, as her sense of her own competence and independence increased, she found ways of resolving what had distressed her.

AO was a candidate in an analytic institute where it was customary for the analyst and former analysand to have social contact after termination and often to co-teach. AO had looked forward to having a collegial relationship with him after ending her 23-year analysis.

> I was twenty when I started analysis. I felt like a child developing into an adult. There was a question in my mind about what kind of relationship I wanted to have with my analyst afterwards. In my institute it's very common for the analyst to become your friend and sometimes to co-teach. I had the idea we'd become friends. ... But, unfortunately, by the time I terminated,

my analyst had become quite elderly and began to develop health problems and also cognitive problems. I hadn't realized the degree of his impairment until we arranged to meet a few times.

I was disappointed in the degree of his vulnerability and the ways he was not able to either protect me from it or manage it better. I felt that my experiencing him as so vulnerable had the potential to ruin the good, strong internalization of him inside of me as a solid, substantial adult role model.

Later AO learned that her former analyst's condition had deteriorated quite quickly. Her disappointment in him faded. She felt compassion for him and a renewed sense of respect and love, while maintaining her own sense of well-being. While she continued to think that trying to have an ongoing, but different, relationship post-analysis might not be so wise given what it could jeopardize, she no longer felt this so adamantly or with such anger.

While I cannot presume to know the thinking of the leaders of her institute, one wonders whether they had failed to consider that a post-analytic relationship that frequently included a social, co-teaching collaboration could disrupt a positive internalization of the transference. Of course, some former analysands find these collaborations enjoyable and beneficial. But if they represented the general expectation in terms of a post-analytic relationship, it might be difficult for the former analysand to take a different stance. As in all the examples, it is important to recognize that individuals react differently.

With the exception of the last reported case, which ended a year and a half before the interview, the analysands who reported disappointment in their social or professional contacts with their former analysts ended treatment between 15 and 30 years earlier. Some former analysts who, for example, asked former patients to participate in this study or to edit a paper, seemed unaware that this was a role-reversal that might be experienced as an imposition. When such situations occurred, former analysands who had appreciated both the impact of analysis and the person of their analyst were angered by the expectation that they should do something for him or her. Often these individuals had felt parentified in their growing up and experienced analysis as a place where they could focus on their own needs.

There were suggestions that these analysts were considerably older than their analysands, and it seems possible they had been trained in an era when it was assumed that analyses were complete and transferences ended with the conclusion of treatment. Therefore, the analysts may have felt free to initiate contact. In contrast, some study participants who are now analysts themselves reported their own inclination to become friends with their former patients as a reaction to the distancing they had experienced from their own analysts after termination. Since I was focused on the experience of analysands, I did not pursue this part of their narrative. Nonetheless, it provides another possible reason why some analysts initiate social contact with their former patients after termination.

Negative representations of self and analyst reinforced by contact

When the analytic experience did not end satisfactorily, later contact might be very uncomfortable because it revived and reinforced negative feelings about the analysands, their analyst and the relationship. Six former analysands reported such experiences. Painful feelings were sometimes understood in the context of transference, and at other times they were not. For example, consider SS, described in Chapter 3 (pp. 68–69), who had had a tumultuous treatment that ended over five years ago. She reported how post-analytic contact contributed to her sense of hurt and lowered her self-esteem.

> I felt my relationship with my analyst was another relationship in which I'd failed. I felt the demands of the analytic setting had forced me to straightforwardly acknowledge feelings of chaos and dependency inside me. I could libidinize them before with great sex, but it affected my personal relationships. After analysis I could look at my feelings and not feel chaotic. … Still I suspect it was a bad match. My analysis was rigid. Friends said that.
>   I had a consultation that was helpful. But most helpful was the writing programme [a national programme developed by the Washington Psychoanalytic Institute]. Through that I met analysts who were not rigid as she was. … After analysis ended, I presented my poems at the psychoanalytic institute in a meeting on poetry and psychoanalysis, and I saw her there. … On an earlier occasion, she had also presented at the institute. I felt part of my being healthy was to talk to her, so when she presented I spoke with her. But when I presented, she didn't speak to me. It was hurtful. It made me feel bad about myself and her.

SS acknowledged both the gains she had made from being in analysis and the limitations she felt due to the specific characteristics of her analyst's way of relating to her. Both in the analysis and in their later meeting, SS felt her analyst had been unable to respond with sensitivity to how she might have experienced the lack of response.

Failure to regain inner stability

Two analysands, DH (pp. 40–41) and UM, both discussed earlier, suffered from past trauma. They had become very dependent on their analysts who, they discovered before being formally told, were moving. As previously reported, DH was an analyst in training who learned about his analyst's intended move three months before it occurred. UM's analyst travelled frequently. When the analyst was available, she met with UM for two to three hours three times a week. UM, who is not a clinician, suspected that the next separation would be permanent, and when this was confirmed, she dissociated and became self-destructive.

Both DH and UM were desperate for any kind of contact and initiated a social relationship with their former analysts. DH went to visit her former analyst in another state. UM stayed as a guest in her former analyst's home. But the social contact neither assuaged their anger nor satisfied their needs. Eventually, both entered another analysis that they found helpful.

The examples of DH and UM represent serious failures on the analysts' part to retain their professional roles. DH and UM felt simultaneously angry and desperate about the fear of being left. Eventually, their former analysts' abandonment of them as patients but attempts to placate them with a social relationship also infuriated them.

Solidifying analytic gains

Positive social and/or professional contact

Sixteen of the 34 former analysands who reported post-analytic social and/or non-clinical contact with their former analysts found the changed relationship a source of pleasure that solidified their sense of self-worth and appreciation of others and their sense of autonomy. This was true although they may have initially worried about the effect of the transition in roles.

Two individuals described the ways their former analysts' post-analytic professionalism helped them put in perspective their disappointment about not having a more personal relationship. This helped in consolidating their analytic gains. Another former analysand collaborated on a paper with her former analyst. This process contributed to her positive sense of her analytic experience and her own identity as an analyst. She knew her former analyst was very ill and welcomed the opportunity to share a different kind of collaborative experience with him as a colleague.

Soothed feeling of loss

GA is an analyst who ended her own analytic treatment 13 years ago:

> My analyst and I live in the same neighborhood and both go to classical music concerts. I wondered what the break would be like, how would it be for me to see him outside in a different way. We talked about that in termination. While never crossing boundaries, we'd meet on committees. It was fine. I'd have felt awful to never see him again.

BA, a clinician who is not an analyst, had ended analysis ten months before our interview. He was still actively working through his feelings about termination. His longing for contact with his former analyst was simultaneous with his wish to mourn and make the analytic experience part of himself. Actually seeing his former analyst in a setting where he was not a patient helped him to feel his analyst as a continued presence and gave him a sense of an inner continuity.

I didn't go back after we terminated, and the first time I saw my analyst was at a conference eight months later. I think about her all the time. I say things to myself that she would say to me. I experience this loss differently from other losses. She made it clear that, though formal analysis was ending, she was still available. She was friendly. It was good to see her.

AJ, an analytic candidate who ended her analysis a year before the interview, elaborated the anxiety and pleasure of integrating post-analytic contact with her analyst. She reported a gradual sense of decreased dependency and delight in increased autonomy.

Seeing my analyst at meetings was very uncomfortable at first, and I was anxious. It was within a few weeks after terminating. She came right up to me and said, 'Hi, how are you doing?' That helped. I loved to watch her. I'm aware of being excited thinking she'll be at a meeting. I chaired a meeting where she was and dreaded talking in front of her, but it was fine. I feel calmer about it. Now I obsess about what I'll wear. I want to look really good in front of her. ... I was working on a paper for graduation, and so that first six months, right around graduation, I saw her. She also came to graduation and gave me a hug. It was the first time we had any physical contact.

I developed the fantasy that I'd go back one time every six months. I thought, I can do that. I'm not sure I need the next six-month visit. We're in meetings together so I see her. I like her and like to see her. I had a crisis a month ago and thought I'd like to see her, but then I felt I didn't need to see her. I've always been capable but didn't feel it, and now I do. It's more than I expected to get.

BA and AJ had both recently ended analyses. They described intense feelings about their analysts, which suggest they were still in a phase of mourning and consolidating their analytic experiences. Both the analysts seemed sensitive to a balance of responsiveness and distance, and the patient–analyst pairs seemed well attuned. For example, AJ experienced her analyst's graduation hug as affirming – neither seductive nor over-stimulating. A different analytic pair might have reacted more problematically to such contact.

Healing post-analytic colleague contact

Two former analysands, HH and AK, both of whom have been described previously, had experienced disappointment in the ending of their treatment, believing their analysts were disappointed in them. Neither of them had been able to tell the analyst what he or she felt at the time.

Both had contact in a non-therapeutic setting that helped them integrate positive internalizations from the analytic experience even as they mourned the loss of the actual analytic relationship. With further self-analysis they each came to understand that their feelings about their analysts' negative representations of them were projections of their own critical feelings about themselves and, possibly, about their analysts.

HH was an analytic candidate at the time of his analysis, which terminated eight years ago.

> It took two years to go back to having positive feelings about my analyst. ... I'm kind of sad that I left without making it okay between us. I saw him afterwards at meetings and parties. I felt he was warm toward me. I could see it in his eyes; he looked kindly toward me. He was trained in an earlier era. ... I saw my contribution – that my negative feelings were partly neurotic. I think I induced a lot in him. I wasn't ready to hear what he was saying, and confronting me then with what hadn't been worked out in analysis would never be good. If you say something in the middle of treatment, you can work it through – but not if you say it in the end.
>
> Since analysis, I'm a better father, husband, teacher and clinician. I'm more active, connected. Problems in intimacy about giving and getting acceptance changed. Analysis helped me with my hostility and ability to express loving feelings without feeling I am crossing boundaries. ... I continued my self-evaluation. I do feel I gained a lot. I'm not living in the past.

AK, also initially an analyst in training, ended analysis two years ago. When she stopped, she felt both disappointed and disappointing. Her former analyst referring patients to her led her to re-conceptualize the ending and understand a transference dimension, which she had not previously recognized. I will repeat the first part of her description to give her report a context:

> When I brought up stopping in six months, she said, 'Why not one month?' We had been talking about terminating for about a year or more. I thought she was miffed I didn't need her. It made me wonder what it was about me. Did I really want to stop? If I disagreed with her, she could never say she had a role in it, so I learned not to bring it up. I thought she was angry, thought I wasn't appreciative enough. When I walked out that day, I asked her something, and she abruptly said, 'I don't know. I'm not involved in that anymore.'
>
> So I thought that was an enactment, but it was a relief because I wanted to stop. ... Since I stopped, life is pretty good. My marriage is good; finances good, practice good. She sends patients to me. I never felt she didn't like me. It's similar to how I felt with my mother. I moved away and felt guilty that she was hurt. I felt it was a belief in my ability that she sent me patients. I feel I do good work. I feel my analyst did good work, but there were a couple of blind spots.

These former analysands found post-analytic contact healing. They used the contacts to counter a sense of injury. HH became able to appreciate that what he had assumed was a rejection was a transference experience. He used the kindness he saw in his analyst's eyes to unlock his negative projection and restore his ability for self-reflection. AK used a concrete action – the affirming post-analytic contact of her analyst's referrals – as healing. This allowed her to make the best of the abrupt ending and, perhaps, protect herself from the full emotional impact of its traumatic potential. She recognized an aspect of transference in her experience of termination – even if her analyst, according to her report, had been curt and was in reality hurt in the ending. The enactment itself was never analysed.

Provided emotional support in post-analytic relationship

CX (pp. 34–37) cited the supportive effect she derived from changing her relationship with her former analyst into a friendship in which they exchanged holiday cards: she writes about her life; he tells stories about his grandchildren. Two other former analysands described more active social contact.

CA, who did community work in an artistic field, had had two long analyses, the last one ending 29 years ago. She had been in her second analysis for five years when her fifth child was born, and she stopped her treatment. She had become severely depressed and thought, 'I can't separate. I have to go back. I was worried my baby would have a depressed mother as I had had.' She decided to continue her analysis.

> It took me a long time to get over my depression. When I finally brought up terminating again, I felt elated. I never thought I would. I set a date for three months off. I had a lot of self-criticism for staying in analysis so long. I wondered if it were me or my analyst holding on. It was a time of acceptance for ending.
>
> Before I actually set the date, it was a long process of terminating – like a repeat of what I did in my first analysis at sixteen – like I had to do it very slowly and let it evolve. I found a way to make a place for myself in the community of analysts. I made a life for myself.

CA used her art as a way of integrating herself into the analytic community, developing programmes that bridged these interests. She also believed she was doing this as a way of staying involved with her analyst, which she thought he was opposed to. She felt she did not see how her life could be without analysis. In reality, her analyst was supportive. He came with his wife to see her act, which gave her a sense of security.

> I couldn't define myself without analysis. Over time I had a friendly relationship with my analyst. When he became ill, I visited him with my

husband. He and my first analyst were my family, but I didn't need analysis any more. I did find an analytic family in the larger analytic community.

FD, an artist, had ended her analysis 31 years earlier.

During the termination period, I had some apprehension about being without analysis, but I knew I was capable of handling it. When we stopped, my analyst said she didn't want to see me for a year. She'd given me the confidence to meet any challenge. I became a real person. I discovered myself. I was a worthwhile person, not dependent on my husband. But my husband left me a month later. I called her. She said, 'You don't need to see me – you have the wherewithal to do this yourself.'

I went to England for four years. When I came back, I was at an art gallery and she was there. She introduced me to the owner of the gallery. This led to my having an art show. (I'd been a glass artist before my husband had pushed me into doing other types of work.) ... My former analyst was giving a talk on film at the art museum and asked if I wanted to go and I did. I'm in a film group now with a group of analysts. So now my former analyst and I have dinner sometimes, and sometimes I drive her places. I enjoy our relationship. My son became her financial advisor.

Both FD and CA have made their former analysts friends in a way that sustains the positive feelings about themselves that developed in the context of analysis.

The friendly feeling conveyed in holiday cards enhances CX's good feelings about herself. Both the cards themselves, and the fact that they continue to be exchanged in the many years after the end of her treatment, made her feel 'warmed and cared about'. While I do not have formal data on this subject, anecdotal accounts suggest that many analysts may exchange holiday greetings after treatment ends.

CA is clear that the social relationships with her analyst and the analytic community are essential to her well-being and sense of identity. Her particular circumstances, together with the length of time since ending, may have made the post-analytic relationship part of her therapeutic healing.

I don't know enough about FD to understand her active friendship with her analyst. It does not conform to usual expectations of post-analytic relationships, but, again, anecdotal reports suggest that such social relationships occur more often than one might expect and that they sometimes work well.

The examples above, which differ in the extent and nature of contact, illustrate Hoffman's point that when a friendship is formed after a therapeutic relationship ends, it can be deeply validating. However, as AO's example described earlier shows, such relationships can also be disappointing. We do not know enough about how the transformation of an asymmetric relationship into an equal one affects the internalization of the analyst over time. This is an area worth further consideration.

Appreciation of post-analytic professionalism

While it should be obvious to us as analysts, I want to underscore that it is usually the meaning of the former analyst's behaviour to the former analysand and not the behaviour itself that determines the analysands' reactions. Some analysands, though they may have wished for less neutrality in the context of their analyses, afterwards appreciate their former analyst not changing his or her role. The following examples illustrate this point.

BF, who is not a clinician, ended analysis 14 years ago.

> When we stopped treatment, I thought maybe I'd check in with my analyst in the next five years, but I never did. We ran into each other one time in a hotel lobby, and we shook hands, 'Nice to see you.' I felt great that he protected the relationship. I'd seen a psychologist in the 1980s who hadn't, and that had been upsetting to me. That brief meeting validated the choice of keeping our relationship more formal. I knew it was a paid relationship. I don't think I intended to make something more of it. I did and do miss the particular opportunity to be and feel understood, but I also know that it had a deprived nature in it. I'm fortunate to have intimacy and deepness in relationships. With my former analyst it was like having a good friend who lives far away.

KE, who is in analytic training, ended analysis two years ago. She felt frustrated by the non-collegial nature of the analytic relationship, but she still viewed the analysis as a valuable experience. As she explained, 'After I stopped, I missed my analyst, the relationship with her and the intimacy it provided.' Some months later, KE saw her analyst at a conference. This experience triggered feelings of longing in her, which, she felt, paralleled the feelings that one of her own patients – an analyst in training – had for her.

> My patient wanted a friendship with me after he completed the treatment. I explained to him that if we had met in another context, a friendship would have been desirable. However, our intimacy was in an analytic context, and I felt the transition into a social context would be complicated for both of us. In particular, I felt his knowing that I had a husband and children would potentially stir feelings of envy and jealousy in him.
>
> In regard to my own analyst, I sometimes longed for her in the same way one might long for a friend/sister/mother. But the relationship with her, after so many years, felt fixed as well as comforting. I suppose I longed for a transformation in the relationship even though I recognized some of the intimacy would be lost in a social context.
>
> My analyst did/does not have this same longing and may not have the same depth of feeling for me as I have for her. I feel the treatment was useful even if she was not able to provide all that I wished for. I also feel I could schedule

an appointment with her in the future if I needed to. But I do not think she would welcome a social call.

Both BF and KE were aware that their unfulfilled yearnings for more personal engagement with their analysts required mourning something they wished for, and they saw the value of accepting a limit. Both came to appreciate that there was a sense of integrity in keeping the analytic relationship and friendship separate. Their feelings about the 'afterwards' of the analytic relationship accord with the traditional theory that real-life relationships can disrupt the internalization of the analytic relationship in which the analysands use the analysts in the way they need. But, as many of these interviews illustrate, this is not what worked well for everyone.

Post-analytic contact as a patient

Of the 82 former analysands in my study, 51 reported that because their previous treatment had been positive, they had sought out their former analyst for subsequent psychological help. Twenty-six of them returned for extended consultations or re-entered therapy. Four returned for a second period of analysis, which they described as expanding and deepening the earlier work.

Twenty individuals reported that they had returned for one or two professional consultations, but they did not elaborate on these experiences. Five of them briefly described the therapeutic contact as mostly focused on consolidating earlier treatment. Five others described the post-analytic experience with their former analysts as disappointing. Ten sought consultations or treatment with a different analyst. AL, described in Chapter 3 on unilateral endings, said she would have returned to her former analyst if he had still been alive. She entered treatment with a different analyst, who failed to help her address the issue that was troubling her.

Enhanced analytic gains

Six study participants provided illustrations of returning to their former analyst in the role of patient, through which the previous analytic work was stabilized, facilitated or consolidated. I will provide an example in which a unique arrangement occurred.

GL, who growing up had suffered many traumatic losses and separations, returned to analysis for a short time each year for three years after stopping. These brief returns supported her ability to separate and sustain a feeling of connection with her analyst. Her analyst had been ill during her analysis and GL felt she needed to keep track of her. The first year she returned for two weeks; the second, for three weeks; and the third time, for one week. The third time the analyst said, 'I don't need you to come back or not come back.' 'She made it clear that if I returned, it related to my need only. Then I didn't have to go back anymore.'

Another former candidate, ER, saw her former analyst for short stints in therapy, 'never more than a few months'. As she explained, 'It's very different. The regressive power of the transference is not there. He really knows me, and we can talk adult to adult. He's wonderful and helpful, but I don't idealize him as I needed to before.'

As I explained earlier, most of the 26 of the 51 former analysands who had positive follow-up treatment described the comfort and ease they felt in returning to analysts by whom they felt known and helped. For the majority, the treatment was brief and was focused on a specific issue – the death of a parent, the illness of a child or partner, trouble or anxiety in a relationship, a work-related concern or consolidation of earlier material. For example, AF, a former analytic candidate, returned 'one or two times' to work on an issue he felt he hadn't sufficiently grasped earlier, 'which had shown up' in his work with patients.

Another former patient, BC, contacted her former analyst a few months after ending analysis, when her writing inhibitions recurred – this had been the symptom for which she had initially sought analysis. In the process of writing to him she came to understand her inhibition, and it dissipated. I will describe her experience in more detail in the next chapter.

BG, an analyst who terminated a year and half earlier, returned one time to talk with her analyst when her child became ill. However, she did not want to feel pulled back into a transference of dependency. For her, both the post-analytic consultation and the social contact supported her positive feeling about what she had gained from analysis and the analytic relationship.

> I didn't want to go back into the analytic thing. My analyst was comforting, and talking to him settled things down in the way I wanted it to. ... He and his wife have offices near me. I run into him. I still feel I want to talk with him, feel foolish, and it's embarrassing ... hard. ... He's quite wonderful about handling it. We both have an interest in art. He saw me at a museum and asked me about my son. Then he wrote me a note saying he hoped he hadn't been intrusive asking about him.

As mentioned earlier, four analytic candidates reported intense depression following termination. One, ST, was contending with intense external stress at the time of stopping and consultation with her former analyst several months later was helpful. For the other three, post-analytic returns were less successful and their post-treatment contact as patients is described in detail below.

Return to treatment seen as disappointing

One of the three candidates, who had had unresolved anger with her analyst in the ending, was unable to shake her depression and eventually entered therapy with a different analyst. The remaining two, QD and DL, were distressed by their former analysts' inability to help them understand their intense grief. Before and after seeking formal consultation with their former analysts, both saw their analysts in social and/or professional settings, which only intensified their feelings of grief and longing about the termination.

QD recognized her tendency to biological depression, and DL to traumatic experiences of repeated losses and deprivation. Both believed that their post-analytic distress was exacerbated by their analysts' failure to help them understand their grief about the termination itself – that is, the actual loss of the analytic relationship. Instead, the focus had been on working through pain from the past and the revival of the transference.

Here is QD's description of the period following her long analysis, which ended ten years ago:

> Four months after I stopped treatment, I went into a terrible depression. I was losing weight. I went back to my analyst a few times. I have mixed feelings about how he dealt with it. I think he was off. I feel critical of him. My internist had put me on an SSRI. My analyst said, 'Go off meds and come back and see me.' I'd seen him for fifteen years. He gave me advice, said, 'Do some research' – which is something he did. It's not what I'm interested in. He didn't help me with the loss, to understand that this was related to termination. It was rigid. I was humiliated about going back, about not doing as well as I expected …
>
> The outcome of this traumatic termination is that I'm less ambitious about analytic work. I thought I'd go on and become a training analyst. Instead I see patients one or two times a week. I feel grateful for the work my analyst and I did, but I never want patients to have the experience of termination that I'd had. … I run into him because his office is near mine. He feels like a stranger. He told me about his grandkids. I wonder what it would be like if I'd been analysed by someone of a different character.
>
> With my own patients, I think maybe I'm too open, too sharing. During analysis I found him inaccessible.
>
> I think there is a strong biological part to my depression. It runs in my family. I went into analysis with him three years after I got married. And the good news is that I married someone who was more 'there'. I think analysis helped my marriage. It allowed me more vulnerability and intimacy with my husband. It did help my depression, helped me keep perspective. When things did not go well with a patient, I blamed myself. My analyst also helped with that.

While QD's feelings about her treatment are not all negative, the post-analytic experience made it harder for her to keep the positive aspects in mind. She was pulled toward disappointment, partly as part of her depressive tendencies and partly from the way she experienced her analyst's response to her post-analytic depression, which she felt was non-attuned and insensitive and now sees as a bad model for her own clinical work. She described how the pain of her termination experience also resulted in her loss of professional ambition.

DL had a traumatic history of loss:

> We had agreed that I was ready to complete my analysis, and I had had a deeply-felt termination process. I felt celebratory on the final day of treatment, which occurred thirteen years ago, but within a few weeks I found that I was suffering a tremendous sense of loss. Upon reflection, I think I was responding to the abrupt loss of my analyst as a self–object. I had let him hold all of my thoughts and feelings. Everything that was important to me I had run through his mind. So when I left, it felt like an amputation, as if I had lost part of myself. Not expecting to feel so bad, I went back to see him for several sessions about seven months after ending treatment.
>
> In hindsight I must have had an illusion that being with him protected me, because I now felt unprotected. Perhaps this self–object transference functioned so well during my analysis that it had never been analysed. I was amazed that I had felt so good during my analysis and then felt so terrible after it ended. The fact that I would run into my analyst at professional events didn't help. Any idea I had had that a real relationship would replace the analytic relationship was dumb.
>
> When I went back to my analyst, he was welcoming and seemed concerned for me. He saw my experience of loss as a recapitulation of past losses. He did not view my grief as a response to losing him or the analytic relationship or the self–object function. He never shared his feelings about losing me. He was trained in the 1950s and 60s, so perhaps he lacked a theoretical framework with which to understand the many dimensions of my loss.
>
> Reading about termination and talking to other people about the end of their analyses helped me digest and recover from my experience. The first year after termination was really awful, the second year was less so. Fortunately, I felt restored after this two-year period of grief and ultimately had a much higher level of happiness and satisfaction in my life than before treatment.

Many former analysands experienced limitations in their former analyst's ability to respond to their distress due to his or her character or theory. When, in what was likely an attempt to be supportive, the analyst reassured the former patient about a difficulty rather than exploring its particular meaning, it often meant that he or she had moved too quickly to a different relationship whereas the former analysand was still consolidating the analytic work. It also suggested that the analyst was relying on the continued influence of a positive transference rather than trying to understand.

When there were constitutional proclivities to depression or a history of loss, analysands were often particularly vulnerable to the ending of analysis. Then a post-analytic return, when it was not attuned, may have exacerbated their suffering. Again, I think it is noteworthy that although these analyses ended many years ago the feeling of pain lingered, and the former analysands wished others to know about it.

After ending their analyses, two other former candidates, SR and IG, resumed contact with their former analysts as patients. SR recognized that her analytic experience had been incomplete in some significant respects. Against her own wishes, IG felt compelled to return by her analyst – a continuation of her struggle to leave the analysis. SR and IG described their post-analytic returns as disappointing.

SR had taught a course at her institute with her former analyst, an experience she believed had contributed to positive feelings about her analytic treatment. Later, at a time of personal distress, she returned for therapy with her former analyst and found it only moderately helpful. It was not clear whether the positive effects of this later contact had been limited because of the co-teaching experience or because of other factors in their therapeutic work. As indicated in Chapter 3, SR had been deeply engaged in her first analysis, which she ended because she relocated for professional reasons. Her second analysis never had the same import for her.

IG had also been in a training analysis, which ended 15 years ago. She believed that her analyst, with whom she was involved in a professional relationship, imposed his need for contact – first by resisting her wish to end analysis, which she had not viewed as satisfactory, and then by insisting on a follow-up visit one month after termination.

> In the one-month follow-up, we sat face to face. It was awful. I wanted to see him but did not want to be there, not be back talking. It was really uncomfortable. *It was for him not for me.* He asked me to make another appointment, and I said, 'Let me see how it goes.' … I run into him. We're in a clinical-case thing together. It's awkward. I'm not comfortable. There are things I'd like him to know, but I don't want to be telling him. I feel what I want is to go talk to a social worker about loss. I'd *never* go back to my analyst. …
>
> The termination really didn't help me deal with this. It was a farce in the way it occurred. It was real in that I was terribly sad, but I was also looking for a way to escape. If I told him, he would have heard it as a criticism and a narcissistic injury. He couldn't let me tell him what it's like to feel you can't get out. He'd too quickly take it to my father and the past. He couldn't let it be between us.
>
> I didn't know it was this bad while I was in it. I thought it was my problem. It was so discouraging. A lot of this became clearer as I became friendly with other people who had been in analysis with him. Others, too, found him very difficult and controlling. Forcing this follow-up visit really confirmed it.

Post-analytic experiences with her analyst and her analytic community enabled IG to gain more perspective on her analysis. As others corroborated her feelings about how difficult her analyst could be, she came to feel better about herself and worse about her analytic experience. She recognized that her negative feelings about her own analysis may have led her, as an analyst, to compensate in the opposite direction, giving her patients 'too much room to figure out things themselves'. Her self-observation points to the idea stated above, that analysts' behaviours could reflect a reaction to their disappointment or anger with their own analyst, leading them to swing in the opposite direction when they related to their own patients in treatment itself as well as in post-analytic contact.

Although IG's analysis ended many years ago, the hurt and anger have persisted, unresolved. Whether due to inexperience or theoretical or character-ological rigidity, her analyst seemed insufficiently attuned to her in both analysis and afterwards.

Disappointment with less-intense treatment after analysis

Two analysands returned for more treatment. LB, a writer, returning for a single visit, was disappointed to find that his analyst was no longer analysing patients. DM, an academic, had had a period of therapy with her former analyst a few years after her analysis ended. She recognized that it was helpful more after the fact than during the therapy itself. A few years later, having serious difficulties with a colleague at work, she requested a return for one week of five sessions.

> It was a peak experience. It boiled analysis down to its essence; each session linked to the other; it was highly focused about siblings. At the end, I felt liberated of a burden.

However, a few years later, having lost her job, several months of analysis proved 'not helpful at all'.

> I had a lot of resistance. He never used that term, but I felt he implied it. I was incredibly needy and at sea. I needed his help, and I felt he didn't do a good job for me. Afterward I blamed him and felt he blamed me as resistant. Now I think my analyst should have said, 'We need something longer, let me refer you to an analyst where you live.' But I also think I really didn't want to do therapy then. I was in a painful spiral of self-blame that I seemed to need to wallow in.

DM seemed to be saying that if, after their last period of working together, her analyst had recommended more analysis – a treatment she had found so effective in the past – she could have freed herself from her depressive state of self-blame. It appeared difficult for her to sort out whether the dissatisfaction she experienced was due to her emotional state at the time, a treatment that was insufficiently intense, or combination of the two.

DM held onto an idealization of what analysis could do and a sense of disappointment in the limits of other or shorter treatment. Undoubtedly, multiple factors influenced her decisions not to seek further help, but she experienced a sense of disappointment that her post-analytic contact had not given her what she needed.

Conclusions

To return to my opening question: How does post-analytic contact affect the internal representation of analysis, the analyst and the analytic relationship? I am convinced there is no clear, generalizable answer. The examples given by the former analysands in my study illustrate Hoffman's point that when a friendship is formed after a therapeutic relationship ends, the change from an asymmetrical relationship to a more equal one can sometimes be deeply validating. Some individuals welcomed and enjoyed their analyst's friendly overtures. They described how such contacts consolidated and supported positive feelings about analysis and helped convert negative self-representations – often projected as negative ideas that they imagined the analyst held of them – to more positive ones. But this was not always the case.

Other analysands gave specific examples of ways that post-termination social contact – as well as their analyst's presumption of being colleagues or friends – threatened to interfere with the positive internalization of the analyst and the analytic relationship that had been achieved in the treatment. It is possible to read these examples as warnings about the need to maintain a distance. Just as each analysis and each termination is unique – dependent on the character and conflicts of the particular analysand, analytic process and relationship with the analyst – there is no one way to respond to former analysands when encountering them in social or professional situations. What can be concluded from the reports is that transferences do not dissolve with termination, that termination has a power and meaning that is always deeply personal, and that the effect of post-analytic contact is always one-of-a-kind.

The interviews also make clear how difficult it can be for an analyst to know the type of contact that would be useful to a former analysand. I am in agreement with Parres and Ramirez (1966), who observed, 'Therapists often can make errors when they attempt to bridge the gap or dissolve the therapeutic atmosphere by either maintaining an "analytic attitude" when it is no longer necessary, or by displaying an excessive amount of intimacy during post-analytic social situations' (p. 241). Their view, offered almost 50 years ago, best summarizes what we can conclude from the present data.

Psychoanalytic candidates and post-termination

Prior to Craige's study (2002), the literature presented a consistent view that termination was easier for analytic candidates than for other patients (Milner 1950; Limentani 1982; Novick 1982, 1997). Although my sample was relatively small compared with social science samples, it was large enough to indicate that in their emotional responses to endings there was no difference between analysands who were themselves analysts and those who were not.

The reports from the former candidates in my study indicated that the boundaries around post-termination relationships are viewed more flexibly in some analytic communities than others. Co-teaching by former analytic pairs seems to be normative in certain analytic institutes, but this is not generally true across North America. Overall, I think, the changed relationship between analyst and analysand is more variable than communities endorsing post-analytic friendships and collaborations seem to assume. For example, while some analytic candidates may genuinely like their training analysts and welcome a transformation of the asymmetrical relationship to a friendship, they do not want to know all the flaws of their former analyst. As one former analysand put it, such perceptions may threaten a beneficial former internalization from the analysis. Analysts, for their part, can and should be friendly to the candidates, but they need not presume that friendship is what is wanted.

Also contrary to expectations created by the literature, the former analysands in this study who established comfortable ongoing friendships with their former analysts were not analytic colleagues but, rather, non-clinicians who shared some other interest with their former analysts. And, in this study, the former analysands who most tenaciously wanted to hold on to an idealization of analysis were also non-clinicians.

For the candidate, talking during termination about what would happen when treatment was ended may have helped smooth the transition from being the analyst's patient to being his or her colleague. A few analysands mentioned discussing with their analysts how it would feel to see each other outside of the office afterwards, how they wished to preserve a relationship that would allow the door to be open for their return if it was desired, and what might occur after analysis ended. They found these anticipatory explorations helpful. But certainly not every analysand wanted to think about 'afterwards' during the ending. As one former analysand put it, social or collegial contact could in no way make up for the loss of the intense and intimate experience of sharing thoughts and feelings in the context of analysis. 'Any idea that I'd had that a real relationship would replace the analytic relationship was dumb.'

No matter what our fantasies or wishes are in relation to our former analysands, we must always remember that we remain their analysts in their minds. The relationship with us is the one they have known and, hopefully, valued. We need to remain available to them as a resource should they wish to return later. This does not mean that, in post-analytic contact, we must forever view them as our patients. Rather, we must manage the tension between having a friendly, collegial contact and being so aloof that they would feel uncomfortable returning for professional help should they wish to do so.

Analysts' own needs, wishes or ideas of how analysis 'should be' or 'should end' or how they themselves 'should behave' toward an analysand after termination must never take precedence over their attunement to the specific analysand – what they know about the individual and what they can observe about his or her current affective state. Trying to determine whether an analyst's behaviour is serving his or her needs primarily (or significantly) or those of the patient is a life-long obligation – part of the identity of an analyst. When analysands recognize that the analyst is attending to something else – a countertransference, a 'rule' – which blocks out what they are trying to communicate, distress and pain are almost inevitable. This is particularly true during termination and its aftermath, when issues of leaving and being left are in the forefront.

The data from my study showed that issues that were not so well understood during analysis often persisted – and were heightened – by post-analytic contact which seemed to corroborate the view that the former analysands could not work out their difficulties with this particular analyst. As one study participant said, 'I think we were a bad match.' Other former analysands, however, were able to use post-analytic contact outside of the consulting room, or within it, to firm and confirm positive changes in representations of themselves and others and the value of analytic work.

My findings suggest that social or professional contact sometimes seemed to disrupt an idealization, opening up negative feelings that might not have been adequately dealt with in the treatment. Such issues might have come to the fore eventually, and post-analytic contact may only have been the precipitant that brought them to consciousness. Sometimes the former analysands could work through these negative reactions on their own – especially feelings of abandonment, hurt or anger. Other times they needed someone else's presence – the former analyst or some other trusted person – to fully grasp what remained unassimilated.

Of course, not everyone needs or wants to return to analysis or even therapy. But the findings in my project support the view that when the previous analytic relationship had been helpful, most returns consolidated it and facilitated understanding of the current distress. But, as several of the interviewees pointed out, just as 'acting like an analyst' in a social setting could be viewed as inappropriate, failing to do so in the consultation room could be disillusioning as well as disappointing.

Finally, it is my belief that the analysand, not the analyst, should initiate post-analytic contact, and that following the analysand's lead is the wisest course. Still, I would hesitate to say always or never in relation to the nature of any particular post-analytic contact, provided it remains within the ethical boundaries of the profession.

Notes

1   Two of the 18 also reported being disappointed with their analysts when they returned as patients.
2   This finding is similar to Tessman's (2003), described earlier.

Chapter 5

As time goes by

Ways of keeping analysis alive[1]

Self-analysis is a process that occurs during analysis in the presence of one's analyst. Development of a self-analytic function has historically been a goal of psychoanalysis. In this chapter, I will reconsider this aim: whether and to what extent self-analysis continues after the analysand and analyst stop meeting; and can there be benefit from analysis if it doesn't?

Can people who are no longer in treatment find ways of maintaining an analytic process that serves some or all of the functions provided by the former analyst: insight, recognition of patterns of defence and conflict, affect regulation, comfort, identifying and working through new problems, remaining curious and self-reflective? If this is possible, what methods do former analysands use and how effective are they?

The capacity to be self-reflective about our inner life – having perspective on the meaning of our thoughts, feelings, fantasies and actions – is both a goal of analysis and a criterion for its termination (Hoffer 1950; Brenner 1976; Gaskill 1980; Schlessinger and Robbins 1983; Kantrowitz, Katz and Paolitto 1990b; Bergmann 2005). Most analysts believe it is a benefit of an analysis that has been successful and a way of continuing to grow from it (Pfeffer 1961, 1963; Schlessinger and Robbins 1974, 1975; Oremland, Blacker and Norman 1975; Norman *et al.* 1976). My own earlier studies (Kantrowitz, Katz and Paolitto 1990b; Kantrowitz 1996) as well as research by Tessman (2003) have also demonstrated that this capacity continues long after analysis ends.

Individual analysts report the ways in which they use self-analysis in their work with patients as a way of understanding countertransference dilemmas and acquiring self-knowledge (Ferenczi 1932; Engel 1975; Calder 1980; Little 1981; McLaughlin 1981, 1988; Gardner 1983; Beiser 1984; Abend 1986; Eifermann 1987, 1993; Jacobs 1991; Sonnenberg 1991, 1995; Silber 1996, 2003; Kantrowitz 2009; Salberg 2010b). While it is assumed that self-analysis is necessary for clinicians, nowhere in the literature is there information about the presence and/or deepening of self-analysis in former analysands who are not clinicians.

In this chapter I will give examples from the former analysands in this project, clinicians as well as those who are not clinicians, showing how they sustain the analytic process and possibly deepen their understanding of themselves after their treatment has ended. Using their reports, I will show how insights gained through the self-analytic process – by, for example, evoking memories of the analysis or using functions that were part of the analytic process – compare to what occurs in analysis itself. I will explain how these reports provide information about the post-analytic experience that our theory would not have predicted – information that also calls into question some of our value-laden and often idealized assumptions.

Throughout my discussion I will be using the term 'self-analysis' to describe the process of self-exploration that leads to the emergence of a new insight or the reawakening of an insight that was once known but, because of the current distress, has been unavailable. This insight may lead to a new solution, but it may also function to reduce emotional distress or modulate affect volatility. As I will discuss, this definition is a very narrow one and excludes other forms of self-reflective activity that may also keep the process alive for former analysands. It also limits our understanding of self-exploration and other post-analytic benefits, which an analytic experience may provide. I will try to show that self-analysis, when so narrowly defined, is another of the idealized notions about psycho-analytic endings.

Self-analysis, as defined above, occurs with less frequency than is usually assumed. But there are other ways to keep analysis alive. Accordingly, I make a distinction between self-analysis and self-reflective activities, which may regulate tension or distressing affect without necessarily leading to insight. I will designate as self-reflection activities of self-exploration that regulate affect tension in the absence of insight, while I will refer to activities that result in insight as self-analysis. Additionally, some former analysands think or talk about their analyses and analysts without a conscious intent of helping themselves, but in ways that evoke the analytic experience. I believe that these too are methods of keeping the analytic process alive.

Development of a self-analytic function

Before the influence of object-relational ideas, when analysts valorized an autonomy that was made possible by a metapsychologically based vision of psychic structure formation, analytic success was thought to depend upon an idealized version of the internalization of an analytic function that theory had determined had to be depersonalized (Hoffer 1950; Ticho 1967; Firestein 1974; Gaskill 1980). It does not seem that Freud adhered to this strict definition.

Freud (1937) believed that an analytic process strengthened patients' egos so that they would be able to continue a process of analysis independently after they terminated. '[W]e reckon on the stimuli that he has received in his own analysis not ceasing when it ends and on the process of remodeling the ego continuing spontaneously in the analysed subject and making use of all subsequent experiences in this newly acquired sense' (p. 249).

Expanding on the way in which the ego was strengthened, Kramer (1959) maintained that the process of transforming unconscious conflicts into insights and new solutions was not always conscious. In her view, once the ego's energy was freed from its defensive functions, it could help stimulate further growth. Such growth was possible even when active attempts to gain insight through self-analysis had failed.

Hoffer's (1950) view emphasized the acquisition of skills to develop insight and containment, and to lift repression. Both the patient's increased ego strength and the development of the self-analytic function occurred through his or her identification with the functions of the analyst. It was the analyst's skill in interpreting the transference that enabled patients to acquire self-analytic abilities: to make interpretations, analyse resistance, contain and tolerate affect, and recover memories of childhood conflict and trauma. Like most analysts at the time, Hoffer believed that this identification was the result of the resolution of the transference neurosis. His description of the self-analytic function as an outgrowth of an internalization of the analyst's analysing functions became the generally accepted definition of this process.

Ticho (1967) further elaborated on the specific functions that were entailed in self-analysis – namely, free association, listening and interpretation – which she also viewed as developing from the resolution of the transference neurosis. She added the idea that successfully working through separation from the analyst is part of this process. Novick (1982), who also believed that the capacity for self-analysis was related to the resolution of the transference neurosis, observed that the patient's ability to internalize a self-analytic function indicated that a mourning process was occurring.

Similarly, Gaskill (1980) stated that a patient's capacity for self-analysis showed that he or she had internalized a representation of the analyst. Once this ability was achieved, the patient was able to respond more realistically and adaptively to internal and external experiences.

And, as I noted earlier, in his summary paper on termination, Firestein (1974) cited the development of a self-analytic function as one of the most agreed-upon criteria for terminating analysis. Over the three and a half decades that followed, authors (Blum 1989; Bergmann 1997; Salberg 2010b) who wrote about termination continued to list the capacity for self-analysis as an accepted criterion for terminating and an indication that a successful analytic process had taken place.

In recounting this abbreviated history of ideas about self-analysis, it is possible to speculate about how certain psychological accomplishments came to be accepted as expectable outcomes of analysis. The strengthening of the ego, the resolution of the transference neurosis and the working through of separation from one's analyst by a process of mourning were not only expected to have occurred at the end of a successful analysis, but they were also viewed as necessary for the achievement of a self-analytic function. These ideas build on one another and likely contributed to idealized views of what analysis could achieve (Firestein 1974; Blum 1989; Bergmann 1997) and how it came to be mythologized (Gabbard 2009).

But even a half century ago, some analysts questioned whether a self-analytic process was necessary for a successful analytic outcome. As indicated above,

Kramer (1959) believed that the integration of the solutions to unconscious conflicts is not always conscious nor does further psychological growth depend on later insights achieved through self-analysis. Her perspective is in line with other writers, such as Ticho (1967), who believed that once defensive mechanisms, which had previously kept conflicts in place, gave way, progressive development would follow.

Continuing this line of thought, Reis (2010) maintained that analytic gains might be assimilated less consciously. Using Winnicott's idea about the fate of transitional objects (1965, 1971), he suggested that the post-termination relationship may not be represented as internalization, identification or replication of the analyst's analysing functions. Rather it could become a 'creative "diffusion", neither lost, nor present, in any recognizable sense other than in creative apperception of continuing experience' (p. 221).

Tessman's (2003) interviews with analysts, about how they have remembered their own analysts over time, explored both their 'remembered engagement and internalization' (p. 2). Her findings suggested that no single outcome could be expected, nor was one desirable. Some former analysands emphasized and took pleasure in thinking of self-analysis as self-generated, while others accentuated the value of connection and described having a continuing internal dialogue with the former analyst. Tessman believed that there was usually an oscillation of subjectively intrapsychic and intersubjective experiences that sustained the analyst within the self after analysis ended.

In addition to the previous ideas about an idealized self-analytic function, some analysts have also made assumptions about which analysands would attain it. Ticho noted that analysands who eventually became analysts were particularly motivated to do self-analytic work – examining their dreams and observing their reactions to countertransference and other scientific and artistic creations. Novick (1982) wrote that the 'criterion of self-analysis may be another ambitious formulation and one that is more applicable to candidates than to patients' (p. 358). Blum (1989) concurred that the development and/or use of a self-analytic function applied specifically to analytic candidates and not necessarily to other patients who may have successfully completed analysis.

Since I very much doubt that any of these analysts would maintain that patients who are not in analytic training cannot have a successful treatment outcome, the implication of their ideas is that achieving a self-analytic function is a desirable – but not an essential – criterion for terminating. In other words, while analysands who do not become analysts may well develop the quality of self-analytic reflection, they are not expected to be motivated to do so. The findings in this project indicate that post-analytic self-exploration is not so directly related to a person's professional background.

Engaging in self-analysis for further psychological growth is one way of keeping an analytic process alive after analysis ends, but it is not the only one. Evoking an image of one's former analyst as a companion in self-reflection and engaging in a process of self-scrutiny that makes use of analytic functions without a mental representation of the analyst are related activities, but they are also different. One way of differentiating these activities is to explicate their purpose: Does the former analysand engage in either of these activities to gain insight into a current conflict? Or does he or she primarily seek to relieve a feeling of affective distress? Is the self-analytic process a substitute for a lost relationship? If insight is achieved, another set of questions follows: Does the insight resolve the conflict? Is it a new insight or a recovery of something previously known but 'forgotten' in the context of the present conflictual feelings?

As I have previously described, research studies about post-analytic experiences have suggested answers to some of these questions. Pfeffer (1959, 1961, 1963), Oremland, Blacker and Norman (1975) and Schlessinger and Robbins (1974, 1975, 1983) all found that the self-analytic function acquired during the analytic process allowed patients to tolerate and master internal and external stress as it arose when treatment had ended. Schlessinger and Robbins further described how some former patients used 'a benign presence' – either a friend or partner in reality, or their analyst in memory – to provide comfort, to help them in self-understanding, or to resolve conflicts. When the analyst's evoked presence was used in the service of self-regulation it seemed to be a mixture of these two experiences. The authors viewed this capacity as an indication of the importance of the alliance in the development of the self-analytic function. They illustrated how the analysis of separation-individuation experiences and tension regulation helped establish and consolidate a self-analytic function (p. 639).

Similarly, Blum (1989) noted that after analysis ended, the analyst's representation may be evoked as an image or a voice, or a specific interpretation may be recalled. These are descriptions of the analyst as an introject, which has historically been viewed as a less assimilated process.

Using narratives about interpersonal aspects of treatment experiences, Geller and Freedman (in press) studied the way former patients continued to make use of their accomplishments in treatment by examining the former patient's representations of the therapeutic dialogue after treatment has ended. They believe there are two complementary ways in which patients access the former therapist's approach to promote self-reflective activities that facilitate insight. One approach is when former patients have representations of the therapists' analysing functions, which they think of as having a conversation with themselves. This is what has traditionally been meant by self-analysis. The other 'takes the form of imaginary conversations with representations of the therapist's "felt presence"' (p. 57).

Schafer (1968), by contrast, maintained that evoking memories of the analyst after termination delayed the work of mourning and the process of assimilation needed for identification to occur. According to classical analytic theory (Dorpat 1974; Giovacchini 1975), unless these analyst-introjects are assimilated as part of the patient's ego, the internalization process has not been successfully completed and the former patients are demonstrating 'dependent' behaviour (Martinez and Hope 1996).

Accordingly, Geller and Freedman (in press) note that analysts, like those cited above, assumed that the 'imaginary conversations' with the analyst were only 'a phase'. In this view, ideally a time would come when patients would no longer need to evoke the analyst's presence, or any other presence, for the process of self-analysis to occur. They add that according to analytic theory, these identificatory processes result in 'psychic structures that de-personify and perform the regulatory functions served by representations of the self in relation to others, some of which were acquired through this process of introjection' (p. 57). Geller and Friedman do not themselves maintain this idealized position. They are only stating how they believe contemporary, or at least classical, analysts would have viewed their findings. Geller (personal communication) believes that after treatment former patients continue to use both processes.

Geller and Freedman remind their readers that, according to research studies, the 'absence of grief was not an indication that nothing of value had been achieved during analysis' (p. 61). I highlight their observation because, as stated before, grief had been presumed to be necessary for the assimilation of the analyst's functions and, therefore, for the development of self-analytic functions. As I have explained in the preceding chapters, the reports of the former analysands in this project have provided further support for the view that grieving is not always a part of analytic termination, nor does its absence signify that the analytic process has been unsuccessful or that self-analytic capacities have not developed.

In my own earlier follow-up study on the outcome of psychoanalysis five to ten years after termination (Kantrowitz, Katz and Paolitto 1990b), the majority of former analysands said they continued to do self-analytic work after their analyses ended. Some reported how they relied on it to acquire insight. Others described how analysing themselves and their dreams or having imaginary conversations with the former analyst helped them relieve affect tensions and find a sense of comfort at times of distress. Still others said they engaged in free association. They might, or might not, imagine another person listening to this process. When present, the listening person was not always imagined as the analyst; he or she could be some other individual perceived as warm or helpful. But many others stated that they engaged in self-analytic activities without describing or illustrating this process.

Over time, many former analysands in the present project actively continued to seek out ways to deal with discontinuities between analysis itself and the process of self-reflection, which might or might not lead to self-analysis as I have defined it. Nonetheless, they found a way of keeping alive an aspect of the analytic experience that they found psychologically important. As we will see, the data from the current project provided additional information about the effect of these various methods.

In my sample, most of the individuals who spontaneously mentioned self-analysis reported having both kinds of internal conversations with themselves, such as when they analysed their dreams or recognized patterns in their behaviour or in their fantasies that stimulated new insights, as well as inner dialogues and imagined conversations with real, external others. These internal conversations occurred when they were aware of conflict or other psychic distress. Their accounts support Geller and Freedman's hypothesis that both processes occur. People who were clinicians and those who were not clinicians engaged in both kinds of inner dialogues. In both groups, some of these people actively grieved in ending analysis; others did not.

Almost all of the respondents demonstrated a self-reflective process as they described their analyses, and some specifically conveyed how much they had learned during the ending. However, only 23 of the participants spontaneously mentioned self-analysis during the interview. Seven of the 23 were not clinicians. I specify this number, because, as noted previously, some psychoanalytic writers (Milner 1950; Novick 1982; Blum 1989) have stated that a self-analytic process is only an expected outcome for analysands who are becoming analysts. I will return to this topic below.

Forms of self-exploration

Toward the end of each interview, I asked each individual in what way he or she had kept the analytic process alive after ending analysis. As stated above, only 23 of the participants offered examples of post-analysis self-inquiry, whereas 59 analysands did not provide examples of continued self-exploration. Nonetheless, most of these 59 analysands reported beneficial changes that had been sustained over time and the desire to share their analytic experience. The wish and ability to retell their analytic experiences reflected its continued presence in their minds. These individuals also focused on the relationship with the analyst. Sometimes their reports of gains included insights that had occurred during analysis: for example, connecting experiences of loneliness with earlier loss, thereby lifting depressive feelings; or understanding how their role in their family impeded their ability to form intimate relationships, which became possible through analysis. At other times, the reports only reflected the change they had experienced, such as a decrease in affect distress and in feelings of helplessness, dependency and self-criticism, and an increase in self-esteem. Some also reported continuing distress about the way their analysis had ended. For this group, there was no report of their continuing self-exploration after analysis ends.

Some analysands reported analytic gains without linking them to insights, crediting the analytic relationship, which they seem to have internalized, with the positive changes that occurred and were sustained. For example, as AR observed earlier:

> I feel better than ever before. It was nice to have more time, money, felt good about myself, my wife, my marriage and that sense pretty much has continued. I'd been very anxious and had trouble forming a lasting relationship with a woman. I was very shame-prone and shame-ridden. I was anxious about being seen and known. That really changed. I got much more comfortable

with my feelings and thoughts. Analysis freed me up in ways that were fabulous. It was something about the relationship. What we established enabled me to grow.

Because analysands like AR consciously thought of the analyst and their relationship, this has been understood as introjection, which, as I said above, has historically been viewed as a less assimilated process. Since for many of these analysands the gains have been maintained in the absence of continuing analytic relationship, I wonder whether we might reconsider these different designations and the value-laden hierarchy they imply.

A few analysands also reported analytic gains with little focus on either insight or the analytic relationships. When there was no report of any continuing self-scrutiny or continued conscious thought of the analyst, it was not possible to assess whether this meant the process had not taken place or that there was a different kind of integration of analytic work. The fact that these respondents volunteered to talk about termination indicated to me that their analytic experiences remained alive.

Some analysands who made no mention of an ongoing process of self-exploration recounted anger or disappointment with their analysis that sometimes persisted over many years. Unwanted self-revelations from the analyst, an illness that was unacknowledged, the mishandling of an analyst's moving or retirement, the inability to accept the analyst's limits, struggles when they wished to end and the analyst's boundary violations (in three instances) marred their experience of treatment.

For example, while MS (pp. 44–45), who had ended her analysis 15 years earlier, reported some gains from treatment, she spoke most compellingly about her anger and disappointment that her analyst 'started talking about herself when we were ending. I didn't want to know that personal information.'

Evoking the analyst

Although not every analysand goes through a process of grieving the loss of the analyst, grief, with varying degrees of intensity, is a frequent experience after analysis ends. In the current study the former analysands explained that these feelings of loss often revived earlier losses, which they dealt with by evoking the image or words of their former analyst. This was particularly true during the year or so after termination. Some examples: 'I refer to my analyst in my mind every day'; 'My analyst is alive within me'; 'She's alive in my head as a comforting presence'; 'I have my analyst's voice – a more rational and calmer voice than my parents'.'

Analysands who had ended their analyses within the last year made references to the frequency with which they thought of their previous analyst: 'I think about her all the time. I say things to myself that she would say to me.' No analysand who had ended analysis more than a year ago spoke of frequency.

SQ, an analyst, had stopped her analysis one year before our interview:

> The process after has been very useful. I refer to my analyst in my mind every day. I think about conversations I had in analysis when I was on the couch – obviously, now, with myself. Sometimes I imagine what he'd say and sometimes just my thoughts – just like analysis – sometimes answers, sometimes just thinking, living with questions – the process of living and growing. I feel my analyst was ambitious and rigorous.

PC, who ended analysis six months ago:

> I maintain the process and reflection by writing regularly – not something I'd done before. In the first few months after stopping, I wrote nearly every day. I miss her. I knew I'd learn things through separating from her and being on my own, and I miss working through that together. Writing helps me process my experiences like I did in our analytic sessions. If I have a compelling dream, I start writing about that. If I'm feeling a strong emotion, I start there. Sometimes I start writing about an event, and sometimes I just sit down and wait and see what comes up.

AJ, an analyst, ended her analysis one year ago:

> She's alive in my head as a comforting presence. I call up her image. When I'm trying to understand something, I let myself wander and listen to myself. I talk to my husband. If I'm feeling stuck, I have two friends I talk to. I also fight that. Because I feel I should be able to analyse things on my own. At times I have a dream and part of me feels I can't analyse it on my own, or it's too much work. It's a real internal struggle about doing it just on my own.

These examples illustrate the previously described process of introjection, where the former analyst is evoked internally as a concrete presence. While other processes are also described – for example, analysing the meaning of 'a compelling dream' – there is no elaboration. Rather the focus is on the absence of the analyst. Evocation of the analyst in the former analysand's minds seems to provide comfort, a way of recapturing both the missing person and the missing experience of analysis itself.

Transition – beginning assimilation of analytic functions

The process of transition from dependency on the analysts for reflection, integration and interpretation to taking on these tasks for themselves is illustrated in the examples that follow.

ZS, a non-clinician, had ended analysis five months earlier:

I feel more rooted and grounded. I've learned that as much work as we accomplished, there's even more that's ongoing. It's hard to understand anything in the moment, so my best shot is to associate, to allow it to come in time.

Since leaving, I had to write a paper for a conference. I had a hard time, since I realized I felt I was trying to write against prohibitions of the father. With this paper I've re-experienced these massive punitive forces. I never doubted that I could finish it, but I had a lot of difficulty, and I thought to write to my analyst. As I wrote, I became aware of working out the meaning of what was happening. I mailed it, but I ended the letter saying I knew I had worked something out and said maybe I'd call him.

We talked on the phone the next week. It was unique in that I told him what I'd figured out, rather than doing that work together. He said he had the feeling it would not be the last time we'd talk, but he would leave it to me to decide when. At that time I was working on – and continue to work on – taking what we did in the analysis outside of the analytic space. For me this has meant coming to terms with the reality of the person of the analyst – being able to experience the analyst as a real person. What would concern me the most would be to de-realize analysis and the analyst, to feel that it was again a secret space [involving secret fantasies about her and her father, which were therefore prohibited and inhibited], a knowledge of myself.

Like the analysands described above, ZS is still keeping her analyst as a participant in her mind. But unlike the others, at one point she actually involves him in the process. Nonetheless, she is aware of being able to reflect on and understand her own experiences by following her associative process – a function she had previously depended on her analyst to perform. Grief over the loss of her analyst does not really seem to be the issue for ZS. Rather, her motivation is to keep him 'real' as a person and not return to inhibitions and prohibitions resulting from her need to hide incestuous secrets and fantasies.

Another analysand, CC, who had ended analysis five months earlier, seemed to be further along in establishing independence from his former analyst. Like ZS, the primary stimulus for continuing the analytic process was not mourning for his analyst; rather, it was resettling internal conflicts when they arose.

One or two times I've thought I'd like to be back talking to my analyst. No crisis but little things I'd like to talk through – like big business decisions or to figure out what's going on under the surface for me. I wonder about being competitive with my dad, that it's not just about business. So I try to weigh out and see which way the scroll is tilted. I talked with colleagues and, eventually, with my dad in reality – that was helpful.

Without analysis I wouldn't have gone through this process – to look at what I can see and figure out what I'm not seeing. Maybe at another stage of life I'll want to go back, but not now. Now I want to do work on my own. I'm pleased with the results. But it was a lot of money. But when I started, I was in a job I hated and in a bad relationship. Now I'm married, expecting a kid and in a job I like. I couldn't have done that without analysis.

I have the voice of my analyst – a more rational and calmer voice than the voice of my parents. The voice of my parents told me what to do. The voice of my analyst asked more questions. It gave me a new way of thinking. I wonder how much would have come with age. I liked the stability, the regularity of analysis. I miss that sometimes. My wife is in analysis. I talk with her – but not about everything. I may not find the possibility of talking freely or thinking in this new way all in one place. I also discuss things with older businessmen – even with my dad and older siblings. I think it will take years to really understand and put things together.

It is not clear to what extent CC uses a process of free association in his self-reflection or a more rational, secondary-process thought. His analyst's approach is still active in his mind, but the questions he raises are his own. Like former analysands cited by Schlessinger and Robbins (1974, 1975, 1983), he turns to other people. He implied that he would feel 'the possibility of talking freely or in thinking in this new way' with colleagues, his father and primarily his wife to help him sort out 'what's going on under the surface'. He seems to be saying that he is aware that he cannot see everything himself. Blind spots remain, and he does not expect any one person to provide an integrative perspective 'all in one place', as his analyst could. Like ZS, he seemed engaged in a process of making his own analytic perspective on himself.

BK (p. 30), an analyst who ended her analysis seven months earlier, illustrates a more integrated process independent of the analyst's presence.

Since stopping, I've found I'm dreaming about patients. I never did before. I can use my unconscious to further analytic work. Amazing! I had a dream about a patient where our roles were reversed. In reality, this patient had a dream of harming me. In my dream I made her my doctor, and I was terminally ill. I realized that the dream was about how she felt in her treatment with me, that she, who had been depressed to the extent that she contemplated suicide, felt she had a terminal condition.

Analysis was a treatment of last resort for her. I saw how she thought I wasn't going to keep her from killing herself. I feel like I've adopted her, and at times I don't want to be in this position. It's that same issue.

BK takes on a vulnerability – a terminal illness – thereby she puts herself in the place her patient had dreamed about. Now BK is vulnerable to the patient's unconscious wish and can be harmed by her. On waking, BK realizes that her representation of the patient's dream wish to harm her was the reversal of her own wish not to feel too responsible for the patient ('adopted her and ... don't want to be in this position'), as well as the patient's anger that the analyst wouldn't be able to stop her from killing herself.

Since her analysis had ended so recently, one could also wonder whether the dream reflected her feelings about her termination – that she had been let go too easily. She may have been wishing that her analyst had wanted to adopt her and simultaneously recognizing the burden this would have created. If my speculation is correct, BK had an internalized curiosity about her own process, an ability to perceive and analyse the transference through an associative process, but did not, at least at that moment, recognize another level of meaning. Therefore she was not performing the function of an analyst to formulate an integrative interpretation from the position of an outside observer of the process, even though in other respects the example illustrates a more integrated process independent of the analyst's presence.

These examples illustrate analysands at different stages of integrating functions of their analyst during the year following termination. Each of them had a unique way of integrating the work of analysis, which was related to specific issues that led them to seek analysis. For some, the evocation of the analyst's presence in their mind was central; for others it was not, though it may have occurred along with other processes in the course of their introspective activities. The question then becomes what happened in the long term: how did the former patients make use of their analysis over time, when they no longer had contact with their analyst?

In raising this question, I realize there is a danger of imposing an idealized expectation of what analysis may have actually provided for any of these analysands. But, as I have explained, that is not my intention. Rather, I want to use former analysands' accounts of their post-termination experiences to learn how they continue the analytic process.

Vicissitudes of life as the stimulus for continuing analytic work

I will begin this section with material from study participants who have been out of treatment for longer periods of time. With one exception they are not clinicians, and they are stirred to return to their analytic experience by the vicissitudes of life. Former analysands who are themselves analysts have the special stimulus of their patients' material to keep their own conflicts alive, and I will discuss their situation in detail later.

We will start with AE, who ended her analysis 24 years earlier.

> I never sat down and deliberately said, 'What would my analyst say?' I had her voice within me – an analogy of hers – and she'd say, 'When negative stuff comes, let it run.' I would do that, asking myself, 'Where is this coming from and why?' I'd find the thread back, and then I'd follow my memory – that's the way my poems come too. Let it percolate and see.
>
> Sometimes I get positive memories. I can still get upset if someone says something negative to me. I try always to be a good girl and do the right thing. I'm still very sensitive to criticism. But I know how to understand my reactions.

AE said she does not concretely evoke her analyst; she referred to having her analyst's words within. Yet these are the analyst's actual words. It is not clear to what extent this is the analyst as an introject or a more assimilated process. AE also used a process of free association. She was aware of old conflicts that can be easily simulated. Still, it seemed she had learned a process that facilitated her awareness that something old was being revived, and that also served her creativity.

AH had been seriously enough depressed to consider hospitalization. At termination, he felt strong and confident as never before and a profound feeling of gratitude. He had not gone back to see his analyst since ending treatment 18 years ago. But he had on occasion called him when he referred people to him, and at times they conversed.

> It's like a homecoming. Like, 'Hey, look at me now. Your work paid off. I'm successful. I'm not suffering with depression anymore.' ... Now [while talking with me] I have the feeling of sadness. He was a powerful father figure. Wouldn't it be wonderful to share with my own father like that? But my father had no sense of what to do. My mother would have to push him forward to even shake my hand. My analyst was a role model for me. He worked and seemed to love it. I worked through a lot of being judged and the fundamental feeling of being neglected and abandoned. 'Unrelated' is how my first analyst characterized my father.

When his oldest son was ten, AH had a dream that his father was raping the child. The dream made him wonder, as he had previously, if his father had sexually molested him. His former analyst lived too far away, so he consulted twice with an analyst in the area where he lived. He got the sense that he could have been abused. But, he added:

> I could put it in a compartment. I didn't feel the need to do more. I'm sleeping, eating and enjoying my family. That dream was six years ago and it still makes me choke up. But I don't let it in to run my life. I understand it and don't have to be run by it.

The interview with me revived AH's feelings about his analyst. He did not indicate that he actively continues an analytic process in a regular way. Rather, he explained, when something stimulated old anxieties he was able to place it in a historical context. He seemed to associate to past events and relationships rather than just employing secondary-process thought.

AH's dream led him to perceive a possible trauma related to his own history, and he sought a consultation to calm the affective disruption that had been aroused in him. The two meetings with another analyst (a substitute for the first one) revived and reinvigorated the transference, and AH was able to restore the adaptive functioning he had earned in his earlier treatment to quiet and settle his anxiety, not for new insight.

BF (p. 94) ended analysis 14 years ago. He explains:

> I did and do miss the particular opportunity to be and feel understood, but I
> also know that in ending I felt deprived. I'm fortunate to have intimacy and
> deepness in relationships; ending was like having a good friend who lives
> far away. Every so often I dig out an old dream and try to recall where I
> was then.
>
> Analysis was important in my life. Everything changed. I can't explain
> exactly what I mean. It has to do with what I feel and how I notice and deal
> with those feelings – something that I wouldn't have done before analysis. I
> used to wake up and hear a dog barking and begin to think paranoid things,
> like someone is breaking into the house. I don't have that anymore. Now I
> know I'm feeling vulnerable for one reason or another.
>
> When I ended analysis, I had a momentary feeling of loss, but it was over
> and I moved on. I play squash with the friend who referred me for analysis.
> We use each other to ventilate on issues. We're buddies. I have a lot of male
> friends where personal things of some depth come up. Sad how it seems that
> so few men have that – sad that some can be wounded and can't talk. I had
> good friends before analysis, but deeper personal relationship is something I
> seek out more since analysis.
>
> I remain very active in trying to understand my behaviour and attitudes
> from an analytic point of view. I try to understand what provokes a dream.
> For example, right now I'm reeling from the knowledge of my sister's and
> my business partner's illnesses. And I dream of my home, a place where we
> would go when I was a child. It was a centre of spiritual experience for me.
> In the dream, the creek poured over, and I picked up the house and moved it
> down the road. It signifies to me something significant has happened. I can
> reflect back on the image and know what happened and move on. It's
> comforting to have a dream that is a confirmation of what I feel.

For BF, using an active process of introspection, a process of free association, had
continued for many years after his analysis. He talked openly with friends, who
were outside observers, but it is not clear whether they offered perspective or
acted primarily as a sounding board for expressing and hearing his own thoughts
and feelings. He was able to recognize precipitants for his distress and he used his
dreams to confirm his conscious understanding. To the extent that he was disrupted
by new events and fears of loss of loved ones, his introspective activities led to
insights about his need to protect himself and ways to do this. These processes
calmed him and enabled him to recover his equilibrium and adaptive functioning.

NP (p. 71) ended analysis 15 years ago.

> I tapered analysis based on realities – a complicated life. I had babies. Even
> when I had help my schedule was crazy. I couldn't figure out how to come
> even one time a week. Even as I was open, I realize now I was holding back.

I wasn't connecting deeply. The ending was abrupt – I only had a two- to three-weeks' notice. I hadn't dealt with the issues really. I hadn't dealt with difficulties with my husband and hadn't been able to do my own work. I didn't understand the pattern that I could help others but not myself. I wanted to be Shakespeare, and I felt I was never measuring up. The realization that I could walk out like I didn't know my analyst – it was a shock that I was like this.

Until my daughter was three and a half or four, I didn't feel so connected to her. I saw her as a pushing-away person too. I didn't understand the extent to which things were difficult for me. Only when I saw it and spoke to her from my heart to her heart did it become clear to me what I hadn't been doing before in connecting. No one would have thought it about me. My daughter was so different from me. It took me twenty years to accept that I have ADD and to take medication as my analyst suggested. It makes me want to cry. I've been very successful in my work, but I could have been more so.

My parents were anti-analysis, anti-introspection. They discouraged us from thinking about anything painful or disturbing. 'Forget about it' was their message. As a kid I always wanted to discuss and analyse everything. But then it seems I actually avoided, just like them. Being able to analyse is like having muscles I hadn't used.

It was hard to hold on to the idea that if I just stayed with what I was feeling or thinking I'd finally understand the situation. I've tried very hard to be very different with my daughter. It was when I felt connected with her that I realized the 'not feeling connected' with her was the same distance I had felt in analysis.

Later NP returned to see her analyst briefly and shared these insights. 'I saw how I had limited myself by not acknowledging my ADD and not being willing to use medication.' Still later, since her analyst was in the process of retiring, she found another therapist.

NP illustrates a process of acquiring a new insight that led to a new adaptation, both personally and professionally. Recognition of her own defensive patterns in her daughter and, it would seem, the experience of loving attachment to her daughter, opened up a process that allowed insight about what had occurred in analysis. Her daughter was the stimulus for the transference in a way she had been unable to allow her analyst to be. She seemed to have made an integrative interpretation for herself, pulling together various threads of conflicts and vulnerabilities.

NP's account does not suggest that she engaged in any continuous analytic process. Rather she called on it when she recognized a pattern. In her case, the process of reflection and free association seemed to follow, rather than precede, her insight. Then she became introspective and understood deeper reverberating issues within herself without needing the presence of another. This independence, while demonstrating integration of analytic functions, may have simultaneously reflected a continuing, though greatly modified, defensive need for self-sufficiency. Nonetheless, her return to therapy suggests that over time she had become more comfortable with seeking and receiving help from others.

The last example in this section comes from AT (p. 63), a former analysand who is now an analyst. Her analysis ended 26 years ago. I am including it here because her insights are not derived from clinical work.

> After analysis, I kept working on my issues, and I was glad to do it on my own. I can talk on a deep level with a friend. We do it mutually. Sometimes I get up and write things down. I've had two really big insights after analysis. When I was in the hospital [for a congenital condition for which she had had many operations since adolescence], I felt like I had lived there for forty years, when actually I was only thirty-nine and had been in the hospital only one year. But when I wasn't in the hospital, I didn't always think I was in the hospital. It was a hospital ego state.[2] I saw that was also true when I was creative. I could write music and then afterwards I was shocked. I didn't know I wrote it. I kept seeing altered states of pain and no pain. Then I understood my mother. She had different states. She was crazy but extraordinary. I realized she'd gotten me through traumatic medical problems, but she also kept me nuts. I realized she had had different ego states I didn't forget my states; they were just discontinuous.
>
> My second insight that came after analysis: I always felt I was a terrible person because of my handicap. My friend said to me, 'This is something that happened to you. It doesn't define you.' I must have done a lot of work before and after that, because I never felt that about myself again. There was the pain and what I couldn't do physically, but not that awful feeling about myself.

AT's recognition of discontinuous affect states enabled her to achieve a new, less judgemental understanding about something between herself and her mother. This less self-critical view also enabled her to take in a more positive view of herself when her friend said she was defining herself with self-blame. As AT noted, it is more than likely that she had already done a great deal of work around this issue for her self-experience to have so totally changed with her friend's intervention.

AT's account suggests that she engaged in this process of introspection on her own, without any thought of her analyst, both when she wrote and when she interacted with a close friend. The friend provided some of the functions of the former analyst by offering an external perspective and an integrative interpretation that catalysed her changed experience of herself. The impact of her observation may also have been fuelled by the extent to which she was also an object of transference for AT.

Patients as the primary stimulus for continuing analytic work

In terms of their commitment to introspection and self-reflection, what differentiates clinicians from non-clinicians is the potential for growth that comes from their work with patients. This avenue for both stimulation and learning is not open to non-clinicians. Because patients bring their conflicts, distress, unmodulated drives and other forms of primitive mental contents to treatment, clinicians are continually confronted with affect and content that stimulates their own residual conflicts and affect intolerance. Distancing, over-involvement, boredom, anger, erotic excitement, blind spots may all occur, leading to responses that have the potential to disrupt their analytic stance and threaten the analytic goal of neutrality.

In order to help their patients, clinicians are pushed to stretch their capacities to contain their patients' vulnerabilities and their own. They also need to probe more deeply at areas of conflict in themselves to differentiate what issues are their patients' and what are their own, as well as how these overlap.

While clinicians' adaptive gains from their own analyses are under siege and made more precarious because of overstimulation from their patients' distress and transference pressures, this bombardment by affect and conflict simultaneously creates an opportunity for them. It also allows them to continue to process, integrate and expand their own understanding of self and others. Their affect becomes more available to them along with their ability to modulate it.

Countertransference reactions are a source of information about both patients and themselves. Racker's (1968) designation of two varieties of countertransference – concordant, an identification with the patient; and complementary, an identification with the patient's objects – are particularly useful concepts to help clinicians organize and contain these reactions.

The examples that follow illustrate various degrees of the former analysands' assimilation of their functions as analyst from their own experiences of treatment. We will begin with HH (pp. 42 and 77), who ended analysis eight years ago.

> When I stopped treatment, I continued with my supervisors. They helped me to look at what was going on with my patients and myself. They gave me what I felt I didn't get from my analyst – the feeling I was a good therapist, a good analyst. I felt appreciated by all three of them. I continued my self-evaluation. I saw that my contribution to analysis was my negative feelings – that they were partly neurotic. I think I induced a lot in my analyst. I wasn't ready to hear what he was saying, and saying it at the end would never be good. If you say it in the middle you can work it through but not in the end.
>
> I do feel I gained a lot. I'm not living in the past. But I'm kind of sad that I left without making it okay between us. I saw him afterwards at meetings and parties. I felt he was warm toward me. I could see in his eyes he looked kindly toward me. He was trained in an earlier era. I try not to hurt the inner self of

my patients. I feel this is good for me to talk through my experience with you. It helps me work through my termination.

For HH, talking both with his supervisors and with me in this interview helped him to work through negative feelings left over from his analytic work and lifted his self-esteem. By using a supervisor to fill the role previously held by the analyst, he used the transference to the analyst more obviously than was the case in most of these interview examples. He also seemed able to interpret aspects of the transference for himself. These processes seemed to represent HH's way of working through some disappointment in his analysis as well as a termination that he felt was incomplete.

AF ended analysis four and half years ago:

> After ending, things came together consciously and unconsciously that hadn't existed before. A lot had happened in my analysis. More happened afterwards. I'd see it with my patients. Sometimes I'd talk to my analyst in my mind, sometimes not. I grieved terribly when we terminated, but not in a way I could think about. I missed him transferentially and supportively. I missed being able to find the personal part. One of my supervisors helped me address things as countertransference. I became friends with her after training, and I do talk with her. … I learn from my patients. I keep discovering more about myself over time after analysis.

AF described the integrative process that took place after her termination. At times, she evoked concrete memories of her analyst as a source of comfort and support, not primarily to promote insight. As with HH, her supervisor took on the role of the outside observer who could help her see aspects of herself of which she was unaware. In her account she did not explain how she used the insights she discovered through work with her patients.

GA ended her analysis 13 years ago:

> My analyst left his mark on me, in the way I function in general. His words come back to me. It's the way I remember people. I have a resistant person in analysis right now. I call up thoughts and images, my analyst's tone, perspective. I think, what would my analyst say to me about this. It was a balance of reassurance and analysing – walking a tightrope of where to be. I know working through this can be helpful. I'm not the most tolerant person, but he helped me be more tolerant. I was very raw with my drives; he helped me temper them – both libidinal and aggressive. … It was a really good fit. Often I can help others in the same way.

GA's analyst remained a living presence in her mind. He influenced how she thought about and worked with patients and in general. She was self-aware. She knew what she still had to struggle with. Her thoughts did not seem to be new insights, and reviving the memory of her analyst seemed primarily to enable her to modulate her reactivity. The memory of him provided a containing function similar to his physical and emotional presence in analysis. But now she could also provide such an experience for her patients.

FM (p. 65) ended analysis 59 years ago.

> I continued to do self-analytic work and learned a lot through my patients. I was treating an adolescent. In his transference to me, I saw the full range of rage that I was missing in myself. I was still avoiding making a fuss. For example, I'd be served terrible meat in a restaurant and never send it back, just walk away. I remember I'd gone away to music camp. My mother wanted me to play the violin. I had my first attachment to a young lady – and it went on for years. I was away for two weeks, and when I returned, she had gone with another guy. Telling all this to my parents as camp ended and we were driving home, I broke out into tears, clearly enraged. I had a crush on this young lady that I felt had been betrayed.
>
> In my analysis, there were episodes involving me and my younger brother that my analyst felt lacked significant anger. I think the anger I felt at the young lady's betrayal is what I felt when my brother was born. I discovered this on my own … over the years my comfort with affects increased.

FM was able to be self-reflective and introspective through an associative process that enabled him to learn more about himself over time. He seemed able to integrate insights about himself, which pulled together various historical events that illuminated aspects of his characterological defences and adaptations. He could recognize affect in his patient that he had previously denied and disowned in himself. His account suggested that these new insights had resulted in more satisfactory adaptations.

FM also had other stimuli that led him to self-exploration:

> I use dreams and music [songs that evoke associations and put him in touch with his feelings] to continue my self-analytic work. Saying goodbye is never easy for me. I form attachments and I keep them. I'm the last one to leave a party. I don't know to what extent I became really autonomous. But I feel I've had a rich, full life.

Former analysands who are also clinicians have had the opportunity to use their work with patients to continue a process of self-reflection. The ways they did this differed, just as their conflicts and defences differed. FM highlighted seeing in his patient what he had been blind to in himself. He recognized how he used a different defence for a similar conflict. Other analysts noted that they had become aware of collusions with patients because of similar experiences or similar defences against different conflicts. Working with patients on conflicts or defences that they have perceived within themselves enabled analysts to explore and understand their own issues in displacement and gradually to assimilate them.

In the following chapter, I will discuss these findings and their implications.

Notes

1   An abbreviated version of the material in this chapter and Chapter 6 were published as 'Afterwards: keeping analysis alive over time.' *Psychoanal. Quart.* 2012, 81: 905–29.
2   AT is describing an experience she came to recognize as a dissociative phenomenon, in which she was disconnected from her usual ego state. When in this 'hospital ego state', it felt like the only ego state she knew.

Afterwards

What we learn

Why do some people have an internalized process that enables them to continue on their own the kind of self-exploration they experienced in analysis and to be consciously aware of what they are doing – while others do not? The data supplies no answer. As I have said, the majority of the 82 people I interviewed for this project did not specify that they had engaged in analytic self-explorations. Yet almost all of them gave evidence of self-reflective abilities after termination, even if they did not label them in this fashion. They retained a sense of their analytic experience that they had been able to revive for themselves and report. Indeed, as I have said, volunteering to talk with me suggests that the interview itself was a way of keeping their analyses alive. A number of them acknowledged that it was helpful, indicating an awareness that talking about their analysis had a beneficial effect on them. Most of the former analysands were deeply reflective about the process, and I think these interviews were probably not the only occasions on which they engaged in such thoughts. But perhaps they hadn't considered what they do on their own as actively keeping their analytic experience alive.

Self-analysis versus self-reflection and other ways of keeping analysis alive

Study participants who explicitly engaged in self-exploratory activities leading to insight after analysis described the emergence of something new. They emphasized different kinds of cognitive awareness, such as 'new ways of thinking', 'a more rational and calmer voice', a way 'to understand my reactions', 'noticing what I wouldn't have noticed before'. They asked questions like, 'What is provoking a dream?' These analysands focused on the method and process of discovery for finding insight. They demonstrated the use of analytic functions.

Other participants primarily used self-reflection to regulate tension. They reminded themselves about what they knew but had been temporarily out of awareness, thought about what their analysts would say, found familiar patterns or associating to other situations that created similar distress but had been resolved satisfactorily enough.

In most respects the subgroup of volunteers who described an active self-analytic process was representative of the sample as a whole: three-fourths had educational degrees beyond a bachelor's; women and men were equally represented; half had had previous analyses; one-third were not clinicians. The age representation for both the large sample and the self-exploration subgroup can be represented as a bell-shaped curve, though there were relatively more people in the younger age ranges for the group describing self-exploration (see Table 4 in the Appendix) than for the group as a whole. More people in the self-exploration group also reported having somewhat shorter analyses,[1] had ended analysis within the last year[2] and had stronger positive feelings about their analyses.[3]

Thinking alone versus thinking with others

Most analysands who engaged in post-analytic self-scrutiny leading to insight sometimes did so with an emphasis on independent self-exploration, such as when analysing their dreams. They thought about themselves using an analytic perspective. At other times, they accentuated evoking an imagined other to accompany them in this quest. Some thought specifically of their actual analyst. On still other occasions, they enlisted real others, such as a spouse or a friend, in their self-scrutiny. Some engaged in all of these processes, sometimes one and sometimes another. What I am emphasizing is the diversity of their methods.

The accounts of these analysands support Geller's and Tessman's observations that internal conversations in relation to self-exploration occurred both with oneself and also with an imagined other long after treatment had ended.

In earlier times, analysts thought that the different ways people integrated an analytic experience reflected a continuum of internalization. On one end was a seamless process of self-analytic exploration that did not include the former analyst or any other person – what Geller and Freedman (in press) refer to as a conversation with oneself. Next came an evocation of the former analyst – Geller and Freedman's 'imaginary conversations with representations of the therapists "felt presence"' (p. 57). At the other end of the continuum was the process of engaging in self-reflection in the presence of a real person – a spouse, a friend, a trusted colleague. A hierarchal perspective was implied: The more independent the process, the more successful the analysis.

Research studies have shown that some people used all these different modalities in their self-exploration, but to the best of my knowledge this perspective was not represented in the analytic literature. My assumption is that these different ways of assimilating analysis probably reflect different types of people in terms of cognitive style, ego organization, or characterological adaptations and defences.

The reports about the self-analytic function after treatment, as given by the participants in this study, provided information that our theory might not have predicted. Specifically:

1   Assumptions that a self-analytic process will be continued because the analysand is in training to become an analyst, but not expected otherwise, needs to be reconsidered. Both clinicians and non-clinicians engaged in an ongoing self-analytic process and believed it was an important and valuable aspect of their treatment.
2   The development of a self-analytic function should not be conceptualized as a necessary precondition for terminating analysis.
3   The absence of a self-analytic process in the aftermath of treatment does not necessarily mean that the analysis was unsuccessful or that its positive effects will not continue.
4   The presence of another person in imagination or in reality when continuing self-exploration does not mean that an analysis has been unassimilated or had an 'unsatisfactory' outcome.
5   While mourning has undoubtedly been part of the analytic process and can be assumed to account for many internal shifts, as previously reported in Chapter 2, grief in the actual ending of treatment and during its aftermath does not always occur.

As I noted at the beginning of this chapter, these findings call into question some long-standing assumptions about our profession. Let me now take them up one by one.

Self-exploration after termination: clinicians compared with non-clinicians

First, it was not surprising that analysts would continue to be engaged in self-analytic exploration after termination, because the nature of their work keeps self-scrutiny, conflict and intense affect alive as a daily occurrence. But it was not the expectation that people who are not analysts, and especially those who are not clinicians, would actively undertake similar efforts of self-exploration after ending treatment (Milner 1950; Novick 1982; Blum 1989). Yet this is what the data shows. The only difference between the clinicians and the non-clinicians with regard to self-exploration is that the clinicians' work with patients stimulated much of their reflections and learning about themselves. I will take up this subject again below.

Development of a self-analytic function

In the past, analysts believed that using a self-analytic function reflected emotional development in so far as it was a way of internalizing the object and of dealing with loss, grief and separation. Post-analytic self-exploration was seen as a way of keeping alive the analytic process as well as the analytic relationship, now as an internalized relationship. Still, we need to question whether those who demonstrated abilities specifically associated with the analyst's functions acquired and internalized those capacities during analysis itself. I will return to this issue later. What this study demonstrates is that the absence of a self-analytic function did not mean that analytic work was not assimilated and kept alive in some other fashion.

The presence of imaginary or real others in continued self-exploration

Those who had recently ended analysis referred to more frequent thoughts of their analyst or analysis. There was more specificity about the evocation of the analyst in whatever process occurred. I agree with Geller (personal communication) that the presence or absence of others in one's thoughts does not indicate a more or a less successful analytic outcome. As many of these former analysands made clear, the presence of others was likely to be a way of continuing an introspective process.

As discussed earlier, the former analysands sometimes referred to the former analyst in their minds, either in imaginary conversations or in recalling what their analyst would say. Or they would talk to another person – a spouse, friend or colleague. While it was once thought that such contacts weakened, or interfered with, the process of internalization (Firestein, panel report 1969), I think most analysts now consider that such contact can be part of a process of working through and mourning and, often, of consolidating changes that have occurred during treatment (Schachter 1992). Moreover, the continued evocation of another in one's mind as a recipient of self-exploration did not mean that there had been a less beneficial analysis. Analysts are now more likely to focus on the individual needs of the patient that facilitate integration of the analytic experience rather than on some ideal of a 'pure' method. Certainly, analytic theorists need to consider the diversity in methods employed by former analysands to sustain their gains. As one former analysand put it, 'I no longer find it all in one place.'

Keeping analysis alive without continued self-exploration

As we have seen, a number of former analysands had other ways of dealing with the separation. Some just thought of their analyst, or recalled experiences from analysis, or evoked certain affect states. Or perhaps the long, intense process was seamlessly absorbed over time as part of a different way of thinking and feeling about the past, as well as about their new sense of self. As Kramer (1959) reminded us, former patients are not required to continue using an analytic method for these changes to be sustained. And as Novick observed (1982), 'We know from work with children that many of them achieve and maintain positive results without developing a self-analytic function' (p. 358).

Stimuli for self-exploration

Both clinicians and those who are not clinicians offered 'strong emotions', 'negative thoughts', a 'compelling' or 'disturbing' dream as examples of stimuli for self-inquiry. For clinicians, affect aroused in relation to patients – 'struggles' and all varieties of countertransference reactions – additionally served to alert them to a need for self-scrutiny. Using songs to evoke affective memories may have developed in analysis, but it also may be a lifelong way of recapturing or recognizing feelings and memories. Like Proust's madeleines, other stimuli could function in a similar manner. Seeing a thing that is a link in a chain of associations can lead to a memory of a happy scene from childhood, a first romance, or losses and tragedies.

An activity such as woodworking, gardening (McLaughlin 1981) or even taking a shower can induce a state of mind that is conducive to self-exploration. Some especially creative individuals and psychoanalysts used writing to articulate and reflect on their inner lives. Thus many possible perceptions or sensations linked to affect-laden memories and fantasies could unleash associations and compelling emotions. The reawakened emotions might be the totality of the experience or they might overcome defences sufficiently to mobilize new, or reawaken, old insights.

Places for self-observation

There seems to be a similarity in all methods used in self-exploration. It is necessary to find some place of observation, to create something outside of oneself to be able to look at oneself more clearly. One former analysand called this 'saying it out loud' – hearing or seeing something internal externalized in order to better comprehend it. Referring to one's former analyst in one's mind and evoking memories of what he or she had said, or might say in the context of an imaginary conversation, are versions of saying it out loud.

Analysing one's dreams may or may not include re-evoking one's analyst's perspective. Dreams, though products of an unconscious process, allow the most hidden and conflict-laden aspects of a person to be viewed and analysed as something outside of oneself. While the person, of course, knows the dreams emerge from within himself or herself, it can be viewed from a perspective that is more objective. Sometimes painful or frightening affect accompanies dreams, but often it is only in deciphering meanings in the dreams that such emotions surface.

Recognition of previously known patterns of behaviour – and the defences used to protect one's vulnerabilities or the re-emergence of formerly known fears and defences against them – can be observed with more distance and perspective. These recognitions are usually more difficult because the patterns are embedded in characterological conflict and defence as part of one's personality. They are aspects of one's self that analysis seeks to make visible. Often they can pose the greatest challenge. Analysis teaches one how to perceive these aspects. Then one can acknowledge them as part of the self and step back from this and look at it as a part of the self that one wishes to have more control over.

NP, the analysand who saw the 'pushing away' behaviour in her child and then in herself, was observing such a pattern. Recognition of discontinuity of self-states involved a similar stepping back and looking at oneself. AT, when grasping her 'hospital ego state', exemplified this kind of recognition. Another variation was the reappearance of a known conflict whose familiarity made its grip less toxic. This was a kind of post-analytic working through. Recall ZS, the writer who experienced the previously dreaded prohibitions as she tried to work. After her termination, she was able to conceptualize them and communicate her experience in a letter to her analyst, thereby lessening their toxic power. In each of these examples, the analysands tried to view themselves as they imagined their analyst had, as an outside observer might. The degree to which they succeeded in this endeavour was variable. Blind spots were inevitable.

As discussed before, talking with trusted others was another method. Although the post-analytic other did not necessarily have the same expertise in listening as the former analyst, and the former analysand was not likely to be as fully disclosing, it partially replicated the analytic situation in that a trusted other was hearing and then reflecting on the person's intimate thoughts, feelings and fantasies. BC (pp. 87–88), for example, said she felt that, in the experience of mutual sharing with another analyst and also talking with her husband, she had 'most things covered'. Often, as BC states, both parties engaged in the process of self-revelation. The mutuality of sharing intimate material tended to reduce the transference, though mutual idealization was often at least a temporary pitfall (Kantrowitz 1999, 2009).

Saying things out loud to another both continued an analytic process and sometimes facilitated further working through of issues insufficiently resolved in the analytic work. One example is HH (pp. 42 and 77), who felt that positive regard from his analyst was too limited but thought he achieved this experience from his supervisors, changing his understanding of his analytic experience in the process. Another example is AT, who had an unresolved self-loathing until an insight crystallized in an interpretation from a friend. Talking to another person, the study participants indicated, was the modality they used more than any other for self-exploration. Two people were engaged in listening and trying to understand what one of them expressed and explored. Perhaps this suggests that actual human contact, the presence of a listening other, often remains central for many who seek self-knowledge.

The presence of an interested and trusted person who wishes to talk about inner processes could also be a stimulus for introspection. Their responses set up a process of continuing engagement in self-reflective activities. This method, unlike the rest, provided the possibility for actual outside feedback. The limits of self-analysis, as Freud (1887) pointed out, are always based on the extent to which one can be objective about oneself. Of course, spouses, friends or colleagues are also not as likely to be fully open in communication about what they see as an analyst would be. The directness and fullness of communication clearly varies depending on the individual characteristics and the relationship of the people involved.

As previously said, for the clinicians in this study work with patients provided an additional avenue for recognition of changes in themselves, as well as stimuli for further self-analysis. Former analysands who were clinicians described having achieved more comfort with specific conflicts, such as separations and endings, which could then be more easily recognized and worked with in the clinical setting with their patients. In addition, perceiving in their patients aspects of themselves that they had disowned or disliked enabled them to struggle with ownership in themselves and served as vehicles for continued self-exploration.

Grief as an indicator of analytic gains

When a person has recently ended a positive experience, they are apt to try to keep its memory alive. In the immediate post-termination period, analysands were highly motivated to continue whatever aspect of analysis had been important to them because the meaningful activity that they had been engaged in with another was no longer taking place. Continuation of the analytic process by oneself was a way of dealing with the separation from analysis and the analyst. It may also have been part of a mourning process – a way of holding on and letting go gradually.[4]

As we have discussed, contrary to theory, conscious experience of grief about loss at the time of termination may not be necessary for an assimilation of analytic gains or for continuing self-exploration when analysis had ended. Indeed, it was clear from the examples in this study that not all analysands consciously experienced grief after ending. In Chapter 2, for example, I reported that a number of analysands expressed a sense of joy and buoyancy in ending; they showed their mastery of a self-analytic process in their interviews, which may suggest that they had worked through the grief during the analysis. For many others who did not describe feelings of grief and mourning, assimilating functions of the former analyst appeared to be a way of dealing with the loss. AH, for example, demonstrated an ability to use his dreams for self-reflection. In every instance, former analysands used some observed phenomenon as the focus for further associations that potentially deepened and expanded self-knowledge.

Return to one's analyst

At times, however, these various venues of self-exploration were insufficient to ease the source of distress. At some point after analysis had ended, almost everyone in this sample sought contact with an analyst again. Most often, the person was their former analyst and the re-contact was relatively brief. As reported in Chapter 4, some analysands re-entered therapy with their former analysts or sought treatment from a different analyst or therapist. For a few, these later treatments were still ongoing at the time of the interview.

Reconsideration of theory

As we have said, except for treating patients, all ways of finding self-knowledge as well as continuing further integration were similar for both clinicians and non-clinicians. As such, we need to consider that modalities of self-reflection, as well as self-analysis itself, are likely to have more to do with an individual's particular quality of mind and sensibilities than his or her professional training. Innate self-exploratory interest and abilities are likely to have become enhanced through subsequent analytic work. People who are introspective and have a push toward intellectual mastery are often – but not always – likely to be drawn to a treatment method that makes use of these attributes. Consideration of individual differences is central to my argument about generalizations and use of theory.

Even though people rarely seek a psychoanalytic treatment for a purely intellectual pleasure, the ability to grasp intellectually the nature of one's difficulties provides a kind of mastery that is satisfying in itself. When insight provides relief through self-understanding, it is likely that people who are drawn to intellectual mastery will continue to pursue a process that can be so satisfying in both respects. There is a functional pleasure in following the working of one's own mind (Hartmann 1939/1958; Schlesinger 2005).

Whether their self-analytic functions were acquired or merely strengthened in analysis, former analysands who engaged in self-inquiry appeared to have employed the functions of an analyst. This may reflect an identification, an internalization, or it may not. In this study, former analysands referred to this similarity with their analyst only in relationship to work with patients. Taking pleasure in this similarity of function may be another way of keeping alive the analytic experience.

Analyses of dreams, as well as new insights about one's own behaviour, are activities that reflect an independence, perhaps a greater interest in ideas themselves, that is different from talking with others or imagining talking to one's analyst. Evoking thoughts of what one's analyst would say is different from having a realization about one's self. As previously said, these methods reflect different cognitive styles. Being more concrete versus more abstract in one's way of thinking and knowing did not seem to indicate a less or more satisfying or beneficial experience in analysis. For example, those who relied only on dreams or independent self-reflection were more self-sufficient, but they were not necessarily as comfortable with intimacy and self-exposure. On the one hand, those who relied exclusively on talking to others may not have developed as great a confidence in their own capacities; on the other hand, there may be hubris in those who believed they could see everything by themselves. Self-knowledge obtained without any interpersonal engagement is always limited by what one is able and willing to see, though exploration in the presence of another always limits one's recognition of one's own capacity and tolerance for working alone. As indicated, some people engage in both processes.

Analysts have tended to place internalization, as reflected in a self-analytic function exemplified by the analysis of one's own dreams, at the pinnacle of the achievement of autonomy. Winnicott's (1965) capacity to be alone could serve as an ideal to be achieved through analytic work. Loewald's ideas about successful separation (1973), an emancipation in the development of autonomy, and Kohut's idea (1977) about a decreasing need to use self-objects following analysis run along similar lines. To know one's separateness from others and be able to tolerate an existential sense of aloneness is indeed an achievement. But both Loewald and Kohut would caution us about making these ideals absolute.

Loewald is explicit in stating, 'If the feelings of mutual abandonment can be analysed, and the relationship rather than the object, is internalized, what results at the end of analysis is emancipation, but to a certain extent this emancipation is always only partial' (1973: 15). Similarly, Kohut is clear that one has a continuing need for self-objects throughout one's life, even though the extent of this dependency may be diminished by analysis. Layton (2010) worries that these views of autonomy are 'cultural pathologizing of dependency and undervaluing of attachment' (p. 192). She is concerned that they perpetuate 'a lonely and omnipotent version of autonomy' (p. 201). Like Kohut (1971), she thinks North American psychoanalysts tend to deny and underestimate the extent of our mutual dependency. Mastery of neurotic dependency should enhance relatedness, not replace it with isolation.

Many of us have tended to valorize the self-sufficiency that a self-analytic function can facilitate. We may do so because, as I stated above, there is so much pleasure in the experience of understanding the working of our own minds and the excitement of discovery. I believe we need to distinguish between the particular benefit we have derived from analysis in the enhancement or development of our analytic functions, abilities we continue to employ and enjoy years after analysis ends, and the changes and stability of gains that analysis can achieve in the absence of these functions.

During most of the twentieth century, psychoanalysis was conceptualized as a treatment process in which insight obtained in the context of an affectively meaningful experience was the exclusive vehicle for its efficacy. Though most analysts would still adhere to a view that insight is central to psychoanalytic success, there has been an increasing appreciation that the analytic relationship is for many analysands perhaps the most significant factor in bringing about change.

Perhaps we need to be more appreciative of the contributions of analysis that are not just about conscious insight and the development of autonomy. Wallerstein's (1986) report of the Menninger study indicates that supportive factors were as central to successful analytic outcomes as were insights. Later, Blatt (1992) distinguished which kinds of difficulties responded most effectively to which kinds of interventions. All the data coming out of the Menninger projects supported the importance of specificity in our considerations of technique and our theoretical conclusions in relation to psychoanalysis (Becall 2010).

Each analyst brings unique personal qualities to the ways he or she provides analytic functions. They are expressed in tone, timing, use of humour and subtle forms of personalized response, which over time become part of what the analysand experiences and anticipates as part of the analytic interaction. Because this factor of personality is unique to each dyad and because the analyst's voice is not represented in this study, I had no way of representing this dimension.

Nonetheless, I believe the former analysands I interviewed were likely to have carried it with them and re-evoked it as a part of a post-analytic process of both mourning and continued self-exploration.

Analysing one's dreams and making further discoveries by reflecting on current behaviour and reactions in relation to the past are valuable ways to keep an analytic process alive. Keeping one's former analyst in mind as a conscious companion in self-exploration seemed to supply comfort and aid in both affect-containment and self-reflection. Having an outside observer with whom one shares deeper and more personal aspects of oneself – a spouse, friends, colleagues – enriched both one's professional and personal life.

Still, not everyone wants or needs to engage in any of these activities after analysis ends. It does not mean that they have not also derived benefit from analysis. The self-analytic function is a source of pleasure and growth, but it may be more of a wishful outcome than a regular occurrence. We need to reexamine our assumptions that it is a criterion for ending analysis or the central measure of analytic success.

Notes

1 Compared with 27 per cent in the overall group, 39 per cent of the subgroup had analyses lasting five and a half years; and 48 per cent compared with 34 per cent in the overall group had analyses that lasted between six and nine years (see Table 5 in the Appendix).

2 This was true for 43 per cent, compared with 24 per cent for the overall group (see Table 6 in the Appendix). It is to be expected that people who ended their analyses within the last year would more frequently think about their analysis than analysands who were more distant from the process.

3 It should be noted that an equal number of former analysands who reported a satisfactory outcome did not provide illustrations of, or describe, a continuing self-analytic process.

4 It is hard to separate the effect of analysands' positive feelings from their continuing to work through the ending of their analyses. Moreover, we do not know whether others in the larger study group might have also provided examples of self-exploratory work and strong positive feelings about their analyses if they had been interviewed in the year or two after their termination.

Chapter 7

Reflections and reconsiderations

As I stated in my opening chapter, I had two major agendas in undertaking a study of experiences of analytic endings. One was to challenge the myth that analyses end in a particular way. I wanted to provide data showing that the specificity of the character and the conflicts of a particular analysand and analyst, their interaction, and the unique issues that came up in termination, overrode all generalizations about endings. We do a disservice to psychoanalysis as a field when we lose this view. My second agenda was to provide the perspective of the analysand who, until recently, has rarely been a voice in the psychoanalytic literature.

Idealization of analysis

When analysts believe they must achieve specific goals with their patients before ending, when they become disappointed with themselves, their patients and, possibly, with analysis itself, their clinical functioning as well as their self-esteem can be harmed. When expectations are idealized and unrealistic, they become inhibiting rather than inspiring.

Perfectionism is a crippling problem. It keeps people from doing what they *can* do because they are always imagining what they should be able to do and can't.

It is reasonable to expect that, to some degree, the process of analysis will facilitate greater freedom and pleasure in an analysand's relationships, work and creativity, as well as in the range and depth of his or her feelings. Nonetheless, the outcome of treatment depends on many different variables, including the patient's capacities prior to analysis, the 'match' between the analysand and the analyst in terms of character and conflicts, and the analyst's abilities and capacity both to become aware of his or her blind spots and to change ways of working based on these insights. Factors in real life can also contribute to a felicitous or a more limited outcome of an analysis: for example, meeting an appropriate mate when the patient is more open to this possibility, or finding an inspiring job when conflicts around working and authority are lessened. The occurrence of such fortunate events is unpredictable, but it is unlikely that anyone will end analysis feeling fulfilled in all ways. As I noted in the Introduction, when analysts write about an analytic gain or benefit at termination, they are usually writing about a specific patient. We should not expect this same analytic gain as a goal for all analysands. Psychoanalysis can make huge differences in the lives of patients, their families and others they encounter. What I am demonstrating in this book is that a schematic view of psychoanalytic endings not only diminishes the diversity of psychoanalytic outcomes but may also interfere with the creativity of individual psychoanalyses.

The vantage point

Analyses begin with an explicit intention that they will end. When the treatment is over, we reflect on what the analysand takes away from the process. In this project my intention was not to evaluate the outcome of the participants' analytic treatment, although their reports often indicated how satisfactory, or unsatisfactory, they felt their analysis to be. As I have indicated, while self-report is not the only way to evaluate success, it is certainly a crucial dimension. If analysands believed that the issues that had brought them to analysis had not shifted in a positive direction, it would be hard to think of the analysis as successful, no matter what else had occurred. My interest, however, was not to assess the analysands' change or lack of change but rather to illustrate the variability of the process and the focus of the analysands at the ending of their treatment.

This book represents the analysands' perspective. Designations of termination, satisfaction, success and benefit all come from them. I have no corroboration from their families and friends, or objective assessments, such as pre- and post-psychological test comparisons. I have presented the patients' stories in their words, with their subjective appraisals.

Throughout the book, I have reminded the reader that we cannot know whether the former analysts would agree with the analysand's version of what happened or, most specifically, with their accounts of the analyst's behaviour. We cannot distinguish whether theory, character, or countertransference predominantly influenced the analyst's behaviour either during treatment or in the post-analytic meetings. We cannot know the extent to which the analysands' accounts are coloured by unmetabolized feelings. We also need to remember that many of these analyses occurred decades ago when analysis was conceptualized differently from today.

As I have emphasized, with few exceptions the literature presents the analytic experiences from the analyst's perspective. Even though today we are less apt to accept ideas just because they are proposed by someone in a position of authority, we often still tend to privilege this hierarchy. So, due to the nature of authority, we are more likely to think that the analysts' accounts of analyses more accurately represent what actually occurred than the other way around. The fact that only the patient's point is presented here means that the reader must keep in mind the possibility of another view.

Unless both the analysand and analyst agreed to it, it would not be possible to present both perspectives. But even with their analysand's permission, I suspect many analysts would not agree to provide their own views about what occurred during treatment. They would be aware that it could have untoward reverberations for the analysand. If such information were different from what the analysand had imagined, it could destabilize and possibly disrupt the analysand's representations of the self, the analyst and the analytic interaction (Kantrowitz 2006). Moreover, as I indicated in the chapter on post-analytic contact, unless the former analysands chose to re-contact their former analysts, they would be left on their own to assimilate a perspective that might be unexpected, painful or confusing. We do not assume that analytic gains are fragile. But we should also not assume that post-analytic input from the former analyst might not cause distress, possibly negatively affecting the analysand's feelings about the analysis itself. The data on post-analytic contact from this project has made that abundantly clear.

So even if I could have made a choice between the scientific gain and the clinical risk, I would have to have chosen, as I have, to represent only the analysands' point of view. My hope is that, reading these accounts of how some patients have been affected by the analyst's words or actions, the analysts will think about their work and post-analytic contacts in ways they had not previously contemplated.

The particular versus the generalization

Although I have continuously emphasized that there is no single way of ending an analysis or having post-analytic contact, my point is not that anything goes. I believe it is always necessary to link what one does as an analyst to a particular patient's conflicts, defences, affect tolerance and internal representations of self and other.

People who enter analysis want to feel better, but they also want to understand themselves. They have chosen a treatment that privileges understanding. While they may not experience insight as the curative factor in their treatment, they often want to find a way to conceptualize what has occurred and why. Some of my colleagues might view this as an intellectualization of the process, a way of keeping the analytic experience at a distance and incompletely integrated. And for some analysands this may, in fact, be the case. But my own clinical experience, as well as the reports of the former analysands in this study, suggests something different: conceptualizations help to organize and contain intense emotional experiences. They are a form of communication that bridges what is unique in the self with universal experiences. By providing ways of thinking about what we share as human beings, theory can sometimes ease the existential sense of aloneness.

As I observed in Chapter 1, our thinking as analysts has evolved over the years. Most of us no longer believe in absolutes. There is no complete analysis, no completely resolved transference, no single developmental phase that characterizes our difficulties, no perfect analyst, no perfect ending. We can better appreciate what analysis can offer without idealizing outcomes. Nonetheless, there is a tendency to want to make it simpler. Disagreements about the nature of therapeutic action have also lessened, but not to the same extent. I suspect this is because we privilege our own experiences and tend to generalize from them. We also tend to see certain aspects of analysis as prominent in our patients because we are more sensitive to these aspects in ourselves.

My experience as an analyst, and I believe most of my colleagues would agree, does not conform to a universal pattern in terminating analyses or in what accounts for therapeutic change. Rather it is specific to the particular dyad. Because it is human nature to impose our subjectivities, it is important to try to broaden the base of information. In these 82 interviews I wanted to test the idea that endings had specificity rather than uniformity.

There is always a danger in finding what we look for. I have tried to be aware of this pitfall and to be open to whatever the interviews revealed. I recognized the possibility that, with a large enough sample, clear patterns could emerge and that what I had seen as the particularity of endings was the exception. Instead, my findings challenged some generalizations in the literature, as well as in the oral tradition of teaching, that for some clinicians have become regarded as facts.

Rethinking old assumptions

In the outcome study of psychoanalysis that I undertook in the 1980s (Kantrowitz et al. 1986, 1987a, 1987b, 1989, 1990a, 1990b, 1990c), I distinguished between an analytic outcome and a therapeutic benefit. Patients might meet many personal goals – for example, to feel better and to function better – and so be thought to have derived therapeutic benefit from analysis. But unless a structural change had occurred and the analyst had conducted the analysis without the need for parameters (Eissler 1953), it was not considered an analytic result. Today, I think none of us would say that treatment was unsuccessful if the patient's functioning in life and self-experience had improved, no matter what we might assume about structural change. Nor do we expect the stringency of abstinence and neutrality on the part of analyst that were required in the 1950s and 1960s in North America.

Structural change is an abstract term, hard to assess and measure. What I believe was meant by it was that the patient had internalized the analytic experience in such a way that his or her psychic organization had been transformed. Self and object and their relationship would be represented more benignly, or affect availability and tolerance would increase, or perceptions of reality would become more consensually validated.

Projective tests, now out of fashion, were thought to assess the patient's pre-analysis psychological organization and areas of dysfunction by assessing the variables just cited. When these tests were repeated after analysis ended, they showed the extent to which these areas had or had not changed. The patient was not always aware of the changes, but analysts assumed these changes would result in better adaptation and greater satisfaction in life.

As previously mentioned, one very important finding in my earlier study in the 1980s[1] was that patient and analyst, and comparisons of pre- and post-analysis projective test results, showed different degrees of optimism about whether, and to what extent, a positive change had occurred (Kantrowitz *et al.* 1987a). Analysts had the most optimistic view about what had been accomplished. The psychological test results gave the greatest indication that problems remained. The analysands' views were neither as sanguine as the analysts' nor as pessimistic as the comparison on the pre- and post-psychological tests. The disparity was troubling.

The implication that one could draw from this finding was that a construct such as the level and quality of object relations was actually represented by various phenomena, which had been assumed to be similar, but were not the same. Each set of observations introduced a different perspective on the effect of analysis. Patients reported their subjective experiences. Psychological tests like the Rorschach, which was central in this project, assessed psychological structure, reality testing, affect availability, tolerance and modulation. It revealed the extent to which thought was integrated with affect – a phenomenon that analysands are often not able to describe as subjective experience. Psychological tests, however, cannot predict what a person will actually think or do. Analysts made inferences about these phenomena based on what patients conveyed in their thoughts and actions.

As I described in Chapter 1, my study of psychoanalytic outcome included the views of 22 former analysands about the effect of their treatment. Analysands were interviewed at two different times after termination: after one year had passed and again five to ten years later. When patients offered negative descriptions of their treatment, they were similar to many of those reported in this book. Four people believed that their analysts had failed to appreciate their vulnerability in self-esteem. In different ways, each described the painful experience of not feeling understood or validated. They also reported that the analysts had not recognized the difficulties they had had in voicing these concerns. Two other individuals believed that their analysts had failed to identify their negative transference. One of these analysands went on to understand and lessen his difficulties with aggression through his work with patients, while the other remained distressed that analysis had not been able to help him. Other analysands reported that their analysts had not adequately addressed certain conflicts or helped contain intense feelings. Because our information about the long-lasting effect of analysis usually comes in the form of later consultations or returns to treatment on the part of former analysands, the data from this project, however incomplete, was relatively unique.

We needed input from former patients to help us see what we had failed to recognize while they were in analysis itself. But this recognition should not be used to support an expectation that analysis could be 'complete' or that analysts will always see and respond with perfect attunement and understanding. As analysts we will inevitably have 'blind spots' – as well as 'hard spots and dumb spots' as James McLaughlin (1981) put it. We should not expect perfection of ourselves any more than that of analytic endings and outcomes. The best we can do is to keep trying to stretch ourselves and our capacities by listening carefully and trying to take in what our patients are telling us about themselves and how we are affecting them. In this book I have tried to expand what can be learned when we have a wider sample of data than our own practices can provide.

Comparison of this study with Firestein's 1982 project

Since Firestein (1982) reported on experiences in terminations from the vantage point of 12 analysts, rather than of 82 analysands who were both clinicians and non-clinicians, it is not possible to make exact comparisons between his study and my own. Still, there are many parallels. As a group, the analysands in this present study showed the same variability in affect as the analysts in Firestein's project reported about their patients. During termination, grief occurred for some but not all, and a few were 'buoyant and optimistic'. The analysts in Firestein's study varied in whether or not they suggested, welcomed, discouraged or were neutral about post-analytic return. None of the analysands in this study, almost 30 years later, seemed to have felt discouraged from making contact again with their former analysts. We can conclude that nowadays analysts believe post-analytic returns may be helpful, and are certainly not viewed as harmful to patients' analytic gains.

Firestein's group of analysts seemed to be attuned to the specificity of their patients' issues and needs, and in this respect at least, most of them did not have an idealized view of analysis nor seem wedded to theories about what *should* occur in termination. While Firestein's report indicated much greater flexibility in analytic beliefs than the literature (reviewed in Firestein 1974) or reports of teaching from that time suggest, the number of participants (12) was very small. It is not possible to know what a larger sample might have shown about adherence to idealized ideas about analysis.

Analysands' reactions to the research interview and my reactions to them

As I explained in the Introduction, I had made clear from the beginning of the project that I would show all the participants what I was planning to publish from their interviews, so I knew I would have at least one more contact with them. After the interviews, 15 analysands called or emailed to say how helpful it had been to talk about their experience. Some of them stated that it had served as a further working through of termination. This specific reaction occurred most often when the former analysand had described negative feelings that had not been fully addressed in treatment. The interviewees often blamed themselves for what had not been resolved and expressed a belief that their analysts shared these negative perceptions of them. Hearing themselves say their negative thoughts out loud to me – some of which had persisted for many years after analysis – and not having these attitudes confirmed by me, may have offered them an opportunity to reappraise their experiencing their analysts as critical of them. As one analysand put it, there was then a recognition that this was probably a projection.

Writing this book has taken a long time and turned out to be far more difficult than I had imagined. So it was several years after we had first spoken that I re-contacted the participants in my study to show them what I had reported. Their responses varied. Most of them thanked me, validated that what I had written accurately reflected what they had told me and said how they still thought about their analysis and its ending. Some added again how helpful it had been for them to talk about their experience. They recognized that in the process of the interview they had been both discharging and working through some of their leftover feelings from analysis. A few reported a new insight based on our conversation. The interviews had left them feeling more settled about things that had disturbed them and more positive about the experience itself. Like analysis, talking about an intense emotional experience and having someone listen and convey understanding can sometimes ease painful feelings.

A few who remained unhappy about their termination wrote that the account I had sent them was, unfortunately, accurate. Some, however, reacted with anger and outrage, maintaining that I had misrepresented their experiences. I have since learned that this feeling is not so uncommon in interview situations and occurs even when material has been tape-recorded and transcribed verbatim.[2] The individuals who felt misquoted said that they did not want the material used.

Having agreed from the outset that I would not publish anything they did not approve, I asked if they wanted to write their own accounts. Almost all of them agreed to do this. In most instances the revised accounts seemed very similar to the one I had written. But as I reread them, I became aware of slight differences. For example, a particular adjective was changed to soften or heighten their affect. I do not know whether this was a mistake on my part, an unintentional misinterpretation, or a change of feeling by the analysand. Also, because some of the analysands who were distressed by what I had written had had struggles with their analysts, they were worried about their analysts' recognizing the account and feeling hurt or angry.

With some former analysands, I felt that their sensitivity to the way I had represented them seemed to echo the sensitivity they may have felt to the way their analysts had worked with them. It is possible that their initial reaction represented a transference to me as a stand-in for their analysts. In almost every case, my willingness to present their accounts just as they wanted them calmed their anger. They then agreed to publication. These experiences focused my attention on aspects of the analysands of which I had not previously been conscious: there is always something more and different from what is initially presented.

Overview of the limitations of the project

As I listened to the former analysands talk about their terminations, I was aware that I was hearing only their point of view, just as I am aware that my own patients only tell me about their world in terms of how they remember and perceive it. With my patients, however, I know that, over time, they and I may come to understand their perceptions differently. So questions of other complexities, back stories or possible contradictions are present in my mind but suspended, not in the forefront of my consciousness. With the volunteers in my study, however, I knew that I would not have the opportunity to explore and rework our understanding of their narratives. My job was to present them as accurately as I could, without trying to shape them or seek points of comparison – just their thoughts and feelings in whatever form they wished to express them.

In retrospect I regret not having structured the interviews more, since it was difficult to organize the material without having asked questions that gave me material that could be compared. Also, the relatively short length of the interviews restricted exploration of many topics and prevented me from learning as much as I would have liked about the complexity of the analysands' experiences. I realized that I had chosen to acquire material of breadth rather than depth, and I regret having made this decision. It was easy to show diversity but hard to link the accounts thematically.

In addition to acknowledging the difficulties imposed by the structure, length and depth of the interviews themselves, I want to address the overall limitations of this project and of the generalizations that can be drawn from it. The data has multiple problems, which stem primarily from the fact that the survey participants were, in many respects, not comparable. As I have already stated, there were considerable differences in their ages and in the length of time they had been in analysis and terminated analysis. Their previous and subsequent histories of treatment were not comparable, nor were their psychological strengths or vulnerabilities. Almost all of them had had different analysts and, of course, different experiences in analysis itself. There was also considerable variation in their reasons for volunteering. I will now consider the effect of some of these variables.

Age

How old a person is at the end of analysis may itself greatly affect his or her perspective on the analytic experience and its outcome. For example, the three former analysands in their thirties who had terminated in the previous year had all been very positive about their treatment and its outcome. They were optimistic about how it would affect the rest of their lives. For each, it was their first and only analytic treatment (though two of them had had previous therapy).

In this sample, it was difficult to separate the effect of the particular life stage for people in their middle years – 40 to 70 – from the experience of previous or subsequent treatment, which most of them had had. Nine people in this sample were in their seventies; six were in their eighties, and one was in his nineties. And when these individuals described their analyses as successful, they were likely to be grateful that they had had an experience that changed them in a way that no previous treatment or life experience had done. On the other hand, when the treatment was disappointing, they tended to feel more despairing of the possibility of change. Older people may be more reluctant to end their analyses and feel more grief in the ending since the experience is probably compounded by the actual or expectable loss of others who are emotionally important to them.

Yet, as noted in Chapter 2, when the participants in this study believed that analysis had gone well, age was not a prominent feature in differentiating those who had optimism about what the future might offer from those less sanguine about their prospects.

Length of time since termination

Twenty people terminated in the year before the interview. For most of them the experience of ending was vivid: they reported more frequent thoughts of their analysts, and for some, grief continued. Twenty-two people terminated more than 20 years ago. For the rest of the participants the length of time since termination fell between 20 and 55 years (Appendix, Table 2).

Comparisons are hard to make between people fresh from the powerful emotional experience of ending, some of whom are still actively grieving the loss of their analysts and the analytic experiences, and people who terminated decades ago, because these provided a retrospective look that was removed from affect intensity. However, the fact that seven of the nine oldest participants – those over age 70 who had ended treatment 29 to 55 years ago – were still thinking about their analysis and wanting to talk about it testifies to its continued importance over time.

Certainly chronological differences make comparisons more difficult, but even if I had been able to have a sample of former analysands who had all ended their analyses 1 year, 5 years, 10 years, 25 years, or 50 years ago, other factors would still limit the comparability. Still, it would have been preferable. Five years from now it is my intention to re-interview the 20 people in this sample who ended analysis within a year of their interview with me. At least the data will suggest how perspectives change or stay the same over time. It will also give me the opportunity to ask specific questions and pursue some topics in more depth.

Previous and subsequent treatment

Whether the interviewee had had previous therapy and/or whether the termination he or she was describing belonged to a first, second or third analysis varied considerably from person to person. Twenty-nine participants had had two analyses; four of these had had three analyses. It seemed that each of them were recounting the analytic or post-analytic experience that had the most affective charge. While an earlier or subsequent experience was likely to affect the individual's perspective on treatment as a whole, it was not possible to untangle the effect of other analyses from the one being reported.

It is usually safe to assume that if a person returned for more treatment, the earlier experience had left unexplored certain issues that he or she now wanted to pursue. But this did not necessarily mean that the earlier experience had been unsatisfactory. Treatments ended for many reasons. Dissatisfaction was only one of them. And, as Freud (1937) stated, life introduces unexpected challenges for which one might seek comfort or further self-knowledge in a return to treatment. Sometimes they returned to their former analyst, sometimes not.

As we know, an analyst can die, retire, move or become ill; the patient can move. In a few instances, the former analysands had had what they felt were profound and satisfactory analyses, but because they had begun analytic training, they had to see a different analyst who was a training analyst. Some of these individuals considered the later analysis pro forma; the real work had been in the initial analysis. For others, the training analysis was the one that most deeply affected them. Therefore, sometimes the former analysand was comparing an analytic experience and its ending to a previous analysis that ended for external reasons; sometimes to a less intense and more limited experience in therapy; and sometimes to a disappointing therapy or analysis. Similarly, the course of the analysands' life experience after treatment – how and in what ways it changed their perspective on their analysis – also varied. My point is the limits in comparability.

Motivations for volunteering

I remind the reader that there are built-in limitations in any sample based on individuals who have volunteered to be interviewed. They all want to tell their story and to have the listener communicate it accurately enough to others. Strong affect, positive or negative, often seemed a motivation for volunteering. But following on from that, ideas of comparability diminish.

The majority of volunteers in this sample conveyed that they had had positive experiences and that they wanted to express their gratitude and appreciation for what occurred. While more personal motivations undoubtedly played a role in their decision to contact me, some volunteers also expressed their wish to participate in the study as a commitment to research in the psychoanalytic field. One can speculate that individuals who are analysts wanted to offer their experiences and their endings to support their belief that analysis 'works'. How and why they believed it had worked for them was a different matter. In that respect, the comparability again dissolved.

On the other hand, negative feelings – strong anger or disappointment – were certainly motivators for some participants in the study. These individuals had had experiences that they considered 'bad' and they wanted them on record – not that analysis itself was 'bad' but that their analyst had behaved 'badly'. Therefore their volunteering was sometimes a pleasurable act of revenge or retaliation, even though their former analysts were unlikely to ever know about it.

The reasons for the intensity of feeling were specific, and no particular theory applied to everyone. But telling another person about negative experiences often helps to discharge an excess of internal pressure. As I said above, the 15 people who reported how helpful it had been to talk about their experience were aware that they were working through some of their leftover feelings from analysis in the process of the interview.

Some participants had a wish for vindication – a hope that I would understand what their former analyst had not, and that I would tell others. For a few, anxiety and guilt followed the articulation of these criticisms. The volunteers feared that the aggressive expression of their dissatisfaction would harm their former analysts.

The way individuals remembered their analysis and their analyst was also affected by their post-treatment contact with him or her, and such encounters generated particularly strong feelings, both positive and negative and with long-term reverberations. Most, but not all, of the volunteers in this category were clinicians. Sometimes they seemed to want on record what could have been done differently and hoped that, through of my writing about their experiences, they could educate other professionals.

While the former analysands who participated in my project are, as I have stressed, different in many respects, one factor unifies them: their wish to talk about their analysis. Even if they have not actively continued to engage in self-exploration, they have kept the analysis, or some aspect of it, alive. Whether their termination occurred a year or two previously or decades ago, they have not stopped thinking about their analysts or the experience of treatment. They volunteered to be interviewed because they wished to share the experience – the satisfaction as well as the disappointment.

Talking about their experience to someone who was interested, who was listening attentively, trying to understand and sharpen their understanding by putting it into words, recreated for them some of what they valued in the process. Others, I think, just wanted a comfortable return to the analytic experience, which they wished to celebrate in the presence of another. Recounting analytic experience also reconnected former analysands with positive feelings associated with their analyst and analysis itself. For them volunteering was, as I said earlier, an act of gratitude.

We cannot assume that everyone who has been analysed continues the process after ending, but it was a characteristic of these volunteers. Telling their personal story was a continuation of their working through, synthesizing and consolidating their analysis; this was true even for those people who had terminated more than three decades ago. For some interviewees, talking to me may also have been a way of continuing to mourn the ending. In all accounts there was vividness. They had kept alive a sense of their analysis, their analyst and the analytic interaction.

For analysands who are themselves clinicians, experiences with patients – as well as with supervisors – provided a specific opportunity to continue to develop psychologically. What they learned about themselves in their clinical work may have deepened insights gained in their analyses, but what they learned about themselves may also have been new. Further insight might change their feelings about – and possibly their memory of – what occurred in analysis.

Memory

Reis (2010) observed that our current understanding of memory, its storage and retrieval, means that to access memory is to change memory. Memory may be cued by affect or affect by memory. I think he was suggesting that the cognitive reshaping that occurs over time is also related to affect states and the way that these may shift and change over time. We cannot account for how memory can affect these reports.

One former analysand, a colleague not formally part of this study, recounted her post-analytic experience and how it shifted and changed over the course of 30 years:

> After I stopped, I missed both my analyst and the analytic experience terribly. To be able to talk to someone who presumably wanted to hear your every thought would not be replaced in real life. I'd learned so much, changed so much. But a year later, following an unexpected ending of a relationship, I found myself angry and disappointed about how we had ended and went back for a few sessions and talked about that. A couple of years later I thought of the analysis as having been extraordinarily helpful, especially in having learned how to analyse my dreams, in recognizing countertransference with patients and helping me be more self-contained and content. But some years later, I was confronted with a major area of conflict in myself that I felt had been completely unaddressed. I was again disappointed and disillusioned. But then I found a way to explore and understand this on my own. It took much time and hard work.
>
> Now some thirty years since I terminated analysis, I have returned to a more balanced view of my analysis. It certainly taught me an analytic method that has personally and professionally enriched my life. It also enabled me to grow up, separate. There's a lot it didn't address, but it gave me tools to keep on learning and changing. But it didn't make me feel that I wanted to return to working that way again. It was too consuming. I suppose too regressive. What would it be if I returned? I don't know. I'm really glad I did it. It changed me profoundly, but I want to live in my life.

As I have stressed, the way a former patient thinks about analysis is likely to change over time. The changes in perspective occur for many reasons and in part they may also have to do with external life circumstances as well as whether the former analysand sustained psychological gains. I remind the reader that an individual's optimism about what has been accomplished can diminish if his or her life goals are not attained. On the other hand, initial disappointment in what analysis had accomplished may sometimes be re-evaluated if one finds unexpected satisfaction in life.

Do these serious limitations in my data mean that nothing of value has been found in this study? I don't think so. I hope I have convincingly demonstrated that idealizations and preconceived ideas about how analysis ends are not supported by data.

Conclusions

1. The importance of specificity

No one phenomenon characterizes endings, nor is there one particular way that analysts should behave during either termination or post-termination. The results of this study certainly confirm that each analysis and each ending is shaped by the nature of the particular issues of the analysand and the particular analytic dyad.

Analysts need to remain attentive to the specific issues and reactions that ending stirs in each analysand. At the same time they must remain acutely attuned to their own countertransference and other personal feelings that may lead them to prolong analysis when a patient indicates a readiness to terminate; or, alternatively, to let the analysand go too quickly without adequate exploration of the meaning of the ending. The material also suggests the importance of being more aware of, and, therefore more sensitive to, analysands' often unspoken reactions and vulnerabilities during both the last phase of analysis and post-analytic encounters.

2. Post-analytic contact

The study does not support the idea that analyses, their endings or the post-analytic emotional reactions of grief are different for former analysands who are now analysts themselves than for anyone else. As I have repeatedly indicated, what is different is the expectation of post-analytic contact. Contrary to expectations from the literature (Milner 1950; Novick 1997), post-analytic experiences of grief and extended periods of mourning were no less intense for analysands who were part of the analytic community than they were for those who were not. Again, I will remind the reader that the four former analysands who described the most protracted experiences of grief after ending were all in analytic training. Later contact with the former analyst does not protect candidates from the loss of the analytic experience; it is an experience that takes place only within the analysis itself.

My findings suggest that social or professional contact with the former analyst after termination is often a mixed experience for the former analysand. As I have just indicated, the data from my study showed that the expectation of having future social or professional contact with their former analysts did not lessen a patient's need to work through and grieve the ending of analysis. Though some analysands clearly felt that later contact was sustaining, in this study those individuals were less likely to be analysts. What is more, the analysands who described a post-analytic social relationship were more often those not in a clinical field. Rather, they were individuals who shared some avocational interest with the former analyst.

3. Grief

The role of grief in analytic ending is a concept that needs to be rethought.

As I have repeatedly emphasized, analytic theory has presumed that analyses inevitably end with grief. Both my study and Firestein's suggest that this is not a universal experience. Sometimes grief, and the process of mourning, occurred in substantial ways earlier in analysis; at other times, grief did not occur because attachment had been defended against. But it is also possible that the experience of grief and the need to mourn have merely been delayed. Perhaps this is why the candidates in Craige's study (2002) reported unanticipated experiences of grief after ending.

Kris's description (1985, 2012) of how resolution of conscious conflict about separation involves a process that is akin to mourning helps us to understand the nature and process of separation and individuation. Two incompatible wishes battle with each other: to retain all the comfort and pleasures of dependence and, simultaneously, to be self-sufficient and enjoy the sense of autonomous mastery. In the actual mourning of a loved one, we wish to not accept that the loved one is no longer in our life; at the same time we know we must accept the reality of loss. Working through occurs by the repeated exploration of each side of the conflict. Tension is discharged through the process and results in assimilation.

Kris helpfully points out that what one needs to mourn is the loss of the loved one in the *future*. It has been mistakenly assumed (Freud 1915, 1917) that one needs to relinquish all connection to what has been previously known and shared. Analysands need to grieve and mourn the loss of the analysing experience itself and the partnership they have had with the analyst in this endeavour. These are the attachments that will not exist in the future.

I am in no doubt that grief and the need to mourn are essential parts of development and change in an analytic experience; it is only whether they must always occur during termination or in the post-termination experience that I have been questioning. When analysand and analyst decide it is time to end, there is a tilt toward the wish for independence from the analysand and an increased ability to transfer attachment and investment into life itself, carrying forward what has been learned and assimilated. For some this was a very hard-won achievement occurring over time in the analysis, but when it occurred, joy, not grief, predominated in their feelings in ending.

4. Unilateral endings

While an ending of analysis that is not based on mutual agreement is never desirable, we need not automatically assume it will disrupt previous analytic gains. The specific reason for the unilateral decision, how it is conveyed and explored, the openness to hearing the patient's distress will make a difference. Like most of the issues discussed in this book, it is the meaning to the analysand and the receptivity and sensitivity of the analyst that will make a difference.

5. Self-analysis and assimilation of therapeutic gains

Finally, my results have provided an expanded view of how former analysands keep their analyses alive in the absence of their analysts. I have described the various methods of self-exploration and offered some ideas about ways in which these activities are both similar to, and different from, what occurs in analysis itself. Of equal interest is my finding that it is possible to retain analytic gains – to keep the sense of the analyst as an internal companion – without fully internalizing an independent self-reflective process in the way it has usually been conceptualized.

Another misconception is that those who are analysts, or in training to become analysts, are more likely to develop and continue a self-analytic function than those who are not. Different ways of assimilating analysis do not seem directly related to one's profession; they more probably reflect variations in people in terms of cognitive style, ego organization, or characterological adaptations and defences.

The interest of former analysands in evoking their analytic experience and the analytic relationship attested to their wish to keep a meaningful part of their past alive. For some, recounting a narrative of their treatment was similar to talking about memorable moments growing up. There was a feeling of happiness in sharing, in actively bringing past pleasure to life. Like childhood memories, these memories can be oversimplified and conflicted experiences may be relegated to insignificance in recollection; alternatively, they may have actually lost their sting over time. If the view of the past interferes with current attachments because the present seems a poor substitute by comparison, then there is more work to be done.

But for many of these analysands who felt satisfied with their treatment, this did not seem to be the case. They felt appreciative of their current lives and grateful to their analysts. I would speculate that an assimilation had occurred. They have separated from their analysts, but the memory of connection is easily and happily revisited. They are taking pleasure not only in remembering what they shared with their analyst but also in their current mastery, their ability to do for themselves. Attachment and autonomy exist simultaneously; one does not cancel out the other. As the interviewer, I am the witness to this process, and having a witness creates an added pleasure.

A number of analysands in this study were continuing to work through analytic experiences that had been less than satisfying. For some, the disappointment was partial: they knew what they gained but continued to regret what was not accomplished. Like many of the examples presented earlier, these feelings may shift and change over time, and sharing the dysphoric affect could sometimes be a way of working it through, as it can be in analysis. For other analysands, their anger and disappointment remained acute.

Previously, I speculated that talking to me might have been, at least in part, an act of revenge. But it may also have reflected the analysands' wish to discharge painful affect by sharing it – to take a step toward lessening the hold of negative affect in their attachment to their analyst and the past. When analysands observed that, after the interview, they were consciously aware that painful affect had been released, this lessening of pain may have occurred. Perhaps the research interview assisted them with mourning that had been interrupted by both their resentment and their self-critical attitude because of the resentment. This too may be a step toward assimilation. That would be my hope.

Notes

1 The overall findings of the study, confirming the importance of the patient–analyst match and the effect of psychoanalysis, would divert us from our present focus.
2 Personal communication from Kitty Ross.

Appendix

This appendix contains the methods, data and tables summarizing distributions of ages, length of time since termination, length of time in analysis and comparisons on these variables between those analysands who engaged in self-exploration and the total sample.

Methods

I posted requests for former analysands to talk with me about their experiences in terminating analysis on the on-line bulletin of the American Psychoanalytic Association, *New Dimensions*, the writing programme of the Washington Psychoanalytic Institute, the newsletters of William Alanson White and the San Francisco Institute of the American Psychoanalytic Association Institute and at some college health services. My notice said that interviews would be conducted on the phone and that the material would be kept confidential and presented anonymously. The former analysands would have the opportunity to read the material, correct any inaccuracies and give permission for its use before it was published. The interviews would last one to two hours. At the completion of the interviews, I asked the participants if they would ask friends and colleagues who had terminated analyses to contact me. So the sample snowballed. Many of the volunteers suggested and/or facilitated some of the posting of the project.

The subjects

I interviewed 82 people over the course of 13 months, 64 women and 18 men. Their ages ranged from 36 to 97. The distribution is roughly bell-shaped, with the majority being in their fifties and sixties (Table 1). Twenty terminations had occurred within the last year; the two longest terminated had occurred more than 50 years ago (Table 2).

Eighteen of the subjects were non-clinicians. Most of them had advanced professional degrees. One was an academic who studied at a psychoanalytic institute but did not do the clinical part of the training. Of the 64 clinicians, 43 were analysts. Of the analysts, 15 were MDs; 17 were PhD psychologists; 6 were social workers; 2 were MA psychologists; 1 was an academic trained in psychoanalysis with waivers to do clinical work. Two others were analytic candidates in training; one of these had a MD and the other one had a PhD. The clinicians who had not had analytic training were comprised of: 6 PhD psychologists; 3 PsyDs; 7 social workers; 2 MA psychologists; 1 family therapist; 1 psychology PhD candidate; 1 PsyD candidate (Table 3).

Previous and subsequent treatment

Of the 82 analysands, 29 had 2 analyses; 4 others had 3 analyses; 12 had had therapy with the person who became their analyst prior to beginning analysis; some of these had also had previous therapy with a different therapist. Twenty-two individuals had had one or more previous therapies with a different person prior to entering analysis. After completing analysis, 25 returned for a consultation or therapy with their former analysts; 4 returned to the former analyst for a second period of analysis; 10 eventually sought therapy with a different clinician. Only 2 of the 82 former analysands had a single analysis and no therapy.

Although my original intention was to report the former analysands' experience of ending a single particular analysis, it became clear that their responses were influenced by all their previous analytic experiences. As a result, while the total sample consists of 82 individuals, the total number of responses in the following categories exceeds this number, as the same person was evaluating different experiences that occurred in different analyses.

Satisfaction with analytic experience

Fifty-two of these former analysands reported that they had at least one analysis that successfully addressed the issues for which they had sought treatment. They also described the termination process itself as successful.

Mixed feelings about outcome

Eight former analysands described their analyses as partially successful but believed that central, crucial areas of themselves remained unaddressed. Four of them believed their analysts had failed to appreciate their vulnerability in self-esteem or recognize their difficulties in voicing these concerns. In different ways, each described painful experiences of not feeling understood or validated. Two other former analysands believed their analyst had failed to identify their negative transference. One of these, a clinician, went on to understand and lessen his own difficulties with aggression through his work with patients. Three continued to feel disappointed with the help the analysis had provided. In one instance, the analysand believed that the analyst had not adequately addressed certain conflicts; in another, the analysand felt the analyst had not adequately helped in containing intense feelings.

Dissatisfaction: belief that analysis failed to help or was hurtful

Twenty-seven former analysands reported that a previous analysis had been either unhelpful or destructive. Eleven of these individuals have had at least one other analysis that they believed was successfully terminated.

Reasons for ending

1 No new insights
Five former analysands described reaching a point of diminishing returns: they were going over familiar material and nothing new was emerging.

2 Desire to have a more varied life
Twenty-one former analysands said they wanted more time, money or ways to be more engaged in their lives and less involved in an analytic process.

3 Confidence about continuing self-analytic work
Twenty-three former analysands believed that they understood themselves and felt they could use a self-analytic process well enough to continue analytic work on their own. Twelve of these individuals provided moving descriptions of how they had internalized the relationship with their former analysts.

4 Analyst becomes ill or dies
Fifteen analysts became ill or died. In two instances, the analytic institute community was secretive about the illness and unsupportive to the then-candidate, who had to deal with both the loss of their analyst and the lack of communication and support. Three analysands abandoned treatment because they believed that their analysts were severely ill and in denial of their illness.

5 Analyst moves
Six analysts moved. In two instances, the former analysands discovered that their analyst was preparing to close his or her practice and had not told them. They felt betrayed that they had not been given adequate time to work through the separation and termination of their analyses. Two analysands were glad about the move, since it allowed them to extract themselves from analyses they wished to end over their analyst's resistance. Two other analysands felt the forced ending facilitated their development.

6 Analysand moves
Eight analysands moved. Six resumed analysis elsewhere; two eventually sought psychoanalytic therapy.

7 Disappointment or anger
Sixteen analysands left their analysis in anger or disappointment. In three instances it related to their analyst's unacknowledged illness and in one instance to the way the analyst had handled the fact that he was moving. Three other endings were

related to sexual boundary violations; three others to a difficulty in accepting the analyst's limits. Six analysands left after struggling with their analysts about their wish to leave treatment.

8 Non-mutual endings
Twenty-five former analysands reported non-mutual endings. Thirteen of the twenty-five subsequently had a successful analysis, which ended by mutual agreement. Three former analysands reported two non-mutual endings, and two others reported three non-mutual endings.

9 Recurrence of symptoms
Eight former analysands stated that the symptoms that had brought them to analysis or had occurred earlier in the analysis recurred during the termination phase. Four of these former analysands also reported a change during the last part of the analysis.

Table 1 Age distribution

30s	40s	50s	60s	70s	80s	90s
3	12	28	23	9	6	1

Table 2 Length of time since termination

1 year or less	5 years or less	10 years or less	20 years or less	Over 20 years	Over 30 years	Over 40 years	Over 50 years
20	16	8	16	10	7	3	2

Table 3 Professions

Non-Clinicians – 23%		Clinicians – 77%	
PhDs	6	**Analysts**	43
Education	1	MDs	15
English	3	PhDs	17
Psycholinguists	1	Social Workers	6
Science	1	MA Psychologists	2
		Academic	1
MDs	3	Analysts in Training	
Nephrologist	1	MDs	1
Rehabilitation	1	PhDs	1
Research	1		
		Psychotherapists	21
MAs	2	PhD Psychologists	6
Business	1	PsyD Psychologists	3
Physical Therapy	1	Social Workers	7
		MA Psychologists	2
Lawyer	1	Family Therapist	1

Table 3 continued

Non-Clinicians – 23%		Clinicians – 77%	
The Arts	3	Therapists in Training	
Film Editor	1	PhD	1
Visual Artist	1	PsyD	1
Writer	1		
Business	2		
Community Volunteer	1		

Table 4 Comparison of age distributions: Total vs self-exploration

Total sample (82)

30s	40s	50s	60s	70s	80s	90s
3	12	28	23	9	6	1

Self-exploration sample (23)

30s	40s	50s	60s	70s	80s	90s
3	3	8	6	1	1	1

Table 5 Comparison of length of analysis: Total vs self-exploration

Total sample (82)

5 years or less	6–10 years	11–15 years	16 years or more
26	33	15	8

Self-exploration sample (23)

5 years or less	6–10 years	11–15 years	16 years or more
9	11	2	1

Table 6 Length of time since termination: Total vs self-exploration

Total sample (82)

1 year or less	5 years or less	10 years or less	11–15 years	16–30 years	31–40 years	over 40 years
20	16	8	16	10	7	5

Self-exploration sample (23)

1 year or less	5 years or less	10 years or less	11–15 years	16–30 years	31–40 years	over 40 years
10	2	2	4	3	1	1

References

Abend, S. (1979). Unconscious fantasy and theories of cure. *J. Amer. Psychoanal. Assn,* 27:579–96.

——(1982). Serious illness in the analyst: countertransference considerations. *J. Amer. Psychoanal. Assn,* 30:365–79.

——(1986). Countertransference, empathy and the analytic ideal: the impact of life stress on the analytic capability. *Psychoanal. Quart.,* 55:563–75.

——(1990). Unconscious fantasies, structural theory, and compromise formation. *J. Amer. Psychoanal. Assn,* 38:61–73.

Alexander, F., French, T.M. *et al.* (1946). *Principles and Applications.* New York: Ronald Press.

Arlow, J.A. (1969). Unconscious fantasy and disturbances of conscious experience. *Psychoanal Quart.,* 38:1–27.

Awad, G.A. (2006). An analyst-suggested termination: does it have a role in the resolution of an interminable psychoanalysis? *Canadian J. Psychoanal.,* 14:232–53.

Balint, M. (1950). On the termination of analysis. *Int. J. Psycho-Anal.,* 31:196–99.

Bass, A. (2009). 'It ain't over till it's over': infinite conversations, imperfect endings, and the elusive nature of termination. *Psychoanalytic Diag.,* 19:744–59.

Beatrice, J. (1982). Premature termination: a therapist's leaving. *Int. J. Psycho-Anal.,* 9:313–52.

Becall, H. (2010). *The Power of Specificity in Psychotherapy.* London, Boulder, New York, Toronto: Routledge.

Beiser, H. (1984). An example of self-analysis. *J. Amer. Psychoanal. Assn,* 32:3–12.

Bergmann, M. (1997). Termination: the Achilles heel of psychoanalytic technique. *Psychoanal. Psychol.,* 14:163–74.

——(2005). Termination and reanalysis. In E. Person, A.N. Cooper and G. Gabbard (eds), *Textbook of Psychoanalysis.* Washington DC: Amer. Psychiat. Publishing, pp. 241–53.

——(2010). Termination: the Achilles heel of psychoanalytic technique. In J. Salberg (ed.), *Good Enough Endings.* Relational Perspective Series. New York, London: Routledge.

Bird, B. (1972). Notes on transference: universal phenomenon and hardest part of analysis. *Amer. Psychoanal. Assn,* 20:267–301.

Blanck, G. and Blanck, R. (1988). The contribution of ego psychology to understanding the process of termination in psychoanalysis and psychotherapy. *J. Amer. Psychoanal. Assn,* 36:961–84.

Blatt, S.J. (1992). The differential effect of psychotherapy and psychoanalysis on anaclitic and introjective patients: The Menninger Psychiatric Project revisited. *J. Amer. Psychoanal. Assn,* 40:691–724.

Blum, H.P. (1989). The concept of termination and the evolution of psychoanalytic thought. *J. Amer. Psychoanal. Assn,* 37:275–95.

Boesky, D. (1982). Acting out: a reconsideration of the concept. *Int. J. Psycho-Anal.,* 63:39–55.

Bonvitz, C. (2007). Termination never ends: The inevitable incompleteness of psychoanalysis. *Contemp. Psychoanal.,* 3:229–46.

Brenner, C. (1976). *Psychoanalytic Technique and Psychic Conflict.* New York: International Universities Press.

Breuer, J. and Freud, S. (1895). Studies on hysteria. *S.E* 2: 1–240.

Britton, R. (2010). There is no end of the line: terminating the interminable. In J. Salberg, (ed.), *Good Enough Endings: breaks, interruptions, and terminations from contemporary relational perspectives.* Relational Perspective Series. New York and London: Routledge, pp. 39–50.

Brunswick, R.M. (1928). A supplement to Freud's 'History of an infantile neurosis.' *Int. J. Psycho-Anal.,* 9:439–76.

Burland, J.A. (1997). The role of working through in bringing about psychoanalytic change. *Int. J. Psycho-Anal.,* 78:469–84.

Buxbaum, E. (1950). Technique of terminating analysis. *Int. J. Psycho-Anal.,* 31:184–90.

Calder, K.T. (1980). An analyst's self-analysis. *J. Amer. Psychoanal. Assn,* 28:5–20.

Calef, V. and Weinshel, E.M. (1983). A note on consummation and termination. *J. Amer. Psychoanal. Assn,* 31:643–50.

Cancrini, T. (1988). The experience of suffering pain in an analytical relationship with special reference to the termination of analysis. *Rivista Psicoanal.,* 34:684–712.

Cooper, S. (2009). Familiar and unfamiliar forms of interaction in the ending phases of analysis. *Psychoanal. Dial.,* 19:588–603.

Craige, H. (2002). Mourning analysis: the post-termination phase. *J. Amer. Psychoanal. Assn,* 50:507–50.

Davies, J.M. (2005). Transformation of desire and despair: reflection on the termination process from a relational perspective. *Psychoanal. Diag.,* 15:779–805.

DeBell, D.E. (1975). In Panel Report by W.S. Robbins: Termination: problems and techniques. *J. Amer. Psychoanal. Assn,* 23:166–76.

De Berenstein, S.P. and De Fondevila, D.S. (1989). Termination of analysis in the light of the evolution of a link. *Int. R. Psycho-Anal.,* 16:385–89.

De Simone, G. (1997). *Ending Analysis: Theory and Technique.* London: Karnac Books.

De Simone Gaburri, G. (1985). On termination of the analysis. *Int. R. Psycho-Anal.,* 12:461–68.

——(1990). Further considerations on the conclusion of analysis. *Rivista Psicoanal.,* 36:340–68.

Deutsch, H. Cited in Bowlby, J. (1960). Grief and mourning in infancy and early childhood. *Psychoanal. Stud. Child,* 15: 9–52.

Dewald, P.A. (1965). Reactions to the forced termination of therapy. *Psychoanal. Quart.,* 39:102–26.

——(1966). Forced termination in psychoanalysis: transference, countertransference, and reality responses in five patients. *Bull. Mennin. Clinic,* 30:98–110.

——(1982). The clinical importance of the termination phase. *Psychoanal. Inq.*, 2: 441–61.

Dorpat, T.L. (1974). Internalization of the patient–analyst relationship in patients with narcissistic disorders. *Int. J. Psycho-Anal.*, 55:183–88.

Eifermann, R.R. (1987). Interaction between textual analysis and related self-analysis. In S. Rimmon-Kenan (ed.), *Discourse in Psychoanalysis and Literature*. London: Methuen, pp. 38–55.

——(1993). The discovery of real and fantasized audiences for self-analysis. In J.W. Barron (ed.), *Self-Analysis: critical inquiries, personal visions*. Hillsdale NJ: Analytic Press, pp. 171–94.

Eissler, K.R. (1953). The effect of the structure of the ego on psychoanalytic technique. *J. Amer. Psychoanal. Assn*, 1:104–43.

Ekstein, R. (1965). Working through and termination of analysis. *J. Am. Psychoanal. Assn*, 13:57–78.

Ellman, S.J. (1997). Criteria for termination. *Psychoanal. Psychol.*, 14:197–210.

Engel, G.L. (1975). Death of a twin: mourning and anniversary reactions. *Int. J. Psycho-Anal.* 56:23–40.

Ferenczi, S. (1927). Letter from Sándor Ferenczi to Sigmund Freud, June 30, 1927. *The Correspondence of Sigmund Freud and Sándor Ferenczi,* vol. 3, 1920–1933, 311–15.

——(1932). *The Clinical Diary of Sándor Ferenczi*, ed. J. Dupont, trans. M. Balint and N. Z. Jackson. Cambridge MA: Harvard University Press, 1988.

Ferraro, F. and Garella, A. (1997). Termination as a psychoanalytic event. *Int. J. Psycho-Anal.*, 78:27–41.

Firestein, S.K. (1969). Panel Report: Problems of termination of the analysis of adults. *J. Amer. Psychoanal. Assn*, 17:222–37.

——(1974). Termination of psychoanalysis of adults: a review of the literature. *J. Amer. Psychoanal. Assn*, 22:873–94.

——(1982). Termination of psychoanalysis: theoretical, clinical, and pedagogic considerations. *Psychoanal. Inq.*, 2:473–97.

Fleming, J. and Benedeck, T. (1964). Supervision: a method of teaching psychoanalysis: Preliminary report. *Psychoanal. Quart.*, 33:71–96.

Fonagy, P. (1998). Psychodynamic approaches. In P. Salkovis, (ed.), *Comprehensive Clinical Psychology*, 6:107–134. Oxford: Elsevier Science.

Frank, G. (1999). Termination Revisited. *Psychoanal. Psychol.*, 16:119–129.

Frank, K.A. (2009). Ending with options. *Psychoanal. Inq.*, 29:136–156.

Freud, S. (1887). Extracts from Fliess papers, Letter 75. *S.E.*, 1:271. Hogarth Press, 1966.

——(1910). The future prospects of psychoanalytic therapy. *S.E.*, 11:139–51. London: Hogarth Press, 1964.

——(1913). On beginning the treatment. *S.E.*, 13:121–44. London: Hogarth Press, 1964.

——(1915). Mourning and melancholia. *S.E.*, 14:243–60. Hogarth Press, 1968.

——(1917). Analytic therapy. In S. Freud, *Introductory Lectures on Psychoanalysis*, Part III. *S.E.*, 16:448–63. London: Hogarth Press, 1964.

——(1918). From the history of an infantile neurosis. *S.E.*, 17:1–122. London: Hogarth Press, 1968.

——(1937). Analysis terminable and interminable. *S.E.*, 23:216–53. London: Hogarth Press, 1964.

Gabbard, G.O. (2009). What is a 'good enough' termination? *J. Amer. Psychoanal. Assn*, 57:575–94.

Garcia-Lawson, K.A. and Lane, R.C. (1997). Thoughts on termination: practical considerations. *Psychoanal. Psychol.*, 14:239–57.

Gardner, R. (1983). *Self-Inquiry*. Hillsdale NJ: Analytic Press.

Gaskill, H.S. (1980). The closing phase of the psychoanalytic treatment of adults and the goals of psychoanalysis. *Int. J. Psycho-Anal.*, 61:11–23.

Geller, J. and Freedman, N. (in press). Representations of the therapeutic dialogue and the post-termination phase of therapy. In N. Freedman, M. Hurvich and R. Ward, with J. Geller and J. Hoffenberg, *Another Kind of Knowing: representations of the therapeutic dialogue and the post-termination phase of psychotherapy*. London: Karnac, pp. 55–63.

Gibeault, A. (2000). In J.M. Quinodoz and E.M.D. Rocha Barros, An IPA Panel Report of the 9th Pre-Congress on Training, Santiago 1999: Clinical approaches to the terminations of the training analysis – clinical dilemmas of training analysts. *Int. J. Psycho-Anal.*, 81:1213–19.

Gilman, R.D. (1982). The termination phase in psychoanalytic practice: a survey of 48 completed cases. *Psychoanal. Inq.* 2:463–72.

Giovacchini, P.L. (1975). Self-projections in the narcissistic transference. *Int. J. Psycho-Anal. Psychotherapy*, 4:142–66.

Gitelson, M. (1962). The curative factors in psycho-analysis. *Int. J. Psycho-Anal.*, 43:194–205.

Glennon, S.S. (2010). Relational analyses: are they more difficult to terminate? In J. Salberg (ed.), *Good Enough Endings: breaks, interruptions, and terminations from contemporary relational perspectives*. Relational Perspective Series. New York and London: Routledge, pp. 257–75.

Glick, R.A. (1987). Forced terminations. *J. Amer. Acad. Psychoanal.*, 15:449–63.

Glover, E. (1955). *The Technique of Psychoanalysis*. New York: International Universities Press.

——(1964). Freudian or neofreudian. *Psychoanal. Quart.*, 33:97–109.

Goldberg, A. and Marcus, D. (1985). 'Natural termination': some comments on ending analysis without setting a date. *Psychoanal. Psychol.*, 54:46–65.

Golland, J.H. (1997). Not an endgame: termination in psychoanalysis. *Psychoanal. Psychol.*, 14:259–70.

Gomberoff, M. (2000). In J.M. Quinodoz and E.M.D. Rocha Barros. An IPA Panel Report of the 9th Pre-Congress on Training, Santiago 1999: Clinical approaches to the termination of training analysis – clinical dilemmas of training analysts. *Int. J. Psycho-Anal.*, 81:1213–19.

Granair, W. (1975). In Panel Report by W.S. Robbins: Termination: problems and techniques. *J. Amer. Psychoanal. Assn,* 23:166–76.

Greenson, R. (1965). The problem of working through. In M. Schur (ed.), *Drives, Affects, Behavior*, vol. 2. New York: International Universities Press, pp. 277–314.

Grinberg, L. (1980). The closing phase of the psychoanalytic treatment of adults and the goals of psychoanalysis: 'The search for truth about one's self.' *Int. J. Psycho-Anal.*, 61:25–37.

Guntrip, H. (1975). My experience of analysis with Fairbairn and Winnicott. *Int. Rev. Psycho-Anal.*, 2:145–56.

Hartlaub, G.H., Martin, G.C. and Rhine, M.W. (1986). Recontact with the analyst following termination: a survey of seventy-one cases. *J. Amer. Psychoanal. Assn,* 34:895–910.

Hartmann, H. (1939/1958). *Ego Psychology and the Problem of Adaptation*. Trans. David Rapaport. New York: International Universities Press.

Hoffer, W. (1950). Three psychological criteria for the termination of treatment. *Int. J. Psycho-Anal.*, 31:194–95.

Hoffman, I.Z. (1998). *Ritual and Spontaneity in the Psychoanalytic Process: A dialectical–constructivist view.* Hillsdale NJ: Analytic Press.

Hoffman, T. (2009). Whose termination is it anyway? *J. Amer. Acad. Psychoanal.*, 37:457–76.

Holmes, J. (2010). Termination in psychoanalytic psychotherapy: An attachment perspective. In J. Salberg (ed.), *Good Enough Endings: breaks, interruptions, and terminations from contemporary relational perspectives.* Relational Perspective Series. New York and London: Routledge, pp. 63–82.

Hurn, H.T. (1971). Toward a paradigm of the terminal phase: The current status of the terminal phase. *J. Amer. Psychoanal. Assn,* 19:332–48.

Jacobs, T. (1991). *The Use of the Self: Countertransference and Communication in the Analytic Situation.* Madison CT: International Universities Press.

Kantrowitz, J.L. (1987). The role of the patient–analyst 'match' in the outcome of psychoanalysis. *The Annual of Psychoanalysis.* 14:273–97.

——(1992). The analyst's style and its impact on the psychoanalytic process: overcoming stalemates. *J. Amer. Psychoanal. Assn,* 40:169–194.

——(1993). Outcome research in psychoanalysis: review and reconsideration. *J. Amer. Psychoanal. Assn,* Supplementary Issue: 313–28.

——(1995). The beneficial aspects of the patient-analyst match: factors in addition to clinical acumen and therapeutic skill that contribute to psychological change. *Int. J. Psycho–Anal.* 76:299–313.

——(1996). *The Patient's Impact on the Analyst.* Hillsdale NJ: Analytic Press.

——(1999). Pathways to self-knowledge: Self-analysis, mutual supervision, and other shared communications. *Int. J. Psycho-Anal.*, 80:111–32.

——(2003). Tell me your theory. Where is it bred? A lesson from clinical approaches to dreams. *J. Clinical Psychoanal.* 12:151–78.

——(2006). *Writing About Patients: responsibilities, risks, and ramifications.* New York: Other Press.

——(2008). Employing multiple theories and evoking new ideas: the use of clinical material. *Int. J. Psycho-Anal.*, 89:355–68.

——(2009). Privacy and disclosure in psychoanalysis. Plenary address at winter meetings. *J. Amer. Psychoanal. Assn,* 57:787–806.

Kantrowitz, J.L., Katz, A.L. and Paolitto, F. (1990a). Follow-up of psychoanalysis five-to-ten years after termination: I. Stability of change. *J. Amer. Psychoanal. Assn,* 38:471–96.

——(1990b). Follow-up of psychoanalysis five-to-ten years after termination: II. The development of the self-analytic function. *J. Amer. Psychoanal. Assn,.* 38:637–654.

——(1990c). Follow-up of psychoanalysis five-to-ten years after termination: III. The relationship of the transference neurosis to the patient–analyst match. *J. Amer. Psychoanal. Assn,* 38:655–78.

Kantrowitz, J.L., Singer, J. and Knapp, P. (1975). Methodology for a prospective study of suitability for psychoanalysis: the role of psychological tests. *Psychoanal. Quart.*, 44:371–91.

Kantrowitz, J.L., Katz, A.L., Paolitto, F., Sashin, J. and Solomon, L. (1987a). Changes in the level and quality of object relations in psychoanalysis: follow-up of a longitudinal prospective study. *J. Amer. Psychoanal. Assn.*; 35:25–46.

——(1987b). The role of reality testing in the outcome of psychoanalysis: follow-up of 22 cases. *J. Amer. Psychoanal. Assn,* 35:367–86.

Kantrowitz, J.L., Paolitto, F., Sashin, J., Solomon, L. and Katz, A.L. (1986). Affect and availability, tolerance, complexity, and modulation in psychoanalysis: follow-up of a longitudinal study. *J. Amer. Psychoanal. Assn,* 34:529–59.

Kantrowitz, J.L., Katz, A.L., Greenman, D., Morris, H., Paolitto, F., Sashin, J. and Solomon, L. (1989). The patient–analyst match and the outcome of psychoanalysis: the study of 13 cases: research in progress. *J. Amer. Psychoanal. Assn,* 37:893–920.

Klein, M. (1950). On the criteria for the termination of an analysis. *Int. J. Psycho-Anal.,* 31:78–80.

Kogan, I. (1996). Termination and the problem of analytic goals: Patient and analyst, different perspectives. *Int. J. Psycho-Anal.,* 77:1013–29.

Kohut, H. (1971). *The Analysis of the Self: a systematic approach to psychoanalytic treatment of narcissistic personality disorders.* New York: International Universities Press.

——(1977). *The Restoration of the Self.* New York: International Universities Press.

Kramer, M.K. (1959). On the continuation of the analytic process after psychoanalysis (self-observation). *Int. J. Psycho-Anal.,* 40:17–25.

Kris, A.O. (1985). Resistance in convergent and in divergent conflicts. *Psychoanal. Quart.,* 54:537–68.

——(1992). Interpretation and the method of free association. *Psychoanal. Inq.,* 12:208–24. See p. 222.

——(2012). Mourning as a psychological principle. Lecture presented to The Boston Psychoanalytic Society and Institute, September 13, 2012. Unpublished.

Lasky, R. (1990). Catastrophic illness in the analyst and the analyst's emotional reactions to it. *Int. J. Psycho-Anal.,* 71:455–73.

Layton, L. (2010). Maternal resistance. In J. Salberg (ed.), *Good Enough Endings: breaks, interruptions, and terminations from contemporary relational perspectives.* Relational Perspective Series. New York and London: Routledge.

Levenson, E.A. (1978). The aesthetics of termination. *Contemp. Psychoanal.,* 12: 338–42.

Levine, H.B. and Yanof, J.A. (2004). Boundaries and postanalytic contacts in institutes. *J. Amer. Psychoanal. Assn,* 52:873–901.

Limentani, A. (1982). On the 'unexpected' termination of psychoanalytic therapy. *Psychoanal. Inq.,* 2:419–40.

Little, M. (1981). *Transference Neurosis and Transference Psychosis.* New York: Aronson.

Loewald, H.W. (1962). Internalization, separation, mourning, and the superego. *Psychoanal. Quart.,* 31:483–504.

——(1973). On internalization. *Int. J. Psycho-Anal.,* 54:9–17.

——(1988). Termination analyzable and unanalyzable. *Psychoanal. Study Child* 43:155–66.

Lord, R., Ritvo, S. and Solnit, A. (1978). Patients' reactions to the death of the psychoanalyst. *Int. J. Psycho-Anal.,* 59:189–97.

Mahon, E. and Battin, D. (1981). Screen memories and termination of a psychoanalysis: A preliminary communication. *J. Amer. Psychoanal. Assn,* 29:939–42.

Martinez, D. (1989). Pains and gains: a study of forced terminations. *J. Amer. Psychoanal. Assn,* 37:89–115.

Martinez, D. and Hope, S.K. (1996). The analyst's own analyst: other aspects of internalization. In *Annual Meeting of the Society for Psychotherapy Research.* Snowberg, Utah.

McLaughlin, J.T. (1981). Transference, psychic reality and countertransference. *Psychoanal. Quart.*, 50:639–64.

——(1988). The Analyst's Insights. *Psychoanal Quart.*, 57:370–389.

Milner, I. (1965). On the return of symptoms in the terminal phase of psychoanalysis. *Int. J. Psycho-Anal.*, 45:487–501.

Milner, M. (1950). A note on the ending of an analysis. *Int. J. Psycho-Anal.*, 31:191–93.

Mitchell, S. (1993). *Hope and Dread in Psychoanalysis.* New York: Basic Books.

Moraitis, G. (2009). Till death do us part. *Psychoanal. Inq.*, 29:157–66.

Muslin, H.L. (1995). Chapter 9 The termination phase in psychoanalysis: a self psychology study. *Progress in Self Psychology*, 11:141–64.

Nacht, S. (1962). The curative factors in psycho-analysis. *Int. J. Psycho-Anal.*, 43:206–11.

Norman, H.F., Blacker, K.H., Oremland, J.D. and Barrett, W.G. (1976). The fate of the transference neurosis after termination of a satisfactory analysis. *J. Amer. Psychoanal. Assn,* 24:471–98.

Novick, J. (1976). Termination of treatment in adolescence. *Psychoanal. Study Child*, 31:389–414.

——(1982). Termination: themes and issues. *Psychoanal. Inq.*, 2:329–65.

——(1988). The timing of termination. *Int. Rev of Psycho-Anal.*, 14:307–18.

——(1997). Termination conceivable and inconceivable. *Psychoanal. Psychol.*, 14:145–62.

Novick, J. and Novick, K.K. (2006). *Good Goodbyes: knowing how to end in psychotherapy and psychoanalysis.* Lanham MD: Jason Aronson.

O'Malley, S., Suh, C.S. and Strupp, H.H. (1983). The Vanderbilt Psychotherapy Process Scale: a report on the scale development and a process–outcome study. *J. Consult. and Clin. Psychol.*, 51:581–86.

Oremland, J.D., Blacker, K.H. and Norman, H.F. (1975). Incompleteness in 'successful' psychoanalysis: a follow-up study. *J. Am. Psychoanal. Assn*, 23:819–44.

Orgel, S. (2000). Letting go: some thoughts about termination. *J. Amer. Psychoanal. Assn,* 48:719–38.

Parres, R. and Ramirez, S. (1966). Termination of analysis. In R.E. Litman (ed.), *Psychoanalysis in the Americas*, New York: International Universities Press, pp. 247–62.

Pedder, J.R. (1988). Termination reconsidered. *Int. J. Psycho-Anal.*, 69:495–505.

Pfeffer, A. (1959). A procedure for evaluating the results of psychoanalysis: a preliminary report. *J. Amer. Psychoanal. Assn,* 7:418–44.

——(1961). Follow-up study of a satisfactory analysis. *J. Amer. Psychoanal. Assn,* 9:698–718.

——(1963). Meaning of the analyst after analysis. *J. Amer. Psychoanal. Assn,* 11:229–44.

Pine, F. (2011). Beyond pluralism: psychoanalysis and the workings of mind. *Psychoanal Quart.*, 80:823–56.

Pulver, S. (2012). Panel on Termination. Winter meetings of Amer. *Psychoanal. Assn.* Unpublished.

Quinodoz, J. (1993). *The Taming of Solitude.* London and New York: Routledge.

Quinodoz, J.M. and Rocha Barros, E.M.D. (2000). An IPA Panel Report of the 9th Pre-Congress on Training. Santiago 1999. Clinical approaches to the termination of training analysis: Clinical dilemmas of training analysts. *Int. J. Psycho-Anal.*, 81:1213–19.

Racker, H. (1968). *Transference and Countertransference.* London: Hogarth.

Rangell, L. (1966). An overview of the ending of an analysis. In R.E. Litman (ed.), *Psychoanalysis in the Americas.* New York: International Universities Press, pp. 141–65.

——(1982). Some thoughts on termination. *Psychoanal. Inq.*, 2:367–92.

Reich, A. (1950). On the termination of analysis. *Int. J. Psycho-Anal.*, 31:179–83.

Reis, B. (2010). Afterwards and termination. In J. Salberg (ed.), *Good Enough Endings: breaks, interruptions, and terminations from contemporary relational perspectives.* Relational Perspective Series. New York and London: Routledge.

Rickman, J. (1957). On the criteria for the termination of an analysis. *Int. J. Psychoanal.*, 31:200–201.

Roose. S.P., Yang, S., Caligor, E., Cabaniss, D.L., Luber, B., Donovan, J., Rosen, P. and Forand, N.R. (2004). Post-termination contact: a survey of prevalence, characteristics, and analyst attitudes. *J. Amer. Psychoanal. Assn,* 52:455–57.

Salberg, J. (2010a). *Good Enough Endings: breaks, interruptions, and terminations from contemporary relational perspectives.* Relational Perspective Series. New York and London: Routledge.

——(2010b). How we end: taking leave. In J. Salberg (ed.), *Good Enough Endings: breaks, interruptions, and terminations from contemporary relational perspectives.* Relational Perspective Series. New York and London: Routledge, pp. 109–29.

Schachter, J. (1992). Concepts of termination and post-termination patient–analyst contact. *Int. J. Psycho-Anal.*, 73:137–54.

——(2005). Postanalytic contacts in institutes. *J. Amer. Psychoanal. Assn,* 53:260–64.

——(2009). Discussion of Craige's 'Termination without fatality'. *Psychoanal. Inq.* 29:188–94.

Schachter, J. and Johan, M. (1989). Evaluation of outcome of psychoanalytic treatment: Should follow-up by the analyst be part of the post-termination phase of analytic treatment? *J. Amer. Psychoanal. Assn,* 37:813–22.

Schafer, R. (1968). *Aspects of Internalization.* NewYork: International Universities Press.

——(2007). The reality principle, tragic knots, and the analytic process. *J. Amer. Psychoanal. Assn,* 55:1151–68.

Schlesinger, H.J. (2005). *Endings and Beginnings: on terminating psychotherapy and psychoanalysis.* Hillsdale NJ: Analytic Press.

Schlessinger, N. and Robbins, F. (1974). Assessment and follow-up in psychoanalysis. *J. Amer. Psychoanal. Assn,* 22:542–67.

——(1975). The psychoanalytic process: recurrent patterns of conflict and changes in ego functions. *J. Amer. Psychoanal. Assn,* 23:761–82.

Schlessinger, N. and Robbins, F.P. (1983). *A Developmental View of the Psychoanalytic Process: follow-up studies and their consequences.* New York: International Universities Press.

Schubert, J. (2000). Give sorrow words: mourning at termination of psychoanalysis. *Scand. Psychoanal. Rev.*, 23:105–17.

Schwartz, H.J. and Silver, A.L.S. (1990). *Illness in the Analyst: implications for the treatment relationship.* Madison CT: International Universities Press.

Schwartz, I.G. (1974). Forced termination of analysis revisited. *Int. J. Psycho-Anal.*, 1:283–90.

Shane, M. and Shane, E. (1984). The end phase of analysis: indicators, functions, and tasks of termination. *J. Amer. Psychoanal. Assn,* 32:739–72.

Sherby, L.B. (2004). Forced termination: when pain is shared. *Contemp. Psychoanal.*, 40:69–90.

Siegel, B.L. (1982). Some thoughts on 'Some thoughts on termination' by Leo Rangell. *Psychoanal. Inq.*, 2:393–98.

Silber, A. (1996). Analysis, re-analysis, and self-analysis. *J. Amer. Psychoanal. Assn,* 44:491–509.

——(2003). Mutual supervision: further thoughts on self-observation, self-analysis, and re-analysis. *J. Clin. Psychoanal.,* 12:9–18.

Silverman, S. (2010). Will you remember me? Termination and continuity. In J. Salberg (ed.), *Good Enough Endings: breaks, interruptions, and terminations from contemporary relational perspectives.* Relational Perspective Series. New York and London: Routledge, pp. 167–89.

Sonnenberg, S.M. (1991). The analyst's self-analysis and its impact on clinical work: a comment on the source of personal insights. *J. Amer. Psychoanal. Assn,* 39:687–704.

——(1995). Analytic listening and the analyst's self-analysis. *Int. J. Psycho-Anal.,* 76:335–42.

Spence, D.P. (1998). Rain forest or mud field?. *Int. J. Psycho-Anal.,* 79:643–47.

Spezzano, C. (1998). The triangle of clinical judgment. *J. Amer. Psychoanal. Assn,* 46:365–88.

Steiner, J. (1994). Patient-Centered and Analyst-Centered Interpretations: Some Implications of Containment and Countertransference. *Psycho-Anal. Inq.,* 14:406–422.

Stewart, W.A. (1963). An inquiry into the concept of working through. *J. Amer. Psychoanal. Assn,* 11:474–99.

Tessman, I. (2003). *The Analyst's Analyst Within.* Hillsdale NJ: Analytic Press.

Ticho, E. (1972). Termination of psychoanalysis: treatment goals, life goals. *Psychoanal. Quart.,* 41:315–33.

Ticho, G.R. (1967). On self-analysis. *Int. J. Psycho-Anal.,* 48:308–18.

Wallerstein, R. (1986). *Forty-two Lives in Treatment.* New York and London: Guilford Press.

——(1988). One psychoanalysis or many? *Int. J. Psycho-Anal.,* 69:5–21.

Weigert, E. (1952). Contribution to the problem of terminating psychoanalyses. *Psychoanal. Quart.,* 21:465–80.

——(1955). Special problems in connection with termination of training analyses. *J. Amer. Psychoanal. Assn,* 3:630–40.

Weiss, S. (1972). Some thoughts and clinical vignettes on translocation of an analytic practice. *Int. J. Psycho-Anal.* 53:505–13.

Westen, D. and Gabbard, G.O. (2002). Developments in Cognitive Neuroscience: I. Conflict, Compromise, and Connectionism. *J. Amer. Psychoanal. Assn,* 50:53–98.

Winnicott, D.W. (1965). The capacity to be alone. In D.W. Winnicott, *The Maturational Processes and the Facilitating Environment: studies in the theory of emotional development.* London: Hogarth and The Institute of Psycho-Analysis.

——(1971). Transitional objects and transitional phenomena. In D.W. Winnicott, *Playing and Reality.* New York: Routledge, pp. 1–13.

Index

Entries in *italics* refer to titles of works.

Abend, S 8, 57, 75, 106
age 143–144, 155
Alexander, F 37
American Psychoanalytic Association 22, 152
analysability 10–11
analysands: age *see* age; analysability 10–11; analytic candidates *see* analytic candidates; analytic experiences 24; anger *see* anger; clinical interviews *see* clinical interviews; dealing with loss 28; disappointment 43–44; effect of unwanted self-revelations 54–55; friendships with analyst post-treatment 94–95, 103; gender 152; grief and mourning 12–14, 24–25, 50–53, 132, 149; individual differences 133; initiating termination 66–73; insights 29–32, 126–127; intolerance at analyst setting limits 41, 68–69; leaving after analyst proposes ending 72–73; leaving after analyst resists the wish to stop 70–71; leaving treatment abruptly, with unfinished work 71; length of time since termination 144; motivations for volunteering 145–146; mutual dependency 15; patient–analyst 'match' 11; post-analytic contact *see* post-analytic contact; previous and subsequent treatment 144–145; professional qualifications 125–153; reactions to research interview 141–142; recognition of separateness 32–34; recovered memory 29; recurrence of symptoms 155; re-entering treatment 97–102; relocation 65–66; response to unwanted self-revelations by analyst 44–45; reworking conflicts 34–37; satisfaction with analytic experience 153; self-analysis *see* self-analysis; sexual boundary violations 39–40; shame 75–76; struggles about ending 41–43; withholding feelings and reactions 75–76
analysis: evaluation 2; generalizations about 1–2; idealization of 136–137; interminability of 7, 16; post-analytic contact *see* post-analytic contact; re-entering 97–102; rethinking old

assumptions 139–141; self-
analysis *see* self-analysis;
timelessness and 78–79;
transference and 7;
unpredictability 1
Analysis Terminable and Interminable
16
analysts: attachment style 11; denial
43–44; disappointment in 43–44;
friendships with analysands
post-treatment 94–95, 103; illness
and death 60–62, 74–75;
initiating termination 40–41,
58–66, 72–73; interpersonal 11,
14; mutual dependency 15;
patient–analyst 'match' 11;
post-analytic contact *see* post-
analytic contact; professional
ethics 66–68, 85; as a 'real
object' 13–14; relational 11, 12,
14, 15–16, 27; relocation 40–41,
58–60; resistance to ending 27,
70–71; setting limits 41, 68–69;
sexual boundary violations
39–40, 66–68; as transference
figure 15–16, 27; unwanted
self-revelations 44–45, 54–55;
withholding information 74–75
analytic candidates: assessment of
patients 10; mourning around
termination 12–13, 20, 32, 53;
mourning during termination 51;
post-analytic contact 81–86,
103–105; self-analysis 109; sexual
boundary violations 39–40;
undermining analytic gains in
post-analytic contact 88–89
analytic experience: effect of non-
mutual endings 74, 76–77; loss of
147, 148; undermining in
post-analytic contact 87–89
analytic goals 9
anger: at analyst setting limits 41,
68–69; disappointment 43–44;

due to analyst moving at short
notice 40–41, 154; recapitulation
of transference 43; sexual
boundary violations 39–40,
154–155; struggles about ending
41–43; unwanted self-revelations
44–45
Arlow, JA 8, 52
autonomy 15
Awad, GA 78

Balint, M 12, 14
Bass, A 15, 78
Battin, D 10
Becall, H 3, 134
Beiser, H 106
Benedeck, T 57
Bergmann, M 4, 9, 10, 15, 16, 27, 106,
108
Bird, B 10
Blacker, KH 106, 110
Blanck, G 9
Blanck, R 9
Blatt, SJ 134
Blum, HP 1, 4, 8, 10, 13, 20–21, 25,
109, 110, 112, 128
Boesky, D 8
Bonvitz, C 15, 80
Brenner, C 57, 106
Breuer, J 7
Britton, R 17
Brunswick, RM 57
Burland, JA 22
Buxbaum, E 10, 19, 20, 81

Calder, KT 106
Calef, V 10
certainty 1–2
clinical interviews: methods 152;
overview 3–4; previous/
subsequent treatment 153;
subjects 152–153; summary of
findings 153–157
communication 74–76

Cooper, S 10
CORST project 10–11
countertransference enactments 44, 87, 105
Craige, H 2, 12–13, 20, 50, 52, 80, 82, 86, 103, 149

Davies, JM 17, 42
De Berenstein, SP 9
De Fondevila, DS 9
De Simone Gaburri, G 8
death: of analyst 60–62, 74–75; analytic institutes and 61–62; anxieties about 15, 27, 47, 48
Debell, DE 14
denial 43–44
depression 48, 99
Deutsch, H 12
developmental theory 9
Dewald, PA 8, 9, 10, 57, 58, 76
disappointment 43–44, 154–155
Dorpat, TL 110
dreams 130

ego activities 8
Eifermann, RR 106
Eissler, KR 139
Ekstein, R 10, 17
Ellman, SJ 11
enactments 38–39
Engel, GL 106

Ferenczi, S 7, 20, 106
Ferraro, F 54
Firestein, SK 1, 4, 8, 9, 18–19, 57, 80, 81, 107, 108, 129, 141, 149
Fleming, J 57
Fonagy, P 22
Frank, KA 2
Freedman, A 57
Freedman, N 110, 111, 127
French, TM 37
Freud, S: chess metaphor 21, 25; definitions of termination 7, 25, 26; interminability of analysis 7, 16, 82; non-mutual endings 57; return to treatment 145; self-analysis 107, 131

Gabbard, GO 1, 22–23, 108
Garcia-Lawson, KA 21
Gardner, R 106
Garella, A 54
Gaskill, HS 9, 106, 107, 108
Geller, J 110, 111, 127
gender 152
generalizations 1
Gibeault, A 20, 83
Gilman, RD 8, 9, 28, 57
Giovacchini, PL 110
Gitelson, M 9
Glennon, SS 15
Glick, RA 65–66, 76
Glover, E 7, 8, 11, 26
Goldberg, A 8, 76
Golland, JH 1, 21
Gomberoff, M 20, 83
Granair, W 13
Greenson, R 10
grief 12–13, 27–28, 50–53, 132, 149
Grinberg, L 9, 12

Hartlaub, GH 4, 81
Hartmann, H 133
Hoffer, W 9, 106, 107, 108
Hoffman, IZ 14, 15, 84
Hoffman, T 76
Holmes, J 11
Hope, SK 110
Hurn, HT 57

idealized assumptions 17–19
insights 29–32, 126–127
interminability of analysis 7, 16
interpersonal analysts 11, 14
interviews *see* clinical interviews

Jacobs, T 106
joy 45–50

Kantrowitz, JL 2, 9, 10, 11, 13, 73,
    106, 111, 131, 138, 139, 140
Katz, AL 9, 106, 111
Kogan, I 9
Kohut, H 9, 15, 133–134
Kramer, MK 52, 107–108, 109, 129
Kris, AO 78, 149

Lane, RC 21
Lasky, R 57, 75
Layton, L 15, 134
Levenson, EA 11, 14
Levine, HB 83, 86
life goals 9
Limentani, A 20, 49, 56, 76, 81, 103
limits 41
Little, M 106
Loewald, HW 9, 12, 15, 25, 49, 133,
    134
Lord, R 14
loss: of analyst as transference object
    13–14; of analytic relationship
    25, 27, 54; anxiety about future
    losses 15; as reason for seeking
    analysis 12; variations in 28

Mahon, E 10
Marcus, D 8, 76
Martin, GC 4
Martinez, D 58, 76, 110
McLaughlin, J 106, 130, 140
memory 10, 29, 130, 147–148
methods 152
Milner, M 12, 13, 27, 37, 53, 81, 82,
    103, 112, 128, 148
Mitchell, S 14, 15
Moraitis, G 12
mourning 12–14, 24–25, 52–53, 132,
    149
Muslin, HL 10
mutual dependency 15

Nacht, S 9
non-mutual endings: abrupt ending by
    analyst 63–64; analysand leaves
    after analyst proposes ending
    72–73; analysand leaving after
    analyst resists the wish to stop
    70–71; analysand-initiated
    66–73; analysands leaving
    treatment abruptly, with
    unfinished work 71; analyst
    ends based on analysand's life
    changes 64–65; analyst-initiated
    58–66; analyst's sexual boundary
    violation 66–68; analytic gains
    and 149; communication 74–76;
    effect of time 77; effect on the
    analytic experience 76–77;
    illness/death of analyst 60–62,
    74–75, 154; overview 56–58;
    past history and 77–78; relocation
    of analysand 65–66, 154;
    relocation of analyst 40–41,
    58–60, 154
Norman, HF 106, 110
Novick, J 4, 8, 9, 10, 12, 13, 14, 27, 37,
    53, 56, 58, 81, 103, 112, 128, 148
Novick, KK 9, 10

Oedipal issues 9, 28
O'Malley, S 2, 73
Oremland, JD 106, 110
Orgel, S 10, 12, 14, 15, 16, 27

Paolitto, F 9, 106, 111
Parres, R 80, 103
partial theories 2
patient–analyst 'match' 11
Pedder, JR 8, 84
perfectionism 136
Pfeffer, A 82, 106, 110
Pine, F 2
positivity 45–50
post-analytic contact: analysts'
    attitudes about 19–20, 80–81;

analytic candidates 81–86,
103–105; disappointment with
98–102; emotional support during
94–95; healing colleague contact
92–94; negative representations
of self and analyst reinforced by
90–91; overview 148; as patient
97–102; positive social/
professional contact 91;
professionalism 96–97; social/
non-clinical settings 86–97;
solidifying analytic gains 91–97;
soothed feeling of loss 91–92;
undermining analytic gains
87–89
professionalism 96–97
progressive development 9
projective tests 139
Psychoanalytic Psychology 22
psychosomatic symptoms 51
Pulver, S 1

Quinodoz, J 19, 20, 49, 53, 83, 84

Racker, H 122
Ramirez, S 80, 103
Rangell, L 8, 9
recapitulation of transference 43
recovered memory 29
Reich, A 7, 12, 19, 20, 81
Reis, B 109, 147
relational analysts 11, 14, 15–16,
27
Rhine, MW 4
Rickman, J 9
Ritvo, S 14
Robbins, FP 9, 26, 106, 110, 116
Rocha Barros, EMD 83
Roose, SP 19, 80
Rorschach tests 140

Salberg, J 1–2, 4, 11, 14, 78, 106, 108
Schachter, J 19, 81, 83, 84, 129
Schafer, R 78, 110

Schlesinger, HJ 1, 12, 15, 25, 50, 55,
84, 116, 133
Schlessinger, N 9, 106, 110
Schubert, J 10, 28
Schwartz, IG 58
self-analysis: alone vs with others
127–132; assimilation of analytic
functions 114–117; clinicians vs
non-clinicians 128; as criterion
for termination 9, 26; defined
106; development of 107–112,
128–129; evoking the analyst
113–114; forms of self-
exploration 112–113, 126–127;
grief as indicator of analytic gains
132; keeping analysis alive
without 129; overview 106–107;
patient as primary stimulus
122–124; places for 130–132;
presence of imaginary or real
others in 129; reconsideration of
theory 132–135; vs self-reflection
126–127; stimuli for 130–131;
vicissitudes of life as stimulus for
117–121
self-reflection 126–127
self-revelations, unwanted 44–45, 54–55
self-sufficiency 49, 54
separateness 32–34
sexual boundary violations 39–40,
66–68
shame 75–76
Shane, E 4
Shane, M 4
Siegel, BL 10
Silber, A 106
Silverman, S 11, 12
Solnit, A 14
song, as stimulus for self-analysis
130
Sonnenberg, SM 106
specificity 148
Spence, DP 22
Strupp, HH 2, 73

Suh, CS 2, 73
symptoms, recurrence of 155

telephone interviews 25–53
termination: anger during 39–45;
    criteria for 8–11, 21–22;
    disappointment 43–44, 154–155;
    dissatisfaction with 154;
    enactments 38–39; genesis 7–8;
    grief and mourning 12–14,
    24–25, 50–53, 149; idealized
    assumptions about 17–19;
    insights discovered during
    transference 29–32; joy during
    45–50; length of time since 144,
    155; and memory of analysis 17;
    mixed feelings about 153; myths
    surrounding 1; necessity 15–17;
    non-mutual *see* non-mutual
    endings; post-analytic contact
    see post-analytic contact;
    recapitulation of transference 43;
    recognition of separateness
    32–34; recovered memory 29;
    reworking conflicts 34–37;
    specificity in 148; theories about
    2; transference moving from
    displacement to the analyst
    37–38, 54; unwanted self-
    revelations 44–45, 54–55
Tessman, I 2, 12, 13, 14, 80–81, 85,
    86, 106, 109

Ticho, GR 9, 107, 108, 109
time 15–17, 77
timelessness 78–79
training analyses 7
transference: analyst as object 13;
    enactments 38–39; insights
    discovered during 29–32; moving
    from displacement to the analyst
    37–38; and process of analysis 7;
    recapitulation of 43; revival 82;
    termination and 15–17, 54
trust 75

unconscious conflicts 7, 11, 39,
    107–108, 109
unconscious fantasy organization 8
unpredictability 1
unwanted self-revelations 44–45,
    54–55

Wallerstein, R 1, 2, 17, 26, 134
Washington Psychoanalytic Institute
    152
Weigert, E 11, 12, 28
Weinshel, EM 10
Weiss, S 58
William Alanson White Institute
    152
Winnicott, DW 109, 133
writing, therapeutic 90, 114, 130

Yanof, JA 83, 86